Ageing in Southeast and East Asia

The **Institute of Southeast Asian Studies (ISEAS)** was established as an autonomous organization in 1968. It is a regional centre dedicated to the study of socio-political, security and economic trends and developments in Southeast Asia and its wider geostrategic and economic environment.

The Institute's research programmes are the Regional Economic Studies (RES, including ASEAN and APEC), Regional Strategic and Political Studies (RSPS), and Regional Social and Cultural Studies (RSCS).

ISEAS Publishing, an established academic press, has issued almost 2,000 books and journals. It is the largest scholarly publisher of research about Southeast Asia from within the region. ISEAS Publishing works with many other academic and trade publishers and distributors to disseminate important research and analyses from and about Southeast Asia to the rest of the world.

Ageing in Southeast and East Asia

Family, Social Protection and Policy Challenges

EDITED BY

LEE HOCK GUAN

INSTITUTE OF SOUTHEAST ASIAN STUDIES
Singapore

First published in Singapore in 2008 by
Institute of Southeast Asian Studies
30 Heng Mui Keng Terrace
Pasir Panjang
Singapore 119614

E-mail: publish@iseas.edu.sg
Website: <http://bookshop.iseas.edu.sg>

The responsibility for facts and opinions in this publication rests exclusively with the authors and their interpretations do not necessarily reflect the views or the policy of the publisher or its supporters.

ISEAS Library Cataloguing-in-Publication Data

Ageing in Southeast & East Asia : family, social protection, policy challenges / edited by Lee Hock Guan.
    "The Chapters in this volume are selected from papers delivered at a two-day workshop, titled Ageing and the Status of the Older Population in Southeast Asia, organized by ISEAS from 22 to 23 November 2004"—Acknowledgement.
    1. Aging—Government policy—Southeast Asia—Congresses.
    2. Aging—Government policy—East Asia—Congresses.
    3. Older people—Southeast Asia—Economic conditions—Congresses.
    4. Older people—East Asia—Economic conditions—Congresses.
    5. Older people—Southeast Asia—Social conditions—Congresses.
    6. Older people—East Asia—Social conditions—Congresses.
    I. Lee Hock Guan.
    II. Institute of Southeast Asian Studies.
    III. Workshop on Ageing and the Status of the Older Population in Southeast Asia (2004 : Singapore)
    IV. Title: Ageing in Southeast and East Asia
HQ1064 A8A263   2008

ISBN 978-981-230-765-1 (soft cover)
ISBN 978-981-230-766-8 (hard cover)

Typeset by Superskill Graphics Pte Ltd
Printed in Singapore by Photoplates Private Limited

CONTENTS

ACKNOWLEDGEMENTS

The chapters in this volume are selected from papers delivered at a two-day workshop, titled "Ageing and the Status of the Older Population in Southeast Asia", organized by ISEAS from 22 to 23 November 2004. The workshop was partially funded with a grant from the Lee Foundation.

The greying of Southeast Asia is becoming a reality at much faster rates than previously experienced by the developed countries. Needless to say, the social, economic and political implications raised by the phenomenon of ageing on a massive scale in the region are enormous. Population ageing, for example, would increase the pressure on governments to increase spending on pensions, health and social welfare provisions. In turn, public provisions and capacity to assist the older population are partly determined by a combination of the size of the absolute numbers of older persons and the level of aggregate wealth of a country. Since all the Southeast Asian countries are in the low to middle-income categories, with the exception of Singapore, it would mean that to meet the socio-economic challenges of an ageing population they would have to ensure substantial economic development as well.

The workshop on ageing was organized in part to raise awareness of the phenomenon of population ageing and in part to stimulate intellectual exchange on population ageing and the status of the older populations in the region and their policy implications. Four areas addressed by the workshop were: 1) comparisons of the formulation and implementation of ageing policies in East and Southeast Asia, 2) the family support system and housing for the older population, 3) economic security, or insecurity, and law and the older persons, and 4) health status and health care financing, and the feminization of older populations.

We would like to thank Mr Kesavapany, Director of the Institute of Southeast Asian Studies, who rendered his full support to this workshop, and to the Lee Foundation for co-sponsoring the workshop. We would like to take this opportunity to also thank the contributors to this volume for their kind cooperation and patience. Last but not least, our appreciation to the Administration staff for their efforts in helping to organize the workshop, and the Publications Unit staff for their assistance in producing this volume.

Lee Hock Guan

CONTRIBUTORS

Ahn Kye Choon is Professor, Department of Sociology, Yonsei University, Seoul, South Korea

Alex Arifianto is Researcher, The SMERU Research Institute, Jakarta

Chia Ngee Choon is Associate Professor, Department of Economics, National University of Singapore

Chung Kyung Hee is Research Fellow, Korea Institute for Health and Social Affairs

Nibhon Debavalya is Senior Research Associate, College of Population Studies, Chulalongkorn University, Bangkok

The late *Sri Harijati Hatmadji* was Director, Demographic Institute, Faculty of Economics, University of Indonesia

Yukinobu Kitamura is Professor of Economics, Institute of Economic Research, Hitotsubashi University

Lee Hock Guan is Senior Fellow, Institute of Southeast Asian Studies, Singapore

Kalyani K. Mehta is Associate Professor, Department of Social Work, National University of Singapore

Josefina N. Natividad is Professor, Department of Sociology, University of the Philippines, Diliman, Quezon City

Nurizan Yahaya is Associate Professor, Head, Biosocial, Cognitive and Functional Laboratory, Universiti Putra Malaysia

Ong Fon Sim is Associate Professor, Faculty of Business and Accountancy, University of Malaya

Tengku Aizan Hamid is Associate Professor, Director, Institute of Gerontology, Universiti Putra Malaysia

Thang Leng Leng is Associate Professor, Department of Japanese Studies, National University of Singapore

Albert Tsui K.C. is Associate Professor, Department of Economics. National University of Singapore

Nur Hadi Wiyono is Researcher, Demographic Institute, Faculty of Economics, University of Indonesia

Grace Wong is Senior Lecturer, Department of Real Estate, National University of Singapore

Yap Mui Teng is Senior Research Fellow, Institute of Policy Studies, Singapore

INTRODUCTION

Lee Hock Guan

In recognition of the situation of older persons in the world, 1999 was declared as the International Year of Older Persons by the United Nations. Following the Second World Assembly on Ageing held in April 2002 in Madrid, Spain, the inaugural ASEAN Senior Officials Meeting on Social Welfare and Development, held in October 2002 in Siem Reap, Cambodia, included in its ASEAN Work Programme on Social Welfare, Family, and Population (2003–06), priorities to take into account with regard to welfare, the family and population, given the emerging challenges arising from demographic developments, particularly population ageing.

Population ageing — the process by which older persons assume a proportionately larger share of the total population — is fast becoming a reality in Southeast Asia, but at much faster rates than previously experienced by developed countries. In part this is due to the huge advances made in the areas of health care knowledge, technologies and services, and as well as their accessibility by an increasingly larger segment of the population. Better control of perinatal and infant mortality, a decline in birth rates, improvements in nutrition, basic health care and control of many infectious diseases have all contributed to a Southeast Asian demographic transition revolution. In 1975, the estimated number of older persons was 18.3 million (or 5.7 per cent of the total population), but by 2000, that number had doubled to 37.3 million (or 7.1 per cent), and was projected to reach 87.9 million in 2025 (12.3 per cent).[1] From 1975 to 2025, or in two generations, while the total Southeast Asian population would increase from 522.1 to 692.2 million, or by 32.6 per cent, the number of older persons would increase by 135.6 per cent. The number of older persons has been projected to reach 176.1 million or close to a quarter of the total population by 2050.

These indicators clearly confirmed that the greying of Southeast Asia is becoming a reality at much faster rates than was previously experienced by developed countries. The increase in the number of elderly people in countries such as Thailand and the Philippines will be up to 15 times higher than in the United Kingdom and Sweden in the period 1985–2020; this is part of the process known as the "compressed demographic transition". As in the case of the developed world, women form the majority of older people, a development usually referred to as the "feminization of later life". In virtually all Southeast Asian countries, this proportion increases with age. As Southeast Asian countries undergo rapid declines in fertility and mortality rates, they are experiencing varying stages of population ageing.

The economic and social implications of ageing are directly connected to the increasing proportion of the elderly in the population as well as the increase in their absolute numbers. For example, in 2000, while Singapore had the highest proportion of the elderly — 12 per cent (170,000) of its population aged 60 years and older — Indonesia had the highest absolute number of 14 million, which was 7.2 per cent of the population. This meant that even though the elderly population in Indonesia was only 7.2 per cent in 2000, it still had an ageing problem because of the large absolute number involved, especially since a disproportionate percentage of the older population are concentrated in the rural areas.

The social, economic and political implications raised by the ageing phenomenon in the region are enormous. Because of the fast speed of ageing, the region, unlike developed countries, cannot afford the luxury of time for the gradual evolution of social and structural support systems and networks for the older population. Southeast East Asian nations will need to formulate and implement without delay comprehensive policies to deal with the impending "age quake". Studies have shown that proper policies are best implemented and the appropriate infrastructure constructed to prepare for the inevitable ageing of the population when the dependency rates are still low. This demographic window is an opportunity that should not be ignored.

Fortunately, evidence suggests that nearly all Southeast Asian governments have recognized the phenomenon of population ageing and have started the processes of formulating and implementing national ageing policies. Chapters 4 to 7 examine the national ageing policies of Singapore, Indonesia, Malaysia and Thailand respectively. However, the existing national policies in Southeast Asia, with the exception of those in Singapore, are inadequate and underdeveloped, and as such would need much more work and commitment. Even in the case of Singapore, its established policies and programmes are being reviewed in view of the changing demographics; in other words, policies need to be dynamic. Several salient points should be taken into account in the formulation of national ageing policies such as: the older population is not a homogenous group, feminization of ageing, equity and sustainability of welfare policies, and the challenge of utilizing the older population as a resource, instead of viewing them as a burden.

Frequently, ageing policies were formulated without sufficient research and available data, consultations with experts, and input from the very people the policies were designed for — the older population; Chapter 3 on Korea shows the need to understand the many sided aspects of ageing as a means to formulate better policies for the older population. Institutions should be tasked, and, if none exist, created, to act as national data collection centres, to conduct and coordinate research on the ageing phenomenon, and to formulate appropriate policies and programmes. In a number of Southeast Asian countries, there are glaring gaps between ageing policies and their implementation and outcomes; this suggests the need for more effective processes and procedures for execution and monitoring of the policies.

The financial expenditure needed to support the older population would increase with the growing proportion of the aged and the longer survival of the aged population. Chapters 1 and 2 evaluate the adequacy of the existing national financial support systems of Japan and Singapore respectively in addressing the retirement needs of their older populations. These two studies illustrate the strengths and limitations of the existing support systems for the older populations and it is worthwhile to consider briefly a fundamental difference between East and Southeast Asian, and European, approaches to public welfare.

Several studies on the existing public pension systems in Western countries have indicated that they were not sustainable if economic growth and productivity could not continue to increase to keep pace with the population ageing process. Indeed, European countries have already begun to rethink their existing policies and programmes in view of a looming crisis of sustainability. The emergence of European social security systems can be traced to the expansion of social rights to include citizens' welfare. In the past, because European citizenship understood human beings as rights-bearing, autonomous individuals, social contracts mainly emphasized the contractual relations between the state and individuals. The question of welfare thus became the responsibility of the state towards the individual, giving rise to a largely public sector-based welfare system. Several European countries appear to be moving from systems where the state plays the major role in welfare provision for the older population, towards greater individual and family responsibility.

In contrast to the European rights-bearing, autonomous individual, the predominant notion of a person in East and Southeast Asian countries is that of a role-bearing individual with an emphasis on concrete interpersonal relationships and interactions. Since a web of relationships and interactions circumscribe an individual's position in society, it is expected that the community — and especially the family — would be apportioned an important role in the social contract. In all East and Southeast Asian countries the family, or more generally, kinship networks, contribute substantially to taking care of the elderly in the society (Chapters 8, 11 and 12). In practice, of course, Asian states also provide assistance to family support, especially in the case of poor families or civil servants' families. However, the sustainability of largely family-based Asian welfare systems has been adversely affected by several trends, such as the changing perceptions of familial roles, the growing number of nuclear families and unmarried individuals, declining fertility and increased population mobility. In effect these trends mean that Asian states will have to play a larger role in caring for the elderly in the future, and these factors have to be considered in developing income security schemes for old age in Southeast Asia.

The Singapore "many hands" model, where the well-being and welfare of the older population are regarded as the responsibilities of the individual and the family first, and then of the community, with the state coming in as a backup, is potentially an example that could avoid the sustainability trap (Chapters 4 and 9). Nevertheless, one has to be cautious with using the family as the primary support base for the aged population, given the increasing trend of migration, and the increasing number of smaller families (two children or fewer) and the singles population (Chapters 8, 11 and 12).

The health status and expenditure for health of the older population are key areas that need more research and carefully thought out and planned policies. The upward trend for health expenditure is invariable with the increasing proportion of the older population and the longer survival of the aged population. To minimize morbidity and disability in old age and thus lower health costs, emphasis should be given to promoting healthy life styles and early health screening and detection. Other ways to ensure cost-effective care include the development of community-based services, the strengthening of family support and home care, the improvement of housing and living arrangements, and the provision of step-down services to hospitals, such as day care, home nursing, hospice and so on. The financing of care should take the following into consideration: family support for home care, personal savings and community services for primary health care, compulsory savings for hospitalizations and acute care, insurance and institutional support for catastrophic and long-term care, and taxation and state welfare as a safety net.

While the full challenge posed by the greying of the region would only be felt at national levels in the near future, older persons in the region are already experiencing various old-age vulnerabilities because of marginalization and exclusion, and inadequate social protection and welfare measures. Old-age vulnerabilities are further accentuated by the socio-psychological perception that conflates old age with illness or disability, instead of equating it with opportunities for positive change and productive functioning. The prevailing learned social and cultural perceptions and attitudes that view old age as a "disability" should be changed to regard it as an "asset" (Chapter 10).

The employment and employability of the older population should be reviewed given that the older population are living longer healthy lives and are better educated. Furthermore, rather than regarding the aged population as a "dependent" population, they should be regarded as "consumers" providing opportunities for the development of a "silver" industry. Initiatives to improve social networks, housing, public services, leisure activities, public safety and the physical environment for the older population should be undertaken to enhance their quality of life and to develop the "silver" market. Hence, for Southeast Asian countries to meet the challenge of the greying of their populations, they should start to formulate and implement long-term policies to address the gradual ageing of their population, and steps should be taken to look at approaches to reduce the health costs of an ageing population.

Note

[1] Most developed countries usually use the age of 65 years and above as the definition of older, or "elderly", person. It has been pointed out that while this definition is suitable for developed countries, it may be problematic for developing countries where the age of becoming "old" could be different. In this volume, authors have used either 60+ or 65+ to refer to the older population.

1

THE PENSION SYSTEM IN JAPAN AND RETIREMENT NEEDS OF THE JAPANESE ELDERLY

Chia Ngee Choon, Yukinobu Kitamura and Albert Tsui K.C.*

INTRODUCTION

Japan is the world's most rapidly ageing country due to its having the longest life expectancy. In 2003, life expectancy at birth for males was 78.36 years, up by 0.04 years from that of the previous year, and that for females was 85.33 years, up by 0.10 years.[1] In 2004, there were 24.9 million elderly (65 years and above), accounting for 19.5 per cent of the total population. The proportion of elderly is expected to increase sharply to reach 25.3 per cent by 2018 and more than 30 per cent by 2033 (Takayama 2004). The aggregate cost of social security in terms of national income is estimated to increase from 17.2 per cent in 2004 to 24.3 per cent by 2025, if there are no changes to the current provisions for benefits. In Japan, nearly 70 per cent of total social security benefits is distributed to the elderly. In 2004, pension payments amounted to 9.2 per cent of GDP and health care expenditure amounted to 5.2 per cent. It is projected that by 2025, pension payment will increase to 11.6 per cent and health care expenditure to 8.1 per cent.

Studies on social security in Japan have focused on issues relating to sustainability of the pension system, the cost of social security, and the need for pension reforms. Takayama (1992, 1998) assessed the effects of a greying

Japan on the government budget and raised the need for a pension reform to address the sustainability issue. Horioka (1997, 2004) has focused on the savings behaviours and portfolio composition of the Japanese elderly and found strong motives for retirement and precautionary savings. Hurd and Yashiro (1997) examined the economic status of the elderly and found that generally the elderly in Japan are much more dependent on public pension, with as much as 80 per cent or more of their elderly income coming from public pension. The elderly in Japan have less financial asset income because they hold a much greater fraction of their wealth in housing assets. The latter stylized fact has led many researchers to examine whether there is a possibility of unlocking housing equity in Japan, for example, Noguchi (1997) and Mitchell and Piggott (2004). However, Ishikawa and Yajima (2001) show that the Japanese elderly tend not to take advantage of accumulated wealth. They do not draw down their assets but instead leave behind assets equivalent to twenty years of consumption.[2] This is in contrast to the elderly in the United States who draw down not only their financial assets, but also their property assets, and move into smaller, owned or rented homes.

Few studies have focused on the financial security of the Japanese elderly that take into account their post-retirement consumption needs, and whether the existing pension system could finance these consumption needs. This paper calibrates the retirement needs of the elderly and look at the expenditure side of the lifetime budget of the elderly. Post-retirement monthly expenses of the male and female elderly starting at age 65 are calibrated based on subsistence consumption and health care expenditure. Besides using the appropriate discount factors, the estimation of the present value of future expenses (*PVE*) also factors in the survival probabilities of the elderly, conditional on survival at age 65. Instead of using deterministic life expectancy forecast, we adapt the techniques introduced by Bourbeau et al. (1997) to derive cohort life tables from the period life tables, and the Lee-Carter (1992, 2000) method to forecast survival probabilities. The estimated *PVE* could be compared with the accumulated retirement wealth to assess the cash flow adequacy of pensioners in Japan. Retirement wealth includes financial wealth, housing, and incomes from social security and pensions.

The rest of this paper is organized as follows. In the next section, we critically evaluate the Japanese pension system, highlighting the major challenges and the recent reforms. Section 3 describes the procedures taken to compute the present value of the estimated retirement needs of the elderly. It contains three subsections. First, we discuss in detail the calibration of two main components of retirement expenditure: subsistence needs and health care expenditure. Second, we use two different interest rate models to generate yield curves to discount the future cash flows. Third, we explain the relevant synthesis in constructing the cohort life tables for the elderly by sex after retirement. Finally, policy recommendations and conclusions are given in Section 5.

THE JAPANESE PENSION SYSTEM

Takayama (1998) asked whether public pension benefits have been too generous and whether there was substantial income transfer from the current young to the elderly. As could be gleaned from Table 1.1 on the international comparison of elderly income, Japanese and American elderly have the highest mean disposable income. Figure 1.1 also shows that, compared with younger Japanese (age 30 to 44), the elderly Japanese enjoy a higher per capita income after income redistribution. Figure 1.1 also shows that for elderly Japanese, aged 65 to 69, the per capita income, inclusive of social security transfer, is roughly 1.2 times that of per capita income before transfer. About 78 per cent of the elderly Japanese income comes from social security and pensions. Hence there was growing concern on inter-generational equity in that the asset-rich elderly were receiving massive income transfers from the younger generation through the pension system. It appears that there is cause for reduction of pensions. Apparently, the promise of a fixed replacement income for retirees under the current pension arrangement has put significant pressure on current and future working populations.

TABLE 1.1
Comparison of Elderly's Income (based on PPP), in US$ for mid-1990s

	Mean Disposable Income of Elderly	GDP per capita	Percentage of Seniors receiving below	
			$7,000	$10,000
Canada	17,000	21,000	1	11
Finland	12,000	19,000	7	41
Germany	14,000	20,000	8	27
Italy	13,000	20,000	20	45
Japan	18,000	23,000	14	26
Netherlands	12,000	19,000	9	51
Sweden	12,000	19,000	4	28
United Kingdom	12,000	19,000	17	53
United States	18,000	26,000	12	27

Source: Casey and Yamada (2002), Table 2.9, p. 43.

FIGURE 1.1
Per Capita Income by Age in Japan, 1989

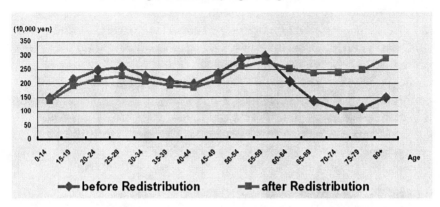

Source: Takayama (2002).

We shall next examine the Japanese pension system, highlighting the major challenges facing the system and the reforms taken to address these issues. The current pension system in Japan has a two-tier defined benefit system which is operated by the government, and is public. A third tier defined contribution plan was introduced in 2001 to complement the defined benefit plans.

First Pillar: The National Pension or Kokumin Nenkin (KN)

The first tier, known as the National Pension or Kokumin Nenkin (KN) or Basic Pension (Kiso Nenkin), has universal coverage and provides a flat-rate basic benefit to all sectors of the population. Participation in the first tier is mandatory to all residents aged 20 to 59. The premium is set at 13,300 yen (US$125) per month. However, low-income persons and non-working spouses of employees are exempt from paying premiums, partially or totally.[3] The full old age pension is payable after 40 years of contribution, provided the contributions were made before 60 years old. In fiscal year 2002, the Basic Pension scheme pays a maximum benefit of 66,200 yen (US$630) per month. Benefit payment under KN is independent of salary and wage earnings and is indexed annually to reflect changes in the consumer price index.

The KN operates as a partial, pay-as-you-go defined benefit (PAYG DB) programme. Two-thirds of the benefits are paid out from the collected premiums from the young and the remaining one-third is financed from the general government budget. In principle, benefit payments begin at age 65. However there is a special legal provision for earlier benefits payment at age 60.[4] Under the pension reform, there is a cut-back on the entitlement to full basic benefits for males aged below 65. The entitlement to full basic benefit is being phased out by stages between 2001 and 2013. The phasing out for female employees started five years later in 2006. Furthermore, as part of the reforms in the first-tier basic pension, pension benefits are no longer indexed to hikes in gross wages, but to net wages instead. Most pensioners will thus have benefit payments shaved by 1 per cent as CPI lags wage inflation by the same percentage.

Second Pillar: Employees' Pension Insurance or Kosei Nenkin Hoken (KNH)

The second tier consists of the Employees' Pension Insurance or Kosei Nenkin Hoken (KNH) and four types of Mutual Aid Pensions (Kyosai Nenkin). KNH provides benefits that are income-related and applies to employees of private companies, and mutual aid pensions apply to public service employees. The second tier operates largely like a pay-as-you-go (PAYG) defined benefit programme. Both employers and employees contribute 8.675 per cent of the employees' salary to the KNH. All workers are subject to the same contribution rate, with no discount given to low-income workers. However employers of female workers who are on maternity leave (up to one year) are exempt from contribution. Contribution to KNH is subject to a monthly salary ceiling of 590,000 yen. Benefits payments are related to the employee's salary, at an accrual rate of 0.5481 per cent for each year of contribution. Thus a subscriber who starts contributing to KNH at age 20 and is fully retired at age 60 would expect to receive 28.5 per cent of the career average monthly earnings after 40 years of contribution.

The career average monthly earnings are calculated over the employees' entire period of coverage, adjusted by a net wage index factor to reflect inflation. Unlike benefit payments under the first-tier KN, which is independent of salary and wage earnings, under the second-tier KHN, subscribers who continue to work after age 60 would have a 20 per cent reduction in benefits. For earnings exceeding 370,000 yen (which is the average salary of a male Japanese worker), the remaining 80 per cent benefit is subject to a negative benefit tax at an effective rate of 50 per cent, or at the rate of 10,000 yen for each 20,000-yen increase in earnings.[5]

Unlike the KN which operates as a partial PAYG, KNH is financed entirely by contributions of current workers with no support from the government's general revenue funds. Since 2001, the KNH has been facing huge current account deficits of 700 billion yen and in 2002, the deficit increased to 4.2 trillion yen. Unless reforms are introduced, the deficit in KNH is likely to persist.

According to Takayama (1998), Japan had a successful story with the PAYG defined benefit system when the economy was enjoying relatively high-speed growth with a relatively young population. PAYG has been effective in reducing poverty among the elderly and providing the elderly with a stable living standard after retirement. Furthermore, the operation of the system was relatively efficient with low administrative costs. However, with the slowing economy and stiffer economic competition, it was difficult to increase the contribution rate. As mentioned earlier, the first-tier, flat-rate basic benefit under KN is currently one third financed by general revenue, with the remaining two thirds by contribution. Sustainability thus becomes a major issue. Indeed in 1999, while social security tax revenue was three times the revenue of corporate income taxes and twice that of personal income taxes, the deficit from all social security programmes amounted to 600 trillion yen, which is equivalent to 1.2 times of the GDP. Putting things in perspective, Takayama (2003a) estimated that in 2003 the aggregate social security benefits was 44 trillion yen, constituting about 9 per cent of the Japanese GDP and was almost the economic size of the automobile industry at 40 trillion yen. It is believed that Japan cannot expect to rely on high growth rates and favourable demographic developments to finance the projected substantial increase in social security benefits in the coming decades. Moreover, there is a limit to the use of public debt to smooth revenue shortfalls without this having macro-economic impact.[6]

Another pension issue concerns the hollowing out of the national pension programme. The growing number of delinquent contributors who fail to pay premiums to the national pension programme has been interpreted as the growing public distrust in the pension system. In fiscal year 2002, delinquent contributors rose to a record number of 8.3 million, bringing the delinquent ratio to a record high of 37.2 per cent. Besides delinquent contributors, 12 million people have opted out of the programme. This implies a hollowing out of the pension programme as one in six members has opted out of financing the pension system. To restore public confidence and sustainability in the public pension system, the Social Security Council has been considering putting in place a system of carrot and stick. The carrot includes raising the government's share of contributions to the basic portion of the public pension system from the current level of 33.3 per cent to 50 per cent by fiscal year

2009. The stick consists of tougher punitive measures to collect premiums, such as, legally enforce the collection of premiums by seizing assets of delinquent members.

Japan has made many parametric changes to its pension system at fairly regular time intervals. Since fiscal year 1999, pension benefits under both KN and KNH are indexed to CPI instead of to wages. Historically, in Japan CPI lags wage inflation by 1 per cent, so indexing to CPI means a fall in pension benefits payments. Other reforms include increases in contribution rates, reduction in benefit payments, and postponing the pensionable age. For example, in March 1999, the government reduced the earnings-related benefits by 5 per cent from an annual accrual rate of 0.75 per cent to 0.7125 per cent. This took effect from fiscal year 2000. From fiscal year 2002, the benefit reduction under the KNH using the earnings-test, applies also to the elderly of age 65 to 69, instead of just the elderly of age 60 to 65. Another parametric reform is the postponement of the pensionable age. In the 1994 pension reform, the normal pensionable age for men under the first-tier KN is being increased in steps from 60 to 63, between fiscal years 2001 and 2013. And between 2013 and 2025, the normal pensionable age for KNH will be increased from age 60 to 65. There were also proposals to extend the contribution period before enjoying full-benefit payments from the current 40 to 45 years. However this proposal was turned down. It is estimated that the 1999/2000 reforms of reducing benefit levels, adopting CPI indexation of benefits, expanding the earnings-test base, and postponing the retirement age — which would cause the KNH obligations to peak at 27.8 per cent instead of the anticipated 34.5 per cent — had things left at status quo (see Takayama 2004).

Third Pillar: Defined Contribution Plan

Besides parametric changes, there is increasing pressure to add another pillar to complement the existing dual-tier defined benefits system: the flat-rate benefits first-tier KN and the earnings-related second-tier KNH. In 1 October 2001, Japan introduced a defined contribution (DC) plan, which is the Japanese version of the US 401(K) defined contribution plan, which pays benefits based on investment returns. As a fully-funded system, a private DC retirement savings account could possibly address the issues of financial sustainability and inter-generational equity and lead to a higher savings rate and labour force participation for the elderly.

Two types of DC pension plans are implemented, namely, the employer-sponsored type and the individual personal type. Under the employer-sponsored DC plan, only employers pay contributions to the plan for workers under the age of 60, with no matching contributions from employees. The contribution ceiling of the DC plan depends on the employers' participation in DB plans. Employers who are subscribers to a DB plan are limited to a ceiling contribution of 36,000 yen, compared with 18,000 yen for non-subscribers. Under the personal retirement account (PRA) plan, each individual could deposit 4 per cent of monthly earnings to the account. The contribution is subject to a ceiling of 68,000 yen and 15,000 yen for self-employed individuals and salaried employees respectively. The PRA is similar to the US 401(K) and employers cannot make matching contributions to the PRA.[7] The PRA contributions are tax-deductible and no tax is levied on the earned income during the phase of accumulation. Participation in PRA could commence at age 25 and continue till age 65, at which time, the PRA is converted to a constant-benefit lifetime annuity and is payable from then on.

However, the inherent advantages of the unfunded defined benefits (DB) system are the disadvantages of the funded DC system. The DC system lacks insurance elements and the accumulated fund depends on contributions, thus giving rise to adequacy issues (see Chia and Tsui 2003). Besides investment risks, the DC system is also subjected to inflation risks.

Other Options

There are numerous other options suggested by pension experts in Japan. The Ministry of Health, Labour and Wealth has shown interest in switching to a notional defined contribution plan (NDC). An NDC plan would mean that benefit payment is equivalent to contribution. However the switch to NDC is possible only after the KNH contribution rate reaches the peak level in 20 years. Others have suggested a partial funding shift to a consumption-based tax (see Takayama 2003).

RETIREMENT NEEDS: CALIBRATION OF PRESENT VALUE OF RETIREMENT CONSUMPTION

In this section we highlight the approaches taken to calibrate the post-retirement monthly expenses of the female and male elderly starting at age 65. The calibration involves forecasting the survival probabilities of these elderly using the Lee-Carter methodology, and choosing the appropriate discount factors. The present value of future expenses (*PVE*) is thus weighted by the survival probabilities of the elderly, conditional on survival at age 65. The *PVE* can be interpreted as the calibrated amount that each of the representative female and male elderly ought to have to support their monthly consumption during the post-retirement period beginning at 65. Assuming a maximum lifespan of 105 years, the present value of a stream of future expenses is given by:

$$PVE = \sum_{j=1}^{492} c_j v_j \, _j P_{65} \tag{1}$$

where

c_j = amount of calibrated expenditure for month j;
v_j = discount factor at month j; and
$_j P_{65}$ = probability of survival of individual starting at age 65 up to age (65 years and j months), respectively.

We note in passing that in our calibration of c_j and $_j P_{65}$, we differentiate the representative female from the male elderly cohorts. But for ease of notation, we do not append gender subscripts to the terms in equation (1). The procedure used to calibrate c_j, v_j and $_j P_{65}$ are discussed in the following subsections.

Calibration of Expenses

It is essential to distinguish the rapid growth rates of medical expenses from that of the relatively stable non-medical expenses. Table 1.2 shows the medical growth rates from 1980 to 1999. The key determinants of medical expenses of the elderly depend on the demographic and health sector-related factors. However, there are no published disaggregated data on the medical expenditure of the elderly by age and by sex. We resort to the recently available 1999 Household survey data covering 15,723 households in Japan. The monthly consumption of the elderly is divided into two major components: non-medical expenses and medical expenses. Non-medical consumption consists of basic necessities such as food, housing, fuel charges, furniture and household utensils, clothes and footwear, transportation and communication, education, reading and recreation, and other living expenditure. Table 1.3 displays the mean expenses of non-medical and medical consumption by age groups and by sex. As can be observed, on average, for all age groups above 65, the male elderly consume more than the female elderly in terms of both medical and non-medical expenses. The data are consistent with the annual medical expenses reported by Chia and Tsui (2003), based on a longitudinal survey conducted in Singapore for the elderly aged 66 and above.

TABLE 1.2
Medical Growth Rates and Sources of Growth

Year	Growth Rate			Sources	
	Medical Costs	Medical costs per capita	Real medical costs per capita	Population ageing	Others Natural increase
1980	9.4	8.6	8.6	1.0	7.5
1981	7.4	6.7	5.0	1.0	3.8
1982	7.7	7.0	7.0	1.2	5.7
1983	4.9	4.2	5.5	1.2	4.3
1984	3.8	3.2	5.2	1.2	4.0
1985	6.1	5.4	4.2	1.2	3.0
1986	6.6	6.1	5.4	1.2	4.1
1987	5.9	5.4	5.4	1.2	4.1
1988	3.8	3.4	2.9	1.3	1.6
1989	5.2	4.8	4.0	1.3	2.7
1990	4.5	4.2	3.2	1.6	1.5
1991	5.9	5.6	5.6	1.5	4.0
1992	7.6	7.3	4.8	1.6	3.0
1993	3.8	3.5	3.5	1.5	2.0
1994	5.9	5.7	3.8	1.5	2.1
1995	4.5	4.1	3.4	1.6	1.7
1996	5.8	5.6	4.8	1.7	3.0
1997	1.9	1.7	1.3	1.8	−0.5
1998	2.6	2.3	3.6	1.8	1.8
1999	3.7	3.5	3.5	1.6	1.9
2000	−1.9	−2.1	−2.3	1.7	−4.0
1980–2000	5.4	4.9	4.5	1.4	3.1

Source: Iwamoto (2003).

In the benchmark calibration, we set the annual growth rate of non-medical expenditure at 2 per cent and the per annum medical expenses growth rate at 4 per cent. In addition, Mayhem (2000), using the past 30 years' experiences of OECD countries, extrapolates the underlying growth rate of medical expenditure to be around 4 per cent. Our choice for the medical growth rate is based on the average growth rates of consumption expenditure of all households reported by the National Survey of Family Income and Expenditure (NSFIE) conducted over the period of 1984–1994.[8] Data from the Ministry of Health, Labour and Welfare show that the real per capita medical expenditure grew at a rate of 4.5 per cent per

TABLE 1.3
Annual Medical and Non-medical Expenditures

Age Group	Medical Expenditure		Non- Medical Expenditure	
	Female	Male	Female	Male
65–69	109.5	151.0	3,039.8	3,554.5
70–74	107.8	138.8	2,729.3	3,253.8
75–79	87.8	11.2	2,337.5	3,012.1
80+	108.4	133.0	2,492.4	2,721.9

Note: Figures are in 1,000 yen.
Source: NSFIE 1999, Japan.

annum from 1980 to 1999 (Iwamoto 2003). Growth in medical cost expenditure could be due to an ageing population or from medical cost growth. The former is estimated by holding the medical cost of each age group constant and allowing population structure to change. Iwamoto reports that the annual growth rate that is attributed to the change in population growth rate was 1.4 per cent from 1980 to 1997 and the residual of 3.1 per cent is attributed to the change in medical technology. Hence population ageing contributed a 27 per cent increase in the real per capita medical cost. The medical expenditure growth rates are incorporated in the calibration of future expenses.

The calibration of future expenses involves two steps. First, we begin with a representative elderly at age 65, who will be 105 after 41 years. The nominal expenditure at age $(65 + t)$ in year $(2004 + t)$, $(t = 0, 1, 2, 3, ..., 40)$ is obtained by the product of the base expenditure corresponding to age $(65 + t)$ and the cumulative factor at a constant annual growth rate of 4 per cent for the medical expenses, and 2 per cent for the non-medical expenses, respectively. Second, we obtain the expenditure in month j at age $(65 + j)$ by taking the monthly average of the calibrated health care expenditure within that particular year. This procedure applies to both the medical expenses and the non-medical expenses using the base expenditures at various age groups. The present value of consumption expenses for the elderly by sex at age 65 is then obtained by discounting the corresponding calibrated stream of future monthly sums of medical and non-medical expenses, weighted by the survival probability of the elderly over the entire post-retirement period. The choice of discount rates and forecasts of the survival probability of the elderly by sex and by age will be discussed in sub-sections 3.2 and 3.3 respectively.

To study the robustness of the estimated *PVE*, we use annual growth rates of medical expenditure of 2 per cent, 3 per cent, 5 per cent, 6 per cent and 7 per cent. The lower rate could be interpreted as the medical growth rate due to population ageing and the higher rates incorporate the medical growth rates due to population ageing and higher medical costs. The growth rates of non-medical expenses are set at 1 per cent and 3 per cent, respectively. Similar to the benchmark case, the stream of future monthly consumption expenditures at alternative growth rates are calibrated accordingly.

Discount Rates

Many studies use constant short-term rates to discount future cash flows. For example, Chen and Wong (1998) take a constant rate of 4 per cent, while Doyle et al. (2001) assume a 5 per cent nominal interest rate. In contrast, Lachance and Mitchell (2002), and Chia and Tsui (2003) employ the one-factor stochastic model developed by Cox, Ingersoll and Ross (1985) to generate discount rates. In this chapter we do not use stochastic models to generate short-term interest rates mainly because an almost zero short-term interest rate policy was implemented in Japan since 1996. Instead, we use two deterministic interest rate models to discount future cash flows. They are the constant yield curve (CYC) model and the fixed yield curve (FYC) model. The CYC uses a flat annual rate to discount all future cash flows. Choices include 1 per cent, 2 per cent, 3 per cent, 4 per cent and 5 per cent, respectively. Alternatively, the FYC is constructed based on the average of historical rates for government bonds across different durations to maturity since 1990. They comprise 0.25 per cent for 1-year bills, 1.63 per cent for 2-year bonds, 2.11 per cent for 3-year bonds, 2.44 per cent for 4-year bonds, 2.67 per cent for 5-year bonds, 1.12 per cent for 6-year bonds, 3.09 per cent for 7-year bonds, 1.49 per cent for 8-year bonds, 1.38 per cent for 9-year bonds, 3.38 per cent for 10-year bonds, 2.56 per cent for 15-year bonds, 3.01 per cent for 20-year bonds and 2.20 per cent for 30-year bonds, respectively. We use the 30-year rate as proxy for spot rates with longer durations. Spot rates for other durations below 30 years are obtained by the method of interpolation. These spot rates are converted into discount factors using the standard formulae for compound interest rates.

Survival Probabilities

Appropriate life tables are required to compute the present value of consumption expenses of the elderly starting age 65. We follow the procedure in Chia and Tsui (2003) to construct the complete cohort life tables using the 41 available life tables in Japan from 1962 to 2002. The construction takes three main steps. First, we have to predict the future mortality rates of the elderly based on the available life tables. Assume that the maximum lifespan of the representative Japanese elderly is 105 years. The elderly who are aged 65 in year 2004 will be 105 after 41 years. The following Lee-Carter (LC) model (1992, 2000) is employed to fit mortality rates for the male and female elderly from age 65 to 85:

$$ln\ m_{xt} = a_x + b_x\ k_t + \varepsilon_{xt} \tag{2}$$

$$k_t = \mu + \varphi\ k_{t-1} + \eta_t \tag{3}$$

where m_{xt} is the central death rate in age class x in year t; a_x is the additive age-specific constant, reflecting the general shape of the age schedule; b_x is the responsiveness of mortality at age class x to variations in the general level; k_t is a time-specific index of the general level of mortality; μ and φ are parameters; ε_{xt} is the error to the actual age schedule, assumed to follow a normal distribution with zero mean and a constant variance; and η_t is the white noise. The long-term patterns of the natural logarithm of central death rates are captured by the single time-specific index of mortality k_t. A lower order autoregressive process is included to absorb the dynamic relationship of k_t between time ($t - 1$) and t. The interpolation procedure developed by Wilmoth (1995) is employed to calibrate the level of mortality for those elderly aged above 85. Second, based on the predicted mortality rates obtained from Step 1, we obtain the cohort life tables using techniques developed by Bourbeau et al. (1997). Third, the annual mortality rates are in turn converted to monthly cohort survival rates by assuming that the mortality rates at fractional ages between age x and age $x+1$ follow a uniform distribution. The survival probabilities conditional on age 65 are computed separately for each representative female and male elderly on a monthly basis. Detailed discussions are provided in Chia and Tsui (2003).

ESTIMATION RESULTS

The amount that the elderly ought to have in order to sustain their post-retirement expenses is estimated using equations (1) to (3). All computations and estimations in this paper are coded in Gauss. We obtain values of the estimated *PVE* under different combinations of interest rates, growth rates of medical and non-medical expenses, and cohort survival probabilities by age and by sex. They include various medical expenditure growth rates, r_m, at 2 per cent, 3 per cent, 4 per cent, 5 per cent, 6 per cent and 7 per cent; and non-medical growth rates at 1 per cent, 2 per cent and 3 per cent. Tables 1.4–1.6 display the estimated values of PVE for the female and male elderly under different medical and non-medical growth rates and under the constant and fixed yield curve models, respectively. As can be observed, the estimated values of PVE using the constant yield curve (CYC) model at flat rate (1 per cent, 2 per cent, 3 per cent, 4 per cent and 5 per cent) decrease when the interest rate increases. The estimated values of PVE by the fixed yield curve (FYC) model for both the female and the male elderly are close to the average of the estimated PVE under the fixed yield model. This pattern is robust across different medical and non-medical growth rates.

As can be gleaned from Table 1.5, the estimated values of PVE for the female elderly are consistently greater than that of the male elderly. For example, under the benchmark scenario (i.e., 2 per cent non-medical growth rate, 4 per cent medical growth rate, and 2 per cent mean interest rate), the estimated PVE for the female elderly is 71.269 million yen, and 66.776 million yen for the male elderly. And under the fixed yield curve model, the estimated PVE for the female elderly is 65.041 million yen, and 61.668 million yen for the male elderly. Such a difference may be partially explained by the longer life expectancy of the female elderly. A similar pattern is observed for the female and male elderly regardless of the non-medical and medical growth rates and the interest rates models.

Besides the female and male elderly, we also calibrate the amount the joint elderly ought to have to sustain their consumption expenses during the post-retirement period. To estimate the PVE for the joint elderly, we adjust two components on the right hand side of equation (1). They are the future cash flows and the survival probabilities conditional on age 65. The stream of future monthly expenses for the joint elderly is approximated by adding those of the individual elderly. The joint survival probabilities for the elderly couple are obtained by the product of survival rates of the female and male elderly. For convenience, we assume that the couples are of the same age and that events of deaths are independent in probability. The estimated PVE for the joint elderly could be interpreted as the weighted average of the estimated PVE for the individual female and male elderly.

Turning to the elasticity analysis, we find relative uniformity in responses of the estimated PVE to a unit change across growth rates of medical expenses and non-medical expenses, and interest rates for the female, male and joint elderly.[9] For example, a 1 per cent increase in growth rates of medical expenses leads to a 0.046 per cent increase in PVE for the female elderly in

TABLE 1.4
PVE for the Elderly under Different Interest Rates Models

Scenario	Model	Female	Male
[a] 1% non-medical growth rate			
Medical growth rates			
$r_m = 2\%$	CYC1	71,275	66,780
	CYC2	62,203	59,496
	CYC3	54,842	53,435
	CYC4	48,811	48,349
	CYC5	43,820	44,047
	FYC	57,141	55,281
$r_m = 3\%$	CYC1	71,955	67,148
	CYC2	62,751	59,798
	CYC3	55,288	53,686
	CYC4	49,176	48,559
	CYC5	44,123	44,225
	FYC	57,617	55,546
$r_m = 4\%$	CYC1	72,794	67,594
	CYC2	63,422	60,162
	CYC3	55,829	53,986
	CYC4	49,617	48,809
	CYC5	44,486	44,435
	FYC	58,198	55,861
$r_m = 5\%$	CYC1	73,836	68,136
	CYC2	64,249	60,602
	CYC3	56,492	54,345
	CYC4	50,153	49,105
	CYC5	44,924	44,680
	FYC	58,913	56,241
$r_m = 6\%$	CYC1	75,137	68,797
	CYC2	65,274	61,134
	CYC3	57,306	54,778
	CYC4	50,807	49,460
	CYC5	45,454	44,973
	FYC	59,798	56,700
$r_m = 7\%$	CYC1	76,765	69,607
	CYC2	66,548	61,783
	CYC3	58,314	55,302
	CYC4	51,610	49,887
	CYC5	46,100	45,324
	FYC	60,897	57,258

Notes: PVE for the female, male elderly are computed using two yield curve models. CYCI (I = 1, 2, 3, 4, 5) is the flat yield curve at 1 per cent, 2 per cent, 3 per cent, 4 per cent and 5 per cent, respectively; and FYC is the fixed yield curve based on the mean spot rates of government bonds with various durations. All figures are in 1000 yen.

TABLE 1.5
***PVE* for the Elderly under Different Interest Rates Models**

Scenario	Model	Female	Male
[b] 2% non-medical growth rate			
Medical growth rates			
r_m = 2%	CYC1	81,756	75,146
	CYC2	70,721	66,473
	CYC3	61,883	59,306
	CYC4	54,603	53,331
	CYC5	48,665	48,308
	FYC	64,565	61,404
r_m = 3%	CYC1	82,436	75,515
	CYC2	71,269	66,776
	CYC3	62,278	59,557
	CYC4	54,968	53,541
	CYC5	48,969	48,485
	FYC	65,041	61,668
r_m = 4%	CYC1	83,275	75,961
	CYC2	71,940	67,140
	CYC3	62,820	59,857
	CYC4	55,410	53,790
	CYC5	49,332	48,694
	FYC	65,622	61,984
r_m = 5%	CYC1	84,318	76,503
	CYC2	72,767	67,579
	CYC3	63,483	60,217
	CYC4	55,946	54,087
	CYC5	49,769	48,940
	FYC	66,337	62,354
r_m = 6%	CYC1	85,618	77,164
	CYC2	73,791	68,112
	CYC3	64,297	60,649
	CYC4	56,600	54,442
	CYC5	50,299	49,234
	FYC	67,222	62,823
r_m = 7%	CYC1	87,246	77,974
	CYC2	75,066	68,762
	CYC3	65,305	61,173
	CYC4	57,403	54,869
	CYC5	50,945	59,585
	FYC	68,322	63,382

Notes: PVE for the female, male elderly are computed using two yield curve models. CYCI (I = 1, 2, 3, 4, 5) is the flat yield curve at 1 per cent, 2 per cent, 3 per cent, 4 per cent and 5 per cent, respectively; and FYC is the fixed yield curve based on the mean spot rates of government bonds with various durations. All figures are in 1000 yen.

TABLE 1.6
PVE for the Elderly under Different Interest Rates Models

Scenario	Model	Female	Male
[c] 3% non-medical growth rate			
Medical growth rates			
$r_m = 2\%$	CYC1	94,612	85,141
	CYC2	81,089	74,750
	CYC3	70,276	66,221
	CYC4	61,545	59,158
	CYC5	54,428	53,260
	FYC	73,575	68,638
$r_m = 3\%$	CYC1	95,293	85,510
	CYC2	81,636	75,053
	CYC3	70,721	66,473
	CYC4	61,911	59,369
	CYC5	54,730	53,437
	FYC	74,051	68,900
$r_m = 4\%$	CYC1	96,132	85,956
	CYC2	82,307	75,417
	CYC3	71,263	66,773
	CYC4	62,352	59,618
	CYC5	55,094	53,646
	FYC	74,631	69,216
$r_m = 5\%$	CYC1	97,174	86,497
	CYC2	83,135	75,857
	CYC3	71,926	67,132
	CYC4	62,888	59,915
	CYC5	55,531	53,893
	FYC	75,347	69,596
$r_m = 6\%$	CYC1	98,475	87,158
	CYC2	84,159	76,389
	CYC3	72,740	67,565
	CYC4	63,542	60,270
	CYC5	56,061	54,186
	FYC	76,232	70,055
$r_m = 7\%$	CYC1	100,103	87,969
	CYC2	85,433	77,039
	CYC3	73,747	68,090
	CYC4	64,345	60,697
	CYC5	56,708	54,537
	FYC	77,332	70,613

Notes: PVE for the female, male elderly are computed using two yield curve models. CYCI (I = 1, 2, 3, 4, 5) is the flat yield curve at 1 per cent, 2 per cent, 3 per cent, 4 per cent and 5 per cent, respectively; and FYC is the fixed yield curve based on the mean spot rates of government bonds with various durations. All figures are in 1000 yen.

the benchmark scenario under the 2 per cent CYC model, 0.044 per cent under the FYC model; a 0.026 per cent increase in *PVE* for the male elderly under the CYC model and 0.024 per cent under the FYC model; and a corresponding 0.025 per cent under the CYC model and a 0.023 per cent under the FYC model for the joint elderly, respectively. Moreover, a 1 per cent increase in growth rates of non-medical expenses leads to a 0.29 per cent increase in *PVE* for the female elderly in the benchmark scenario under the CYC model and 0.28 per cent under the FYC model; a 0.25 per cent increase in *PVE* for the male elderly under CYC model and 0.23 per cent under the FYC model; and a corresponding 0.21 per cent under the CYC model and a 0.20 per cent under the FYC model for the joint elderly, respectively. Furthermore, a 1 per cent increase in the flat rate of the CYC model leads to a 0.25 per cent decrease in *PVE* for the female elderly in the benchmark scenario; a 0.24 per cent decrease in *PVE* for the male elderly; and a corresponding 0.21 per cent decrease in *PVE* for the joint elderly.

CONCLUSION

In this paper we have computed the present value of expenses that the female and male elderly Japanese will probably ought to incur to cover their consumption needs in the post-retirement period. Our estimation consists of three components: the subsistence needs and the health care expenditures, the survival probabilities conditional on living at age 65, and two deterministic term structure of interest rates serving as discount factors. Comparing the *PVE* with preliminary calculations of the retirement wealth indicates that the existing pension provision is indeed generous and is more than adequate to meet retirement needs. However, the Japanese government faces two major economic challenges: a relatively generous, unfunded pension system with a rapidly ageing population requires policy changes; large fiscal deficits have driven the stock of government debt up sharply, and in a way that is not sustainable. For example, in a recent paper, Miles and Cerny (2003) assess the macro-economic impact of deficit financing and pension reform, and analyse how the interaction between these bears on the welfare of different cohorts. Future research works on Japanese pension reforms should focus on sustainability issues.

Notes

*   Acknowledgements:
     This paper was presented on 22–23 November 2004 at the Workshop on Ageing
     and the Status of the Older Population in Southeast Asia, organized by the

Institute of Southeast Asians Studies, Singapore. We would like to thank Kyosuke Kurita for statistical assistance; the Japanese Society for Promotion of Science and Sumitomo Foundation for providing research support. All remaining errors are ours.

1   Ministry of Health, Labour and Welfare, Japan, website.

2   Takayama and Kitamura (1994) also find evidence of substantial inter-generational transfers from micro data in the National Survey of Family Income and Expenditure.

3   1,000 yen = US$9.5 = Euro 7.3

4   Basic pension may be claimed at any age between 60 and 70 years, subject to actuarial reduction (increase) if a claim is made before (after) age 65 years.

5   For details see Takayama (2003*a*).

6   Miles and Cerny (2003) use calibrated overlapping generations to examine the impact of deficit-financed policy reforms in the pension systems on different cohorts, particularly if the pension contribution rates are not raised sufficiently to balance pension revenues and spending.

7   Civil servants and full-time housewives are not eligible to participate in the DC pension plans.

8   The consumption expenditure of all households aged 65 and above based on the NSFIE are reported in Table 3 of Kitamura, Takayama and Arita (2001). We assume that the consumption expenditure consists of medical and non-medical expenditure and that the non-medical expenditure grows rather slowly. Hence we may approximate the growth rates of medical expenses by the growth rates of consumption expenditure. The average rate is 3.8 per cent per annum.

9   We expect a positive relationship between *PVE* and the growth rate of medical and non-medical expenses; and a negative relationship between *PVE* and the interest rate used to discount a stream of future expenses. The latter is due to the time value of money.

References

Bourbeau, R., J. Legare and V. Emond. "New Birth Cohort Life Tables for Canada and Quebec", *Demographic Document* No. 3, Demography Division, Statistics Canada, 1997.

Casey, B. and A. Yamada. "Getting Older, Getting Poorer? A Study of Earnings, Pensions, Assets and Living Arrangements of Older People in Nine Countries". Paris: OECD, 2002.

Chen, R. and K.A. Wong. "The Adequacy of the CPF Account for Retirement Benefits in Singapore". *Singapore International Insurance and Actuarial Journal* 19, no. 2 (1998): 1–16.

Chia, N.C. and A.K.C. Tsui. "Life Annuities of Compulsory Savings and Income Adequacy of the Elderly in Singapore". *Journal of Pension Economics and Finance*, March 2003.

Cox, J.C., J.E. Ingersoll and S.A. Ross. "A Theory of the Term Structure of Interest Rates". *Econometrica* 53 (1985): 385–407.

Doyle S., O.S. Mitchell and J. Piggott. "Annuity Values in DC Retirement Systems: The Cases of Singapore and Australia". NBER Working Paper 8091, National Bureau of Economic Research, Cambridge, Massachusetts, 2001.

Hurd, M.D. and N. Yashiro. *The Economic Effects of Aging in the United States and Japan*. Chicago: The University of Chicago Press, 1997.

Horioka, C.Y. *Are the Japanese Unique? An Analysis of Consumption and Saving Behaviour in Japan*. Osaka University, The Institute of Social and Economic Research, Discussion Paper No. 606, 2004.

———— and W. Watanabe. "Why do People Save? A Micro-analysis of Motives for Household Saving in Japan". *Economic Journal* 107 (1997): 537–52.

Ishikawa, T. and Y. Yajima. "Savings, Consumption and Real Assets of the Elderly in Japan and the U.S. — How the Existing Home Market Can Boost Consumption". NLI Research Institute, No. 149, 2001.

Iwamoto, Y. Issues in Japanese Health Policy and Medical Expenditure, mimeo, 2003.

Kitamura, Y., N. Takayama and F. Arita. "Household Saving and Wealth Distribution in Japan". In *Life Cycle Savings and Public Policy*, Axel Boersch-Supan, ed., pp. 147–201. San Diego: Academic Press, 2003.

Lachance, M.E. and O. Mitchell. Guaranteeing Defined Contribution Pensions: The Options to Buy-back a Defined Benefit Promise. *NBER Working Paper 8731*, 2002.

Lee, R.D. "The Lee-Carter Method for Forecasting Mortality with Various Extensions and Applications". *North American Actuarial Journal* 4, no. 1 (2000): 80–91.

———— and L. Carter. "Modeling and Forecasting the Time Series of U.S. Mortality". *Journal of the American Statistical Association* 87 (1992): 659–71.

Mayhew, L. "Health and Elderly Care Expenditure in Aging World", International Institute for Applied Systems Analysis, Laxenburg, Austria, 2000.

Miles, D. and A. Cerny. "Managing Japanese Pension and Debt Liabilities: Reform with and without the Use of Fiscal Deficits". <http://www.esri.go.jp/en/prj-rc/macro/macro14-e.html> (2003).

Ministry of Health, Labour and Welfare, Japan. <http://www.mhlw.go.jp/english/database/db-hw/lifetb03/1.html>.

Mitchell, O.S. and J. Piggott. "Unlocking Housing Equity in Japan". *National Bureau of Economic Research,* Working Paper 10340, 2004.

Noguchi, Y. "Improvement of After-Retirement Income by Home Equity Conversion Mortgages: Possibilities and Problems in Japan". In *The Economic Effects of Aging in the United States and Japan*, Hurd M.D. and N. Yashiro, eds., 1997.

Takayama, N. *The Greying of Japan: An Economic Perspective on Public Pensions*. Tokyo: Kinokuniya, and Oxford: Oxford University Press, 1992.

————. *The Morning After in Japan: Its Declining Population, Too Generous Pensions and a Weakened Economy*. Tokyo: Maruzen, 1998.

————. *Never-ending Reforms of Social Security in Japan*, 2003*a*.

————, ed. *Taste of Pie: Searching for Better Pension Provisions in Developed Countries*. Japan: Maruzen Co. Ltd, 2003.

————. A Balance Sheet Approach to Reforming Social Security Pensions in Japan. A paper presented at the joint PBC-IMF Seminar on China's Monetary Policy Transmission Mechanism, Beijing, 12–13 April 2004.

———— and Y. Kitamura. "Household Saving Behaviour in Japan". In *International Comparisons of Household Saving*, Poterba, ed., pp. 161–89. Chicago: University of Chicago Press, 1994.

Wilmoth, J.R. "Are Mortality Rates Falling at Extremely High Ages? An Investigation Based on a Model Proposed by Coale and Kisker". *Population Studies* 49 (1995): 281–95.

2

THE CENTRAL PROVIDENT FUND AND FINANCING RETIREMENT NEEDS OF ELDERLY SINGAPOREANS

Chia Ngee Choon

INTRODUCTION

Many Singaporeans depend exclusively on a fully funded mandatory defined contribution (DC) social security system. The system, which is based on individual accounts, is administered and managed by the Central Provident Fund (CPF) Board, a statutory board under the Ministry of Manpower. The advantage of a DC system is that it links benefits closely to contributions, hence minimizing the disincentive effects of evasion and early retirement. Not only does this explicit link make the social security system less sensitive to demographic changes, it also avoids the problems of sustainability and the political costs of unrealistic benefit promises. Besides, it ensures individual equity and avoids intergenerational inequity. While there are fiscal advantages, savings available for post-retirement consumption expenses depend on the total accumulated amount and its returns. Moreover, the absence of mandatory annuitization exposes the individual elderly to the risk of outliving resources due to longevity. This risk is exacerbated as savings are allowed to be withdrawn before retirement for housing finance and other investments.

To assess the adequacy of retirement savings, it is important to investigate the accumulation and de-cumulation mechanism of these mandatory savings under the Central Provident Fund System. In the next section, the main features of the CPF system are critically reviewed. Section 3 examines the adequacy of the accumulation of the mandatory savings to finance the retirement needs of the elderly.[1] Instead of emphasizing the mechanism of accumulation, the expenditure side of the lifetime budget of the elderly is modeled and the retirement needs in terms of the present value of retirement consumption (PVRC) is estimated. The estimation is obtained by simulations through three major components: calibration of subsistence and medical expenses of the elderly; forecast of cohort survival probability by age and by sex; and generation of yield curves to discount future cash flows. The simulation study indicates that the existing CPF-decreed minimum sum is inadequate to meet the future consumption needs of the female elderly. The inadequacy becomes more severe at higher medical expense growth rates.

The unique way of financing housing through the mandatory savings system in Singapore has created a class of "asset rich and cash poor" Singaporeans. The question that begs analysis is whether there is a mechanism to unlock housing equities. In section 4, we attempt to examine reverse mortgages (RM) as an alternative financing instrument.[2] We will draw policy implications from simulation results in Chia and Tsui (2004), which show that RM instruments are likely to replace about 50 per cent of the median salary of 4-room public housing dwellers. However, the market may be missing from the supply side, thus suggesting a transformed role for the government from being a public housing provider to a RM supplier.

SOME UNIQUE FEATURES OF CPF

The CPF was instituted in 1955 as a mandatory retirement savings scheme for all employees, both public and private, in Singapore. It is mandatory for both employees and employers to make monthly contributions to the Fund.[3] The contribution amount is set in proportion to the employees' monthly wage, with lower rates for older workers. Table 2.1 shows the CPF contribution rates as of January 2005. The employers' CPF contribution rate is currently set at 13 per cent of monthly salary for workers aged below 50, while rates for workers above 50 range from 3.5 per cent to 11 per cent. The employee's contribution is set at 20 per cent of the monthly salary for workers below 50 years old and range from 5 per cent to 19 per cent for those above 50. Contributions by both the employers and employees are exempted from the employee's personal income tax. The salary ceiling for CPF contributions

TABLE 2.1

Rates of Contribution and Allocation of Contribution as of January 2005

Employee Age (years)	Contribution By Employer (% of wage)	Contribution By Employee (% of wage)	Total Contribution (% of wage)	Credited Into		
				Ordinary Account %	Special Account %	Medisave Account %
35 & below	13	20	33	22	5	6
35 – 45	13	20	33	20	6	7
45 – 50	13	20	33	18	7	8
50 – 55	11	19	30	15	7	8
55 – 60	6	12.5	18.5	10.5	0	8
60 – 65	3.5	7.5	11	2.5	0	8.5
Above 65	3.5	5	8.5	0	0	8.5

Notes: All figures are in percentage of wage for workers with a wage of at least $750 per month. Contribution rates are subject to a salary ceiling of $5,000 in January 2005.
Source: CPF website at http://www.cpf.gov.sg

from monthly salary is currently set at $5,000. It will be reduced to $4,500 from 2006 onwards.[4]

Given the high compulsory savings rate, one issue is whether CPF has crowded out private savings. Lim et al. (1988) held that "private saving is mainly CPF saving". Various authors have estimated that CPF contributions roughly constituted a quarter of the Gross Domestic Savings (GDS).[5] Singapore has one of the highest GDS to GDP ratio in the world, which stands at around 50 per cent for the 1990s. In general, in East Asian countries, between 1984 and 1993, savings averaged almost 30 per cent of disposable incomes. In the OECD countries, savings declined from more than 25 per cent of gross national disposable income in 1965 to less than 20 per cent in 1995 (World Bank 1999).

An individual's contribution to the CPF is credited into three accounts: ordinary account, special account, and medical savings (Medisave) account. Table 2.1 shows the apportionment of the contribution to the various accounts. The ordinary account earns a CPF interest rate which is pegged to the average of 12-month fixed deposit rates of local banks' rate. The special and Medisave accounts enjoy an additional 1.25 per cent above the normal CPF rate. Savings in the three accounts are earmarked for different uses. Savings in the ordinary account can be used to finance housing purchases, investments in approved shares and stocks, and to finance children's tertiary education. The special account is earmarked for retirement. Medisave account is used to meet hospitalization and medical expenses, and for paying premiums for health insurance, such as the national catastrophic health insurance under Medishield and other private medical insurance.

The utilization of savings by CPF members has evolved and liberalized over the past three decades. Prior to 1977, all CPF contributions were credited into one account. In 1977, the special account was set up for retirement and cannot be withdrawn before retirement. However, although the total contribution rate was 31 per cent in 1977, only 1 per cent was earmarked for the special account. This amount increased steadily and reached a maximum of 6 per cent in 1983. Thereafter the rates dropped and stabilized at 4 per cent in the 1990s. Ironically, although CPF was initially designed for retirement, only a small proportion was allocated to the special account which seems to suggest that savings for retirement had been accorded the lowest priority. In addition, during the economic recession of 1985–1986 and the subsequent economic adjustment period of 1987–1988, and more recently during the Asian financial crisis from 1997–1999, contribution to the special account was suspended. Furthermore, savings from the special account was liberalized and could be withdrawn even before retirement to finance housing mortgages. It has also been acknowledged that the pre-retirement withdrawal scheme for properties has led to over-investment in these assets. The key role of CPF to finance old age needs to be revisited. The use of one instrument to achieve multiple social objectives has eroded its primary objective of providing for retirement.

Unlike the special account, savings in the ordinary account are allowed to be withdrawn even before retirement. Since 1968, CPF savings have been allowed to be withdrawn for mortgage payments of public housing. In 1981, the pre-retirement withdrawal was extended to mortgage payments for private residential properties. Presently, about 80 per cent of the population lives in public housing developed by the Housing Development Board (HDB). In the initial years in the 1960s, HDB borrowed from the CPF for its development expenditure budget, thus solving the financing problems on the supply side. Allowing CPF savings to be used as down-payments and payments of housing mortgages helped resolve some of the financing problems on the demand side. It is therefore not surprising that about 72 per cent of the total CPF balance has been withdrawn by individuals to finance home mortgages (CPF, 2003). Table 2.2 compares the annual total amount contributed to the CPF with the amount withdrawn to finance home mortgages for both public housing and private residential properties. Indeed, in 1999, the amount withdrawn (S$15,720m) was higher than the amount contributed ($12,827m)

TABLE 2.2
Withdrawals for Housing and Contributions to CPF, 1999–2003 ($ million)

Year	Withdrawals under Public Housing Scheme	Withdrawals under Residential Properties Scheme	Total Withdrawals for Housing	Total Contributions to CPF
1999	10,235.0	5,485.8	15,720.8	12,827
2000	8,208.5	4,237.9	12,446.4	14,093
2001	8,330.7	3,676.5	12,007.2	18,322
2002	8,219.5	3,693.8	11,913.3	16,166
2003	6,849.5	3,069.3	9,918.8	15,870

Source: CPF, Annual Report 2003.

to the fund. This is because given the economic hardship at that time, savings in the special account were used to meet housing mortgage obligations caused by a shortfall in the ordinary account due to unemployment. As can be gleaned from Table 2.2, following economic recovery, contributions to CPF now exceed the total withdrawals for housing.

Besides being allowed to be used for housing payments, as part of asset enhancement, CPF savings in the ordinary account are also allowed to be withdrawn for investment in approved shares, stock, unit trusts and gold. Initially, the full amount in the ordinary account could not be withdrawn for investment as it was necessary to set aside a minimum amount. However, as of January 2001, this rule was relaxed. Moreover, further liberalization allows savings in the special account to be used for investment in retirement-related financial instruments such as fixed deposits, unit trusts, insurance products and Singapore government bonds.

Not only are CPF savings used to finance housing and investments, they are also harnessed to finance health care. In anticipation of the rising public sector burden from health care financing because of an ageing population, an individual medical savings account, also known as Medisave, was introduced in 1984. Medisave operates as a pre-funded savings scheme for financing health expenditure and is basically a self-insurance scheme without risk-pooling. In 1990, this was supplemented by a health insurance for catastrophic illnesses under Medishield. Premiums for Medishield can be paid out from the medical savings account.

As funds in the CPF accounts can be withdrawn even before one retires, the CPF scheme is no longer a mere savings vehicle for old age security and maintenance. Indeed, this unique feature of pre-retirement withdrawal has transformed the retirement scheme into an instrument to achieve other social objectives: such as enhancing an individual's asset holdings, financing merit goods and fine tuning the economy. For example, during the economic recessions of 1985/1986 and 1997/98, in order to maintain economic competitiveness, the mandatory employers' contribution rate was cut to lower labour costs. In addition, savings in the retirement account were allowed to be withdrawn to make up for the shortfall or non-contribution to the ordinary account due to reductions in employers' contributions to CPF, wage cuts, and job losses, etc.

Because of longer life expectancy and increased dependency ratio, the mandatory retirement age was raised from 55 to 60 in 1993 and was further lifted to 62 in 1999. When CPF was instituted in 1955, the withdrawal age was set at the mandatory retirement age of 55. With the subsequent lifting of the retirement age, one policy debate was whether to put the CPF withdrawal age in tandem with the retirement age. A compromise reached is to keep the withdrawal age at 55, but to create a Minimum Sum Scheme. Under this scheme, members have to set aside a CPF-decreed minimum to ensure an adequate subsistence living upon retirement. As of July 2005, the decreed minimum is set at S$88,000. The minimum sum will be raised by $4,000 yearly to reach $120,000 (in 2003 dollars) in 2013. Members may use their properties to pledge up to 50 per cent of the minimum sum, with the remaining in cash. Married couples can jointly set aside 1.5 times the decreed sum if they nominate each other as beneficiaries for the remaining amounts upon death, and such nominations cannot be revoked. Once the member reaches 55 years old, the minimum sum can be invested in three different ways: [1] to buy life annuity from an approved insurance company, which will yield monthly income for life; [2] deposit the amount with approved banks; or [3] let the CPF Board keep the amount, which will yield monthly payouts until the minimum sum is exhausted. According to published data in the CPF Annual Report, of those who turned age 55 in 2000, 16 per cent bought life annuity, 19 per cent left the sum with the banks or the CPF Board. A significant 30 per cent had to pledge their property since all their retirement savings were fully "plastered on the walls", and the remaining 35 per cent either did not have the minimum sum to set aside or had other reasons not to do so (CPF, 2000a).

In July 2003, when the decreed sum was set at $80,000, 61.4 per cent of those CPF members who were aged 55 and above at that time, had CPF balances of more than S$80,000 (see Table 2.3). The picture portrayed thus seems not so pessimistic — only 38.6 per cent had balances below S$80,000. However, the numbers presented in Table 2.3 are regrossed balances which do not exactly represent the resources available for retirement. The regrossed

TABLE 2.3
Distribution of Regrossed Balances (include withdrawn amounts)
by Age Groups

| Balance | % of members | | | | | Active |
	>40–45	>45–50	>50–55	>55–60	60+	Members
Below 1,000	0.2	0.1	0.1	0.3	2.4	2.0
1K to below 5K	0.7	0.6	0.6	2.2	9.7	4.2
5K to below 10K	0.9	1.0	1.2	2.3	9.2	3.6
10K to below 20K	2.2	2.4	2.5	4.5	12.6	5.9
20K to below 30K	2.4	2.7	2.8	5.4	11.9	5.3
30K to below 40K	2.7	2.9	3.0	5.0	8.6	4.9
40K to below 50K	2.8	2.9	3.0	4.7	8.2	4.6
50K to below 60K	2.8	2.9	2.9	4.6	7.0	4.4
60K to below 70K	2.7	2.8	2.9	4.8	6.0	4.2
70K to below 80K	2.8	2.7	2.8	4.7	4.9	4.0
80K to below 90K	2.9	2.7	2.7	4.5	3.7	3.9
90K to below 100K	2.9	2.6	2.6	4.9	2.9	3.8
100K to below 150K	16.1	12.8	11.9	18.8	6.3	15.7
150K & above	58.2	60.9	61.1	33.2	6.5	33.5
All Groups	100.0	100.0	100.0	100.0	100.0	100.0

Source: CPF Annual Report, 2003.

balances include amounts that have been withdrawn by CPF members either for financing housing or for investment in financial assets.

Even if CPF members do have an accumulated sum of $80,000 at retirement, the decreed amount may not be able to finance retirement.[6] Chia and Tsui (2003) have assessed the adequacy of the CPF-decreed minimum savings for retirement needs of the elderly in Singapore. Instead of emphasizing the mechanism of accumulation, they studied the expenditure side of the lifetime budget of the elderly by estimating the present value of retirement consumption (PVRC) for an elderly at age 62 till death. PVRC is thus the calibrated required cash flow in terms of consumption needs during retirement. Assuming a maximum lifespan of 105 years and a retirement starting at age 62, the estimated present value of retirement consumption (PVRC) is given by:

$$PVRC = \sum_{j=1}^{528} c_j v_j \,_j P_{62} \tag{1}$$

where c_j is the benchmark expenditure for month j, v_j is the discount factor at time j and $_jP_{62}$ is the probability of survival of the individual starting at age 62 up to time $(62 + j)$.

The estimation of PVRC is obtained by simulations through three major components: calibration of subsistence and medical expenses of the elderly; forecast of cohort survival probability by age and by sex; and generation of yield curves to discount future cash flows. The stream of retirement consumption under different scenarios of subsistence levels, growth rates of consumption, medical growth inflations, and interest rates are obtained by calibration. The survival probabilities are based on the stochastic forecasting of cohort tables, which include the improvement of life expectancy and different mortality experiences between the males and females. Chia and Tsui showed that the existing CPF-decreed minimum sum is inadequate to meet the future consumption needs of the female elderly. For the male elderly, because of his relatively shorter life expectancy, the decreed sum would be sufficient and the PVRC for male elderly is below the CPF-decreed $80,000. However, the corresponding PVRC for the female elderly under similar scenarios is consistently above the CPF-decreed amount. Under the benchmark scenarios, the spread of PVRC between the female and male elderly is about 12 per cent. The inadequacy for the female elderly is approximately 2 per cent of the decreed sum of $80,000 (see Table 2.4). It becomes more severe when higher rates of medical inflation are assured. For instance, the average of the estimated PVRC for the female elderly amounts to $81,425, $86,304 and $90,807 when the medical inflation is set to 3 per cent, 4 per cent and 5 per cent, respectively, thereby yielding an average of $86,178. The simulation results suggest that gender differences in longevity need to be considered when setting the minimum sum. Based on the simulation results, it appears more appropriate to raise the minimum sum for the female elderly by at least $6,000.

As for married couples, the mean PVRC using the benchmark scenario is also above the CPF decreed amount. If however, deterministic interest rate paths are assumed, then the computed PVRC will be slightly below the decreed amount. If medical and general price inflation are factored in, the decreed amount of $80,000 would be insufficient to meet the retirement consumption needs of elderly Singaporeans. For married couples, the inadequacy is most severe when stochastic interest rates models are used.

Table 2.4 indicates that the inadequacy is most severe when medical expenditure grows at 7 per cent. This implies that the rates of return of compulsory savings must compensate for inflation rates, particularly for medical inflation. Other policy implications include the need to contain medical costs and to design alternative health care financing schemes.

TABLE 2.4
Comparison of PVRC for the Elderly Against the
CPF-decreed Minimum Saving

Scenario	Female	Male
Case 1: Benchmark scenario using life table with $c_s = \$300$, $m_g = 3\%$, $c_g = 1\%$, $r_a = 4\%$	$68,620 (14.2%)	$60,636 (24.2%)
Case 2: Benchmark scenario using cohort table with $c_s = \$300$, $m_g = 3\%$, $c_g = 1\%$, $r_a = 4\%$	$81,425 (–1.8%)	$72,494 (9.4%)
Case 3: Benchmark parameters but setting medical expenditure growth rate at		
i. $m_g = 4\%$	$86,304 (–7.9%)	$76,001 (5.0%)
ii. $m_g = 5\%$	$90,807 (–13.5%)	$80,394 (–0.5%)
Case 4: Benchmark parameters but setting discount rate (r_a) at:		
i. 3%	$92,940 (–16.2%)	$81,366 (–1.7%)
ii. 5%	$72,083 (9.9%)	$65,236 (18.5%)
Case 5: A higher subsistence expenditure (c_s) at $400 per month	$101,384 (–26.7%)	$90,176 (–12.8%)
Case 6: Cost of living growth (c_g) at 2% per annum	86,612 (–8.3%)	$78,292 (2.1%)

Note: Figures in parentheses denote the percentage deviations of the monthly payouts from premiums paid under the CPF-decreed sum of $80,000 for each female and male elderly. A negative sign indicates inadequacy while a positive sign indicates adequacy.
Notations and parameterization used in Chia and Tsui (2003) are as follows:
[1] Subsistence consumption (c_s) = $300 per month, Growth rate (c_g) = 1% per annum.
[2] Health care consumption (c_h) differs across gender, age groups and household types. (See Table 4 of Chia and Tsui.)
[3] Growth rate of medical expenditure (m_g) = 3% per annum.
[4] Cox-Ingersoll-Ross model of stochastic interest rates: Initial interest rate = 3%; average interest rate (r_a) = 4%.
Source: Chia and Tsui (2003).

Chia and Tsui (2003) have assessed adequacy by comparing the retirement needs of the male and female elderly with the minimum sum as decreed by the CPF. However, in reality, not many elderly have the decreed amount in their CPF accounts. The average balance of males aged 50–55 in 2003 was $69,347.[7] The average balance for females in the same age group was even lower, at $45,176. This implies that the average balance of the male elderly was 13 per cent lower than the decreed sum and for the female elderly, it was 44 per cent lower. Indeed, this implies that the inadequacy was more severe for the female elderly than for the male since the simulated PVRC was 12 per cent higher for the female elderly. Hence, even lifting the minimum sum will not solve the adequacy problem as what matters is the actual accumulated balance, which is substantially below the decreed sum.

Simulation results from Chia and Tsui also demonstrated that the inadequacy was more severe for the elderly in 1-, 2- 3-room public housing than those in larger public housing units. This implies that to achieve the other objectives of social security of income redistribution and social insurance, there is a need to examine the existing single-tier mandatory savings scheme to finance retirement needs. Although a single-tier social security system based on a personal savings account helps avert financing crisis, it is unable to address the problems of adequacy and poverty. Parametric changes to the current system of personal retirement accounts will not suffice; there seems to be a need for structural changes. As ageing becomes more prevalent, to address poverty among the elderly, it may be necessary to include a basic tax-financed, defined-benefit social security that ensures a minimum subsistence income. There was also an attempt to introduce a self–arranged, tax-sheltered supplementary retirement savings (SRS) scheme in April 2001. However, the take-up rate for SRS has been disappointing.

Alternatively, reverse mortgages (RMs) may be introduced to augment retirement incomes. We next proceed to examine whether such an instrument could be harnessed as a source of financing retirement income for homeowners who have withdrawn their savings in the CPF accounts for housing mortgage payments.

UNLOCKING HOUSING EQUITY

Reverse mortgages (RMs) essentially are designed to allow property owners to obtain loans in the form of retirement annuities, using their residential assets as collaterals; and repaying the loans by selling the house upon their death. It thus affords an alternative means for elderly homeowners to borrow against the financial equity embodied in their homes, while sparing them from the emotional disruption of moving out of, or selling their abodes. There are many forms of RMs, but the basic design is that the property will be reverted to the RM supplier at the end of a specified period or upon the death of the reverse mortgagor. In conventional mortgages, the loan quantum is dependent on the borrower's ability to pay. However for RMs, the loan quantum depends on the appraised value of the property, the projected rate of house price appreciation, the age and sex of the homeowners, the levels of interest rates and the required loan.[8] There are also costs involved in taking out these RM loans. RMs differ in terms of the types of loan advance and the time frame. Loan advance can be taken as a lump sum or as a regular income stream. The terms of the RM can either be fixed-term or tenure. In a fixed-term RM, the period of loan advance is fixed, usually 10, 15 or 20 years.

Empirical study by Kutty (1998) indicates that the use of home equity conversion mortgage products in the United States could possibly raise about 29 per cent of poor elderly homeowners above the poverty line. In addition, Gibbs (1992) shows that the equity released could potentially help to finance long-term care among the elderly in the United Kingdom, where relatively large sum of money are required. More recently, Stucki (2004) examines the use of reverse mortgages to manage the financial risk of long-term care in the United States. The usefulness of such a RM scheme is conceivably greater in countries where land prices are extremely high (for example, Japan) or where there is a skewed investment portfolio towards home ownership (for example, Australia) or where there are deliberate public policies towards home ownership (for example, Singapore).[9]

In the RM feasibility study by Chia and Tsui (2004), 4-room public housing dwellers are used as the benchmark household. This is supported by the empirical evidence that the greatest proportion of HDB dwellers (about 39 per cent) in year 2002 were in 4-room flats. In fact, 68 per cent of the residents were living in HDB 4-room or larger flats or private housing, up from 52 per cent in 1990. A decade ago, the greatest proportion of the HDB dwellers were in 3-room flats. Because of greater affluence, 42 per cent of these 3-room HDB dwellers had moved to 4-room or larger flats or private properties in 2000.[10]

Table 2.5 shows that for an initial property value of $240,000 and a monthly annuity level of $1,500, the probability of loss for the supplier is only 0.0367, with a later first breakeven month, occurring at $m^* = 478$.[11] However, when the monthly annuity payout is increased to $1,600, the probability of loss to the supplier will be much higher at 0.5374, with the first breakeven month occurring sooner at $m^* = 350$. If the private RM supplier is risk averse and prefers a smaller probability of loss, then he will

TABLE 2.5
Present Value of Profit, Probability of Loss for Private Suppliers

Level of Annuity	Breakeven month (m*)	Probability of loss	Present value of profit (PVP)			
			Mean	Standard deviation	5th percentile	95th percentile
1000	528	0.0000	62899	961	61189	64460
1200	528	0.0000	60245	4451	54238	72215
1300	528	0.0000	48439	5173	41585	62930
1400	528	0.0000	33835	5386	27037	48980
1500	478	0.0367	18061	5429	11473	33240
1520	455	0.0871	14783	5423	8279	29965
1540	429	0.1742	11507	5414	5064	26660
1560	403	0.2911	8209	5403	1828	23332
1580	375	0.4203	4892	5391	−1431	19986
1600	350	0.5374	1557	5378	−4709	16620
1650	301	0.7226	−6850	5339	−12949	8115
1700	273	0.8024	−15338	5295	−21242	−498
1800	233	0.8747	−32486	5192	−37970	−17962
1900	206	0.9121	−49818	5100	−54859	−35638
2000	186	0.9350	−67265	5004	−71854	−53447
2200	157	0.9595	−102377	4833	−106052	−89302
2400	136	0.9716	−137664	4702	−140397	−125352

Source: Chia and Tsui (2004).

set a lower level of monthly annuity, say at $1,000. But in this instance, there may be no demand for the RM as the replacement ratio will be at 33 per cent, which is much lower than the expected 70 per cent.[12] Hence, the completeness of the RM market depends on setting an annuity payout that is adequate to finance retirement expenditure, while minimising the probability of loss to the supplier.

Table 2.5 also indicates that when the monthly payout is increased to $1,700 to reach a replacement ratio of 46 per cent of the pre-retirement average income, the probability of loss to the supplier is very high at 0.8024. This is in stark contrast to the negligible probability of loss when the monthly annuity payout is $1,400. Hence, the difference of $300 may be interpreted as the loading factor levied by the RM supplier. The loading factor can be as high as 21 per cent ($300/$1400). Hence, their findings are consistent with

Caplin (2002) and others who accord the incompleteness of the reverse mortgage market to high loading factors.

Chia and Tsui (2004) then went on to evaluate the RM market if the supplier is a non-profit motivated supplier, for example the government. In this case, in computing the accumulated loan value, risk-free interest rate is used, instead of the risk-embedded rate. The latter rate incorporates both the risk premium and profit margin. It is assumed that profit is not a major consideration for the public provider, and that the provider has access to lower cost of capital and is more able to pool risk. The *breakeven annuity* in Table 2.6 refers to the annuity which would yield a zero mean present value of profit for the private supplier. A similar procedure was used to obtain the new breakeven month for the public provider while setting the monthly payout at the breakeven annuity.

Table 2.6 presents simulation results which compare the adequacy of the RM instruments provided by profit and non-profit motivated suppliers. These include the mean monthly payout at the breakeven annuity, its standard deviation, the 5th and 95th percentiles profit, the probability of loss, the first breakeven month, and the replacement ratio based on the mean and median monthly income of the household. The simulations were repeated using different initial property values assumptions, ranging from $220,000 to $300,000.

The simulation results indicate that the viability of the market depends crucially on the size of the monthly payouts and keeping the interest rates used to accumulate total loan values. The choice of cost of capital yields important policy implications — the viability of the RM hinges on the different costs of capital facing the private supplier and public provider. As can be observed from Table 2.6, for a given property value of $220,000, the mean breakeven annuity is $1,475. This level of breakeven annuity represents a replacement ratio of 49 per cent of the average household income; there may be a demand for RM. However, there could be no private supplier as the probability of loss is close to 58 per cent, implying that it is highly probable that the accumulated loan balance is higher than the net value of the property at the time of repayment. If a lower annuity is set, say at $900, it would mean a negligible probability of loss for the private supplier. (See Table 2.5). But then set at $900, it is unlikely to draw a positive demand as the replacement ratio is a meagre 20 per cent. Hence the RM market fails. Can the government intervene in this market? Table 2.6 indicates that at the same average breakeven annuity, the probability of loss for the public provider is now almost negligible as the public provider has a lower cost for funds and is able to charge the loan balance at a risk-free interest rate.

TABLE 2.6
**Probability of Loss and First Breakeven Month under Private and Public
Reverse Mortgage Suppliers Using Different Initial Property Values**

	Initial property value				
	$ 220K	*$ 240K*	*$ 260K*	*$ 280K*	*$ 300K*
Mean payout of breakeven annuity	1475	1609	1743	1876	2011
Standard deviation	5010	5472	5894	6260	6675
5th percentile	−8106	−9091	−9752	−10233	−11274
95th percentile	8368	8913	9448	9791	10887
Probability of loss					
Private supplier	0.581	0.586	0.585	0.584	0.586
Public provider	0.004	0.004	0.004	0.004	0.003
Breakeven month					
Private supplier	339	338	338	338	338
Public provider	511	511	511	511	514
Replacement ratio[a] (3000 per month)	49%	54%	58%	63%	67%
Replacement ratio[b] ($3719 per month)	40%	43%	47%	50%	54%

Note:
a. Replacement ratio based on the median monthly income of HDB households.
b. Replacement ratio based on the average monthly income of HDB households.
Source: Chia and Tsui (2004).

At a higher initial property value of $300,000, the homeowner can expect to unlock the housing equity to yield an income which is almost 67 per cent of the pre-retirement average income. But again there may be a missing market as the probability of loss for the private supplier is still high at 0.586. However, the probability of loss is only 0.004 if the supplier is a public provider. Furthermore, compared with the private supplier, the first breakeven month for the public provider occurs 172 months later.

If profitability is vital for private RM suppliers but not so for the public supplier, then the simulation results suggest a transformed role for HDB from a public housing provider to a RM provider. This is because HDB possibly has access to lower-cost funds at a risk-free interest rate, thereby making it more able to function as a supplier of RM in cases when the private supplier fails.

CONCLUSION

The existing CPF schemes with its pre-retirement withdrawal features have serious limitations in addressing income maintenance, health care issues and poverty at old age. Under the current arrangement, the accumulation of savings depends on the economic well-being of CPF members in terms of their ability to work and to stay employed. It also depends on the overall investment health of the CPF Board and its ability to pay higher rates of return.

Our analysis shows that there are significant gender differences in retirement needs among the elderly. The inadequacy is more severe for the female elderly than the male as the retirement needs for the female is higher than for the male, with the retirement need of the female at 12 per cent higher than that for the male. Based on our simulation results, it seems more appropriate to raise the decreed minimum sum for the female elderly by about $6,000 more. However, even lifting the minimum sum level will not solve the adequacy problem as the actual accumulated saving is substantially below the decreed amount.

Retirement needs of the elderly also depend on the growth in medical inflation and the general price inflation. This implies that the rates of return of compulsory savings must compensate inflation rates, particularly medical inflation. Other policy implications include the need to contain medical costs, designing health care financing schemes to address medical inflation, and long-term medical care.

The issue of inadequacy is more pressing for elderly in smaller 1-, 2-, 3-room public housing than those in larger public housing units. This implies that besides parametric changes to the current social security arrangement, to achieve the other objectives of social security of income redistribution and social insurance, it is imperative to re-examine the current single-tier mandatory savings scheme. As ageing becomes more prevalent, it is necessary to include a basic tax-financed, defined-benefit social security to address poverty among the elderly.

Given the inadequacy of accumulated savings to finance retirement needs, this chapter then suggested the annuitization of residential equity through RMs to enhance old-age financial security. However, the RM market in most countries has remained thin. This is in line with our analysis that the RM market tends to be incomplete. To ensure profitability, if the monthly annuity payout is set too low, there will be no demand for the RM instrument. However, if the monthly payout is set at a level that would ensure an acceptable replacement ratio, it is highly probable that the supplier will make a loss. Hence the supply of RM will not be forthcoming. We suggest that for the case of Singapore, perhaps a public provider is necessary. Our analyses indicate that high loading factors and provision costs of RMs have inevitably led to an incomplete market, hence hampering the proper functioning of RMs. Future studies should focus on lowering the transactions costs and provision costs, so that RM could be harnessed as an adequate and viable retirement financing instrument for "asset-rich and cash-poor" Singaporeans.

Notes

[1]   This section draws on simulation results from Chia and Tsui, 2003.

[2]   This section draws on simulation results in Chia and Tsui, 2004.

[3]   According to the CPF Annual Report 2001, at the end of year 2000, the balances which are left with the CPF Board that is not in the insurance pool amount to $90.3 billion. Of this, about 2/3 is invested in Singapore government bonds and 1/3 as advanced deposits with the Monetary Authority of Singapore. The latter is to be converted into government bonds at a later date. The issues relating to the deployment and the returns of CPF savings are beyond the scope of this chapter.

[4]   All dollars in this chapter are in Singapore dollars (US$1 approximates S$1.75). The median monthly income from employment in 2001 is $1,875. (Statistical Highlights, 2002). The household income distribution is given in Appendix 1, which shows that the average monthly income for the fourth quintile is $5,770 and that the salary ceiling cap is binding for the top 20 per cent households of Singapore. The average monthly household savings (inclusive of CPF savings) is $1,576.

[5]   See Peebles (2002) for an excellent survey of empirical studies on savings and investments in Singapore.

[6]   See Chia and Tsui (2003) for the methodology used to compute the present value of retirement consumption and the assumptions made in the choice of the parameters.

[7]   Calculated from the CPF Annual Report, 2003 Annex H. The age group 50–55

instead of the age group above 55 is used as the latter group would have withdrawn their balances.

[8]   For RM, age is a positive factor — the older the homeowner, the greater the RM as the expected number of payments is smaller. For example, in the United States the minimum qualifying age is set at 62 years, and the average age is around 72 years. In Singapore, the average qualifying age is 62. Gender plays a role as males and females have different life expectancy.

[9]   The share of land assets in real assets is 83.4 per cent in Japan and 36 per cent in the United States. (See Noguchi 1997.) Australian home ownership is in excess of 70 per cent (Beal 2001), whereas home ownership in Singapore is in excess of 90 per cent.

[10] See Singapore Department of Statistics, 2001, Table 10.

[11] The first breakeven month is defined as the first month when the accumulated loan amount exceeds the property value. For details on the computation procedure, refer to Chia and Tsui, 2004.

[12] There is no single acceptable replacement ratio. McGill et al. (1996) recommend using a replacement rate of 73 per cent. In Canada, financial planners typically set a ratio of 70 per cent of post-retirement income to maintain a comparable standard of living experienced before retirement.

References

Beal, D.J. "Home Equity Conversion in Australia — Issues, Impediments and Possible Solutions". Manuscript, University of Southern Queensland, 2001.

Caplin, A. "Turning Assets into Cash: Problems and Prospects in the Reverse Mortgage Market". In *Innovations in Retirement Financing*, O.S. Mitchell et al., eds. Philadelphia, PA: University of Pennsylvania Press, 2002.

Chia N.C. and A.K.C. Tsui. "Life Annuities of Compulsory Savings and Income Adequacy of the Elderly in Singapore". *Journal of Pension Economics and Finance* 2, no. 1 (2003): 41–65.

———. Reverse Mortgage as Retirement Financial Instrument: An Option for Asset-rich and Cash-poor Singaporeans, manuscript, 2004.

———. "Medical Savings Accounts in Singapore: How Much Is Adequate?" *Journal of Health Economics*, forthcoming, 2005.

Gibbs, I. "A Substantial but Limited Asset: The Role of Housing Wealth in Paying for Residential Care". In *Financing Elderly People in Independent Sector Homes: The Future*, J. Morten, ed. London: Age Concern Institute of Gerontology, 1992.

Hancock, R. "Can Housing Wealth Alleviate Poverty among Britain's Older Population?" *Fiscal Studies* 19, no. 1 (1998): 249–72.

Kutty, N.K. "The Scope for Poverty Alleviation among Elderly Home-Owners in the US through Reverse Mortgages". *Urban Studies* 35, no. 1 (1998): 113–30.

Lim, C.Y. et al. *Policy Options for the Singapore Economy*. Singapore: McGraw Hill, 1988.

Noguchi Y. "Improvement of After-Retirement Income by Home Equity Conversion Mortgages: Possibility and Problems in Japan". In *The Economic Effects of Aging in the United States and Japan*, Michael D. Hurd and N. Yashiro, eds. Chicago University Press, 1997.

Peebles, G. "Saving and Investment in Singapore". In *Singapore Economy in the 21st Century*, A.T. Koh et al., eds. Singapore: McGraw Hill, 2002.

Singapore, Department of Statistics. *Census of Population 2000: Households and Housing: Statistical Release 5*. Singapore National Printers, 2001.

————. *Statistical Highlights 2000/01*, Singapore National Printers, 2003.

Singapore, Central Provident Fund. *Annual Report*. Singapore: CPF Board, 2003.

Stucki, B.R. "Using Reverse Mortgages to Manage the Financial Risk of Long-term Care". Presented at Managing Retirement Assets Symposium. Organized by Society of Actuaries, Las Vegas, 2004.

World Bank. "Why do Savings Rates Vary Across Countries". *World Bank Policy and Research Bulletin* 10, no. 1, January–March 1999.

3

AGEING AND AGEING POLICIES IN THE REPUBLIC OF KOREA[1]

Ahn Kye Choon and Chung Kyung Hee

INTRODUCTION

In the field of Korean sociology, little attention has been paid to ageing and the problems of older persons. By 1995 only three of the many articles published in the Korean Journal of sociology were on ageing, and only a few members of the Korean Sociological Association were also members of the Korean Gerontological Society or the Population Association of Korea. The reason for this dismal situation was that ageing was not a serious social problem and therefore it did not receive much attention from the academic world and society in general.

In recent years, however, as Korea has become an ageing society, increasing attention has been paid to the problem of ageing by academics and policy makers. More scholars are now engaged in research on the problems of ageing in related fields such as demography, sociology, social welfare, economics, and public health. The government has also expanded organization support for ageing policies in the Ministry of Health and Welfare, and increased the budget to deal with the problems of ageing. Newspapers and television stations are also paying more attention to the problems of an ageing society. As a result, the ageing problem is becoming a matter of great public concern.

Despite these efforts and favourable changes, a lot of problems still exist in this field. The government budget towards solving the problems of older persons is still limited, and the manpower allocated is not enough to solve the problems. There are still considerable gaps between the results of research and government policies. This chapter will focus on identifying the basic characteristics of older persons and their needs, and then examining whether the government's ageing policies are specific enough to meet the different needs of the various subgroups of older persons.

DEMOGRAPHIC TRENDS OF AGEING

While there are various ways to measure the degree of ageing, the proportion of the elderly population and the ageing index are the most common methods. Generally people aged 60 and above or people aged 65 and above are regarded as older persons. In this paper, older persons refer to those aged 65 years and above.

As shown in Table 3.1, the pace of population ageing was very slow until 1980, both in terms of the proportion of older persons, and the ageing index. Since 1985, however, it accelerated at faster rates than before. In the year 2000, the proportion of older persons reached 7.1 per cent, and the ageing index increased to 32.9.[2] According to the new population projection of Korea National Statistical Office (KNSO), the ageing process will continue to accelerate in the future.

TABLE 3.1
Trends in Population Ageing in Korea: 1960–2020

Year	Percentage of Older Persons	Ageing Index
1960	3.7	9.2
1970	3.3	7.9
1980	3.8	11.2
1990	5.1	20.0
1995	5.9	25.2
2000	7.1	32.9
2010	10.7	62.0
2019	14.4	102.0
2020	15.1	109.0
2030	23.1	186.6

Source: 1960–2000 Population and Housing Census Reports, KNSO/ROK 2010–2020 Population Projection 2001, KNSO/ROK.

It is expected that the proportion of older persons and the ageing index will reach 15.1 per cent and 109.0 respectively in the year 2020. Korea will become an aged society, when the percentage of older persons is over 14 per cent, in the year 2019 and thereafter. It is noted that the process of ageing will go on much faster in Korea than in Western aged societies.

The ageing process is a reflection of changing age structure, and in turn, changes in the age structure are mainly due to the changes in fertility and mortality. It is a fact that fertility in Korea has declined very rapidly since 1960. The total fertility rate was 6.0 in 1960 and has continuously decreased since then to reach 1.17 in 2002. On the other hand, mortality also declined very fast during the same period, mainly due to improved living standards and advancements in medical technologies and public health services. The life expectancy at birth was 53 years in 1960, but increased to 76 years (male: 72.8, female: 80.0) in 2001. These remarkable changes in fertility and mortality occurred during the last 40 years. This is the reason the ageing process has been very rapid in recent years.

BASIC CHARACTERISTICS OF OLDER PERSONS AND THEIR NEEDS

Demographic Characteristics

As shown in Table 3.2, the proportion of the age group 65–69 is decreasing, from 42.8 per cent in 1980 to 40.8 per cent in 2000. If we were to divide

TABLE 3.2
Age and Sex Composition of Older Persons: 1980–2000

Age	1980		1990		2000	
	Proportion	Sex ratio	Proportion	Sex ratio	Proportion	Sex ratio
65–69	42.8	72.5	41.7	71.6	40.8	75.9
70–74	29.4	61.5	27.5	64.5	27.2	61.1
75–79	15.9	47.8	17.4	51.3	17.8	54.3
80–84	8.2	36.4	9.0	39.1	9.0	44.9
85+	3.7	26.9	4.4	24.9	5.2	29.8
Total	100.0	59.5	100.0	60.0	100.0	61.8

Note: Sex Ratio = (No. of Male Population/No. of Female Population)*100
Source: KNSO (2000j, Korean Statistical Information System (KOSIS).

older persons into two groups, namely the young-old (under 75) and the old-old (over 75 or more), we would note that the proportion of the old-old group has increased slightly. We would also see that the sex ratios of age groups above 65 has remarkably declined as they age (from 75.9 to 29.8 in 2000). Of course this is due to the longer life expectancy of the female.

Imbalance in sex ratio is clearly reflected in the marital status of older persons. The proportion of the currently married has continuously declined with age, from 67.0 per cent in the 65–69 age group to 15.3 per cent in the 85+ age group for the year 2000 (see Table 3.3). In particular, there are huge differences in the proportions of the currently married between men and women; 85.4 per cent of older males have wives compared with only 31.3 per cent of older females with husbands. Since female older persons live longer, and their husbands have passed away, they tend to keep the status of unmarried, and are likely to live alone.

The place of residence is also an important factor in considering ageing policies. The overall trend of urban migration is reflected in the distribution of older persons by place of residence. While more older persons lived in the rural areas in 1980, in contrast in 2000, more older persons were found in urban areas (see Table 3.4). Also in 2000, the percentage of older population living in rural areas (38.5 per cent) was higher than the percentage of the total population residing in rural areas (20 per cent). It means that more older persons tend to live in rural areas compared with the younger population. Although the proportion of rural older persons has become smaller, we cannot ignore them because they are living in poorer living conditions.

TABLE 3.3
Proportion of the Currently Married: 2000

Age	Total	Male	Female
65–69	67.0	91.0	48.8
70–74	52.0	86.7	30.8
75–79	40.0	80.5	18.0
80–84	28.3	70.1	9.5
85+	15.3	53.2	4.0
Total	52.0	85.4	31.3

Source: KNSO (2002j, KOSIS).

TABLE 3.4
Distribution of Older Persons (60+) by Place of Residence: 1980–2000

	1980	1990	2000
Urban	39.1	54.7	61.5
Rural	60.9	45.3	38.5
Total	100.0	100.0	100.0

Source: KNSO (2002j, KOSIS).

Living Arrangements

According to the 1998 KIHASA (Korea Institute for Health and Social Affairs) survey,[3] 21 per cent of households with older persons live alone, 22 per cent live only with their spouses, and 5 per cent live with others (See Table 3.5). More than half of the households with old persons live with their children. Although the proportion of the traditional stem family among total households has decreased from 19 per cent in 1970 to 8 per cent in 2000, it is still the dominant pattern of living among households with older persons. That is one reason people tend to regard the ageing problem as a family affair. Nevertheless we should pay attention to the fact that the proportion of older persons living alone or with spouses only is rapidly increasing in recent years.

TABLE 3.5
Living Arrangements of Older Persons: 1998

(Unit: %)

Area	Household With Older Persons				Total (Households)
	Older Persons Living Alone	Elderly Living With Spouses Only[1]	Elderly Living With Children	Others	
Whole	20.1	21.6	53.2	5.1	100.0 (1,958)
Urban	18.1	18.3	57.6	6.0	100.0 (1,253)
Rural	23.6	27.5	45.4	3.5	100.0 (750)

Note: 1) Includes households where both the husband and wife or where just one person in the couple is 65 years old or over.
Source: KIHASA Survey, 1998.

We can also observe that there are considerable differences in the distribution of living arrangements between urban and rural areas. The proportion of older persons living alone or with spouses only are higher in rural areas, while the proportion of elderly people living with their children is higher in urban areas due to the migration of young persons to urban areas.

ECONOMIC SECURITY

Employment Status

The labour force participation rate of older persons was 29 per cent in year 1998 (See Table 3.6). The labour force participation rate of the male elderly was much higher than that of the female elderly. There is a big difference in the labour force participation rate between rural and urban areas; almost half of the older persons in rural areas are still working on the farm, while 83 per cent of the urban elderly do not work. As we can easily imagine, the labour force participation rate decreases as age increases.

Sources of Income

As shown in Table 3.7, the most important source of income for older persons is financial support from their children. In 1998, two thirds of older persons received financial support from their non-co-resident children, and 23 per cent from co-resident children. Only one third of older persons had income from their own or their spouses' employment. It is important to note that only a small proportion of older persons cited social pension (3 per cent) and public assistance (9 per cent) as their sources of income. Despite these sources of income, more than half the older persons perceive that they suffer from economic hardships, considering their expenditures.

HEALTH STATUS

Chronic Diseases

The proportion of older persons with at least one chronic disease was 87 per cent in 1998 (See Table 3.8). Female elderly showed a rate of 92 per cent, meaning that only a very small portion of female elderly did not have a chronic disease. As the age of respondents increases, so does the prevalence rate of chronic disease. Overall the prevalence rate of chronic diseases in the rural area is higher than in the urban area.

TABLE 3.6

Labour Force Participation Rates and Occupations by Area, Gender, and Age: 1998

(Unit: %)

Employment Status & Occupations	Total	Area		Gender		Age		
		Urban	Rural	Male	Female	65–69	70–74	75+
Employment Status								
Employed	29.0	17.1	49.1	39.8	22.6	40.2	28.5	16.3
Unemployed	71.0	82.9	50.9	60.2	77.4	59.8	71.5	83.7
Occupation								
Legislators, Senior Officials & Managers	(2.0)	(4.9)	(0.2)	(3.5)	(0.4)	(2.9)	(0.7)	(1.2)
Professionals	(1.9)	(4.7)	(0.3)	(2.9)	(0.9)	(1.9)	(0.6)	(3.8)
Technicians & Associate Professionals	(1.1)	(2.6)	(0.1)	(1.9)	(0.2)	(0.8)	(2.2)	(0.0)
Clerks	(1.2)	(2.9)	(0.2)	(2.3)	(0.0)	(1.6)	(0.7)	(0.5)
Service & Sales Workers	(8.8)	(17.5)	(3.6)	(7.8)	(9.9)	(9.8)	(10.0)	(4.0)
Agricultural & Fishery Workers	(60.4)	(21.6)	(83.4)	(62.5)	(58.3)	(55.4)	(65.6)	(66.8)
Craft	(2.7)	(6.4)	(0.6)	(3.4)	(2.1)	(3.4)	(2.3)	(1.6)
Machine Operators & Assemblers	(0.4)	(1.2)	(0.0)	(0.9)	(0.0)	(0.8)	(0.0)	(0.0)
Unskilled Laborers	(21.5)	(38.3)	(11.6)	(14.9)	(28.3)	(23.2)	(17.9)	(22.2)
% member	100.0	100.0	100.0	100.0	100.0	100.0	100.0	100.0
Total	(685)	(255)	(431)	(347)	(338)	(362)	(196)	(126)

Source: KIHASA Survey, 1998.

TABLE 3.7
Sources of Income by Area, Gender, and Age: 1998

(Unit: %)

Sources of Income[1]	Total	Area		Gender		Age		
		Urban	Rural	Male	Female	65–69	70–74	75+
Employment	33.7	23.1	52.0	48.2	25.2	46.5	32.3	18.0
Real Estate/Rental	12.0	13.2	9.8	13.6	11.0	12.8	13.4	9.4
Savings	5.7	6.8	3.7	8.1	4.3	6.7	4.3	5.8
Social Pension	2.8	4.0	0.9	5.1	1.5	1.8	4.2	0.2
Retirement Annuities	0.9	1.0	0.7	1.7	0.4	1.6	0.5	0.3
Private Pension	0.2	0.3	0.2	0.2	0.3	0.3	0.4	0.0
Support from Non-coresident Children	66.3	64.0	70.3	64.2	68.6	62.5	68.3	69.2
Support from Coresident Children	23.3	24.8	20.8	16.3	27.5	20.2	22.7	28.3
Support from Other Relatives	1.2	1.8	0.2	0.7	1.5	1.1	0.9	1.6
Public Assistance	8.5	8.6	8.3	6.8	9.5	6.5	10.0	9.7
Support from Organizations	0.7	0.8	0.3	0.6	0.7	0.4	1.0	0.6

Note: 1) The total percentage is more than 100 because multiple choices were allowed.
Source: KIHASA Survey, 1998.

TABLE 3.8
Prevalence Rate of Chronic Diseases by Age and Gender
(Unit: %)

	Total	65–69	70–74	75+
Total	86.7	85.2	87.6	87.8
Area				
Urban	85.3	82.9	88.1	85.8
Rural	89.1	89.6	86.8	90.7
Gender				
Male	77.4	75.8	79.4	78.0
Female	92.2	92.0	92.0	92.5

Source: KIHASA Survey, 1998.

Of the various chronic diseases, arthritis is the most prevalent. Lame back, high blood pressure, gastric ulcer, and cataract are the next most prevalent chronic diseases. Whatever the chronic disease, those who suffer from them have difficulties in performing the activities of daily living (see Table 3.9).

Activities of Daily Living and Instrumental Activities of Daily Living

As for daily living activities, 10.5 per cent of older persons had at least one difficulty in the activities of daily living and 1.3 per cent had difficulties in all 6 items in 2001 (see Table 3.10 and Table 3.11). 70–90 per cent of respondents answered, by each item, that they were able to maintain their daily lives without assistance.

There were no substantial gender differences in difficulties of the Activities of Daily Living (ADL). 12.5 per cent of elderly women had at least one difficulty in ADL. Among elderly men, 10.5 per cent had at least one difficulty in ADL.

Table 3.11 shows dependency rate using 10 items of instrumental daily living activities in 2001. Among those 10 items, the highest proportion of older persons was found to have difficulty in financial management (35.8 per cent). The second and third highest proportions were in telephone use (23.3 per cent) and public transport (21.4 per cent) respectively.

In all, 30.8 per cent of older persons had limitations only in Instrumental Activities of Daily Living (IADL), 10.5 per cent had at least one difficulty out of 6 ADLs, and 1.3 per cent had restrictions in all ADLs. In the case of the

TABLE 3.9
Prevalence Rate and Limitation in Daily Living by Disease and Gender: 1998

(Unit: %)

Diseases	Prevalence Rate			Limitation in Daily Living		
	Total	Male	Female	Total	Male	Female
Neoplasm	0.9	1.7	0.5	70.3	64.8	81.4
Arthritis	43.4	26.6	53.3	84.4	76.1	86.8
Lame back	29.2	15.9	37.1	88.2	83.8	89.3
Herniation of						
Intervertebral disk	5.4	4.9	5.6	87.0	76.0	92.7
Gastric ulcer	15.9	11.7	18.3	63.5	58.0	65.5
Hepatitis, Liver cirrhosis	1.6	3.3	0.7	65.7	60.7	80.4
Diabetes	9.0	8.6	9.2	62.9	50.6	69.7
Thyroid	1.3	0.6	1.6	64.4	73.4	62.5
High blood pressure	23.5	17.5	27.0	55.7	45.3	59.6
Paralysis	4.4	4.5	4.3	82.9	81.8	83.6
Angina pectoris	5.1	4.7	5.3	74.9	66.7	79.1
Tuberculosis	0.5	1.1	0.1	58.0	49.3	100.0
Chronic Bronchitis	6.3	9.1	4.7	66.2	58.6	74.9
Asthma	5.1	6.2	4.5	72.4	66.4	77.2
Cataracts	10.6	6.0	13.4	74.3	61.3	77.7
Chronic otitis media	1.0	1.3	0.8	83.5	94.6	73.7
Chronic heart disease	1.1	0.4	1.5	88.6	35.0	96.4
Sequela of bone fracture	5.4	6.6	4.7	89.6	92.5	87.3

Source: KIHASA Survey, 1998.

oldest elderly, aged 75 and above, the numbers respectively increased to 43.6 per cent, 18.6 per cent, and 2.4 per cent.

SOCIAL WELFARE NEEDS

Awareness and Utilization Rates of Welfare Policies for Older Persons

There are many kinds of welfare policies that will be presented in the next section. Here we are going to look at awareness and utilization rates of welfare polices and the intention to utilize them.

While 19 per cent of the respondents were aware of the policy for Old Age Allowance, only 7 per cent of them were covered as of May 1998. After being told about the Old Age Pension, 62 per cent expressed the wish to

TABLE 3.10
Activities of Daily Living by Gender and Age: 2001

(Unit: %)

	Total	Gender		Age Group		
		Male	Female	65-69	70-74	75+
Dressing						
No Assistance Needed	95.8	95.0	96.3	97.3	97.1	92.8
Little Difficulty	2.4	3.1	2.0	1.6	1.6	4.1
Always Need Assistance	1.8	1.9	1.7	1.1	1.2	3.1
Washing						
No Assistance Needed	95.0	94.8	95.1	97.1	97.1	90.6
Little Difficulty	3.1	3.0	3.1	1.8	1.8	5.7
Always Need Assistance	1.9	2.1	1.8	1.1	1.1	3.7
Bathing						
No Assistance Needed	90.5	91.3	90.0	95.4	93.3	82.1
Little Difficulty	5.9	4.8	6.6	2.7	4.8	11.0
Always Need Assistance	3.6	3.9	3.4	2.0	2.0	6.9
Eating						
No Assistance Needed	96.8	96.5	97.0	98.0	98.0	94.3
Little Difficulty	2.4	2.8	2.1	1.5	1.8	4.0
Always Need Assistance	0.8	0.6	0.9	0.5	0.2	1.6
Moving						
No Assistance Needed	97.7	98.0	97.5	98.8	98.5	95.6
Little Difficulty	1.0	0.8	1.1	0.5	0.7	2.0
Always Need Assistance	1.3	1.2	1.3	0.6	0.8	2.4
Toilet Use						
No Assistance Needed	96.9	96.8	96.9	98.2	98.1	94.2
Little Difficulty	1.5	1.8	1.4	1.0	0.9	2.7
Always Need Assistance	1.6	1.4	1.7	0.8	0.9	3.1
Total	100.0	100.0	100.0	100.0	100.0	100.0
(N)	(5,058)	(1,911)	(3,147)	(2,049)	(1,368)	(1,641)

Source: Sunwoo, D., et al. *2001 Survey of Long-term Care Service Needs of Older Persons in Korea,* KIHASA.

receive it when it replaced the Old Age Allowance in July 1998. The awareness rates for the Elderly Workplace and Elderly Job Placement Centres were also quite low. Only a few older persons had actually utilized them, while 24 per cent and 16 per cent wanted to use them respectively in the future (see Table 3.13).

TABLE 3.11
Instrumental Activities of Daily Living by Gender and Age: 2001

(Unit: %)

	Total	Gender		Age-group		
		Male	Female	65–69	70–74	75+
Grooming						
No Assistance Needed	93.1	94.1	92.4	96.5	95.5	86.8
Sometimes Need Assistance	4.1	3.1	4.8	1.8	2.8	8.1
Always Need Assistance	2.8	2.8	2.8	1.7	1.8	5.1
Housework						
No Assistance Needed	90.1	89.8	90.2	95.0	93.1	81.4
Sometimes Need Assistance	5.1	5.1	5.1	2.4	4.2	9.1
Always Need Assistance	4.8	5.0	4.7	2.6	2.7	9.5
Food Preparing						
No Assistance Needed	87.6	86.3	88.4	94.3	91.8	75.7
Sometimes Need Assistance	6.5	7.3	6.0	2.9	4.5	12.6
Always Need Assistance	5.9	6.4	5.6	2.8	3.7	11.7
Cleaning and Laundry						
No Assistance Needed	87.9	87.1	88.3	94.5	92.3	75.9
Sometimes Need Assistance	6.2	5.8	6.5	2.4	4.5	12.5
Always Need Assistance	5.9	7.2	5.1	3.1	3.3	11.6
Walking outside						
No Assistance Needed	89.0	92.1	87.1	95.3	93.2	77.6
Sometimes Need Assistance	8.1	5.3	9.8	3.3	5.1	16.5
Always Need Assistance	2.9	2.6	3.1	1.4	1.7	5.9
Use of Public Transport						
No Assistance Needed	78.6	87.1	73.4	89.4	84.9	59.8
Assistance Needed in using public transportation	13.0	6.8	16.7	7.0	9.9	23.1
Assistance Needed in using private transportation	6.6	4.9	7.7	2.9	4.2	13.3
Always Need Assistance	1.8	1.2	2.2	0.7	1.0	3.8
Buying Living Goods						
No Assistance Needed	89.6	92.1	88.0	95.7	93.7	78.4
No Assistance Needed in buying some items	4.8	3.2	5.8	1.8	3.8	9.5
Possible with Assistance	2.1	1.6	2.4	0.9	0.9	4.7
Impossible	3.5	3.1	3.7	1.6	1.5	7.4
Financial Management						
No Assistance Needed	64.2	82.9	52.8	77.6	66.5	45.5
Sometimes Need Assistance	30.6	12.7	41.5	20.2	30.9	43.4
Always Need Assistance	5.2	4.4	5.7	2.1	2.6	11.2

continued on next page

TABLE 3.11 — *cont'd*

	Total	Gender		Age-group		
		Male	*Female*	*65–69*	*70–74*	*75+*
Telephone use						
No Assistance Needed	76.7	89.0	69.3	88.8	81.7	57.3
Can make specific phone calls	8.4	3.3	11.5	5.9	9.5	10.8
Can answer the phone but						
cannot make a phone call	10.6	3.9	14.7	3.8	7.1	22.1
Always Need Assistance	4.3	3.8	4.5	1.5	1.8	9.8
Medication Use						
No Assistance Needed	94.0	94.3	93.8	97.4	96.6	87.6
Sometimes Need Assistance	3.0	2.6	3.3	1.1	1.9	6.3
Always Need Assistance	3.0	3.1	2.9	1.5	1.5	6.1
Total	100.0	100.0	100.0	100.0	100.0	100.0
(N)	(5,058)	(1,911)	(3,147)	(2,049)	(1,369)	(1,640)

Source: Sunwoo, D., et al. *2001 Survey of Long-term Care Service Needs of Older Persons in Korea,* KIHASA.

TABLE 3.12
Dependency Levels among Older Koreans, 2001

(Unit: %)

	Healthy	*Limitation only in IADL*	*With restrictions in 1-6 ADLs*	*With restrictions in all ADLs*	*Total (N)*
Total	57.5	30.8	10.5	1.3	100.0 (5,058)
Gender					
Male	75.8	13.8	9.3	1.2	100.0 (1,911)
Female	46.3	41.2	11.2	1.3	100.0 (3,147)
Age group					
61–69	73.9	19.8	5.6	0.7	100.0 (2,050)
70–74	59.3	31.9	8.0	0.8	100.0 (1,368)
75+	35.4	43.6	18.6	2.4	100.0 (1,640)

Source: Sunwoo, D., et al. *2001 Survey of Long-term Care Service Needs of Older Persons in Korea,* KIHASA.

The awareness of the Elderly Cafeteria was relatively high (40 per cent), but only 6 per cent of the respondents had used it. 18 per cent of the respondents wanted to use it in the future.

TABLE 3.13
Awareness and Utilization Rates of Welfare Policies for Older Persons: 1998

(Unit: %)

	Awareness Rate	Utilization Rate		Want to Use in the Future
		Currently Using	Utilized in The Past	
Old Age Allowance	192	6.8	0.7	61.9
Elderly Workplace	16.0	0.3	0.7	23.6
Elderly Job Placement Centre	15.1	–	0.1	15.5
Free Elderly Cafeteria	39.9	1.8	4.0	17.8
Geriatric Hospital	20.6	0.2	0.5	40.1
Health(sub) Centre	97.2	24.1	40.7	67.2
Elderly Activity Centre	95.4	28.1	19.5	45.8
Elderly College/School	75.4	2.0	7.1	18.2
Community Elderly Welfare Centre	42.1	2.3	3.3	21.6
Free Elderly/Nursing Home	61.0	–	–	13.7
Low-cost Elderly/Nursing Home	31.0	–	0.1	6.7
Charged Elderly/Nursing Home	53.4	–	–	5.7
Exemption of Inheritance Tax (Residential)	14.1	–	0.2	11.6
Exemption of Inheritance Tax (Personal)	12.0	–	0.1	10.1

Source: KIHASA survey, 1998.

As for the Geriatric Hospital, only 21 per cent of the respondents knew about it, and very few older persons had utilized it. However, 40 per cent of the respondents expressed their willingness to use it. What this indicates is that there is considerable latent demand for Geriatric Hospitals. On the other hand, almost all older persons knew about Health Centres that provided health/medical services to the public. More than two-thirds of the respondents had utilized Health Centres and expressed their willingness to use them in the future.

Most of the respondents were aware of the Elderly Activity Centres, the most popular leisure centres for older persons. Almost half the older persons had used them and wanted to use them in the future. The awareness rate for elderly colleges or schools was relatively high, but the utilization rate and the percentage intending to use them in future were very low.

The awareness rates for free, low-cost, and charged elderly nursing homes were 61 per cent, 31 per cent, and 53 per cent, respectively. But only a few older persons had used them, and the percentage intending to use them in future were relatively low.

Regarding the exemption of Residential Inheritance Tax and Personal Inheritance Tax, only a few respondents were aware of it, and almost none benefited from it. The proportion of those who wanted to use it in the future was also very low.

Social Care Services

There are three components in social care services for older persons, namely, home help services, day care centres, and short-term care centres. Only 19 per cent of the respondents were aware of home help services, and less than 1 per cent had used them. But one fourth of the respondents wanted to use them in the future, and two-thirds of them wanted to use only if services were free (see Table 3.14).

As for day care and short-term care centres for older persons, only a few respondents knew about them, and none of them had used them. But the proportion of those who wanted to use them in the future was relatively high.

Needs for Housing

Respondents were asked whether they wanted to live in special houses for older persons if they were constructed. Only one third of older persons wanted to live there (see Table 3.15).

The proportion of those who wanted to live in special house was a little bit higher in the urban area and among those in the age group 65–69. Even among those who did not live with their children, it was only 27 per cent. The major reasons for not wanting to live in elderly/nursing homes were "the objection of children", "bad perception of facilities", and "too expensive". These imply that the need for the housing of older persons is still family-oriented in Korea.

POLICIES AND PROGRAMMES RELATED TO OLDER PERSONS

Development of Welfare Policies for Older Persons

Development of welfare policies

The Welfare Law for older persons was enacted in 1981 to establish legal grounds for the improvement of the welfare of older persons. It was amended in 1990, 1993, and 1997. The law is based on three basic principles. First, since older persons have devoted themselves to bringing up their children and to the development of society, the nation should guarantee them a sound and stable life with dignity. Second, older persons should be guaranteed opportunities for jobs, depending on their ability, and of participation in social activities. Third, older persons themselves should try to maintain their health and contribute to social development through effective utilization of their knowledge and experiences. Following this law, various welfare programmes have been developed and expanded for older persons (see Table 3.16). In 2000, in recognition of the increasing demand for long-term care services among older persons, the government organized the Policy Planning Committee for Long-term Care for Older Persons. The Presidential Committee

TABLE 3.14
Awareness and Utilization Rates of Social Care Services By
Area and Gender: 1998

(Unit: %)

	Total	Area		Gender	
		Urban	Rural	Male	Female
Home Help Services					
Awareness Rate	18.5	22.4	11.7	22.6	16.1
Utilization Rate	0.6	1.0	–	0.2	0.9
Want to use in Future					
Want to use only if free	15.9	6.9	14.2	15.1	16.4
Want to use	9.3	10.9	6.5	13.4	6.8
Not willing to use	74.8	72.2	79.3	71.5	76.8
Day Care Centres for Older Persons					
Awareness Rate	2.0	2.7	1.0	3.9	0.9
Utilization Rate	–	–	–	–	–
Want to Use in Future	18.2	19.7	15.6	22.5	15.6
Short-term Care Centres					
Awareness Rate	1.8	2.4	0.8	3.2	1.0
Utilization Rate	–	–	–	–	–
Want to Use in Future	15.7	17.6	12.4	19.2	13.6
Total	100.0	100.0	100.0	100.0	100.0
(person)	(2,217)	(1,403)	(814)	(814)	(1,395)

Source: KIHASA Survey, 1998.

TABLE 3.15

Special Housing for Older Persons by Area and Age: 1998

(Unit: %)

	Want					Do Not Want	Total	(Person)
	Sub-total	Urban Areas	Sub-urban Areas	Near Famous Resort Areas	Rural Areas			
Total	33.6	6.8	9.1	1.0	16.7	66.4	100.0	(2,208)
Area								
Urban	39.0	9.4	12.4	1.1	16.1	61.0	100.0	(1,395)
Rural	24.3	2.3	3.3	0.8	17.9	75.7	100.0	(813)
Age								
65–69	41.6	7.5	12.5	1.0	20.6	58.4	100.0	(879)
70–74	33.2	7.2	8.1	1.4	16.5	66.8	100.0	(665)
75+	23.3	5.3	5.6	0.6	11.9	76.7	100.0	(663)

Source: KIHASA Survey, 1998.

TABLE 3.16

Welfare Programs and Policy Development of Older Persons, 2004

Year	Programs and Policy Development
1980	Special Treatment Program for Older Persons established
1981	Welfare Law for Older Persons enacted
1981	Elderly Job Bank implemented
1982	Special Treatment Program for Older Persons established
1982	Charter of Respect for Older Persons established
1983	Free Health Check-up Program for Older Persons established
1986	Elderly Workplace Program started
1990	Division of Welfare for Older Persons amended
1990	Welfare Law for Older Persons established
1990	Old Age Allowance provided to Low-Income Elderly
1991	Elderly Employment Promotion Program started
1998	Old Age Pension provided for Low-income and Lower Middle Class Elderly
2000	Policy Planning Committee for Long-term Care for Older Persons organized
2004	Presidential Committee on Aging and Future Society established
	General Law for Aged Society in the process of enactment

Source: Ministry of Health and Welfare, Guidebook for Programs and Policies for the Elderly, 2004.

FIGURE 3.1
Organization of the Ministry of Health and Welfare

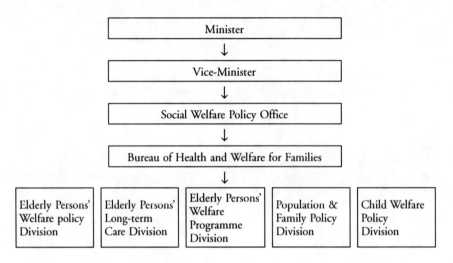

on Ageing and Future Society was established in February 2004, and the General Law for Aged Society is in the process of enactment.

The division of Elderly Welfare was newly established in November 1990 under the Ministry of Health and Social Affairs. Before 1990, affairs on elderly welfare had been mainly dealt with by a division of the Family Welfare. Also, the Elderly Persons' Long-term Care Division (former Elderly Health Care Division) was established in May 1999, and the Elderly Persons' Welfare Programme Division in December 2003 to address increasing policy needs.

Budget for Elderly Welfare

The Korean government has put steady effort to develop elderly welfare policies. As shown in Table 3.17, however, the budget for elderly welfare is only less than 5 per cent of the budget for MOHW and only 0.37 per cent of the total government budget in 2003. Moreover, more than three quarters of the budget for elderly welfare was used for old age pension, while only less than one fourth was used for leisure activities, health and medical care, and home care services.

TABLE 3.17
Budget for Elderly Welfare: 1982–2003

(Unit: million won)

Year	Total Budget of Government (A)	Budget of Ministry of Health and Welfare (B)	B/A %	Budget for Elderly Welfare (C)	D/B %	C/A %
1982	9,313,725	232,521	2.5	702	0.03	0.01
1990	27,455,733	1,151,823	4.2	37,861	3.29	0.54
1995	51,881,113	1,983,896	3.8	61,807	3.11	0.12
2000	86,474,007	5,310,021	6.1	280,867	5.29	0.32
2003	111,483,098	8,351,072	7.5	407,767	4.88	0.37

Source: Ministry of Finance and Economy, Government Finance Statistics in Korea, Each Year.

POLICIES FOR OLDER PERSONS

Income Maintenance System

Public Pension programmes, public assistance based on the National Livelihood Security Law, and Old-age Allowance are the three main components of the public policy aimed at enhancing income security of older persons in Korea. Currently, 6.6 per cent of older persons are covered by Public Pension and 9.5 per cent are receiving National Livelihood Security benefits. To be eligible for Old-age Allowance, one must be a recipient of National Livelihood Security benefits (non-public pension recipient), aged 65 years or above, and living below the government-announced minimum income and asset levels per year.

For National Livelihood Security recipients, the amount of Old-age Allowance benefit is 50,000 won for a person aged 80 and above and 45,000 won for people aged between 65 and 80. In the case of a low-income older person, only 35,000 won of Old-age Allowance is provided; for married couples, each spouse is entitled to a benefit reduced by 25 per cent of 35,000 won. From 1991 when it was introduced until 1998, the Old-age Allowance scheme had been restricted to Livelihood Protection Recipients aged 70 and above. However under the Old Age Pension scheme, which replaced it in 1998, coverage was expanded to low-wage earners as well as Livelihood Protection Recipients aged 65 and above, providing the former with monthly assistance of 30,000 won per person, and the latter with 50,000 won per

TABLE 3.18
Old Age Pension Recipients: 1999–2003

	1999	2000	2001	2002	2003
Recipients (thousand)	660	715	924	891	859
Amounts (thousand won)					
Livelihood Protection Recipients	40–50	50	50	50	50
The low income persons	20	30	40	50	50

Source: Ministry of Health and Welfare (1999 Livelihood Protection Data, 2000).

person. The total number of recipients under the Old Age Pension scheme was 715,000 (21.2 per cent of the total elderly group) in 2000. The Old Age Pension provides its "non-contributory old-age pension benefits" to the low-income elderly who are excluded from the National Pension Scheme, functioning as a complementary mechanism to the public pension scheme.

As of 2003, the Old Age Pension scheme provided benefits to a total of 859,000 recipients, 22 per cent of the total number of older persons above the age of 65. Currently, the Korean government is planning to expand the coverage and raise the benefit levels of the Old Age Pension.

Policies for Employment Opportunities

There are three job placement programmes that provide older persons with opportunities to earn money by making use of their free time. These are the Elderly Job Placement Centre, the Elderly Workplace and Elderly Employment Promotion (based on the Employment Promotion Law).

The Elderly Job Placement Centre (formerly the Elderly Job Bank) was established in 1981 to provide older persons with opportunities to earn money. In 2001, 70 centres were operated by local branch offices of the National Association of Senior Citizens. The government provides each of these centres with 500,000 won monthly to cover their operational expenses. And Community Senior Clubs Programmes were started from 2001 to encourage older persons to start community-based small businesses. In addition to these programmes, the Elderly Employment centre was established as a branch of the National Pension Corporation in January 2004.

The Employment Promotion Law, enacted in 1991, encourages business firms to hire older persons aged 55 or above for at least 3 per cent of their employee pool. In addition, this law stipulates that 160 occupation categories (attending to parking lots and public parks, translation, etc.) should be preferentially allocated to older persons.

Policies for Healthy Life

Free Health Examination

To diagnose and stop geriatric diseases at an early stage, medical check-ups are provided for older persons covered by health insurance. Free health examinations are also provided to older persons under the Livelihood Protection scheme. Free health examinations were extended to cover various geriatric diseases such as diabetes and cataracts in 1992. In 1996, they were also expanded from covering just general examinations, including blood test and X-rays, to include special geriatric diseases such as cancer, depending on the demand of older persons.

Community Visiting Nurse Services

There are two types of community visiting nurse (CVN) services for older persons in Korea. One is the CVN service provided under the Community Health Care Act by nurses working at public health centres. These public health centres are operated by corresponding local governments — Si (cities), Gun (counties), Gu (districts) — scattered throughout the country. There were 242 public health centres and 1,267 public health clinics as of December 2001. Medical services are provided free of charge by these public facilities, which are mainly targeted at low-income groups.

The role of community visiting nurses at public health centres had been largely confined to providing simple or routine health care services such as bathing/dressing patients and providing health checks. But recently, more sophisticated medical care services, including ulcer treatments, are being delivered.

The other type of CVN services is delivered under the Medical Care Act by home visiting nurses working at hospitals. As of 2000, 45 hospitals were providing these services. The target group consists of early discharged patients, those who have experienced inpatient (or outpatient or emergent patient) treatments and need re-admission to hospitals, patients with chronic diseases or cerebrovascular diseases, women who are delivering a child, newborn babies, etc. The cost of those services is covered partly by health insurance and partly paid by the patient.

Policies for Social Welfare Service

The public provision of long-term care in Korea is still in its early stage. Therefore, the main policy concern at present are not qualitative aspects such as autonomy, privacy, and consumer rights of older persons, but how to respond to the increasing demands for long-term care.

As the elderly population increases, the number of frail or disabled elderly Koreans who need assistance with day-to-day tasks also increases. In Korea, the physical care needs of older persons have traditionally been provided mostly by family caregivers. The concept of family care for older persons is still prevalent, but the role of the family in supporting older persons is no longer taken for granted. It is also becoming more difficult to take care of frail older persons within the family. This may be due to several factors such as changing values of family life, changes in family type, the decrease in family size, and women's increasing participation in the workplace and social activities. Based on these changes, the government has recently begun to devote attention to providing public long-term care services for older persons.

Institutional Care Services

There are 7 types of welfare facilities for older persons in Korea. In 2003, 20,439 people (0.51 per cent of those aged 65 and above) were cared for in 357 facilities. As of December 31, 2003, there were 119 elderly homes — no charge, part charge, or full charge — for the aged. The number of nursing homes will increase in line with a deliberate plan to cover old-older persons with profound disabilities living in private dwellings.

Home Care Services

In recognition of the difficulty of caring for frail older persons in the family, the government has begun to devote attention to home care services for older persons. 228 home help service centres, 211 day care centres for older persons, and 66 short-term care centres are in operation at present. Around two-thirds of these centres are receiving financial support from the central government. The programme will receive major budgetary support, and is thus expected to increase rapidly in the coming years.

Home help services, day care centres for older persons, and short-term care centres are available free of charge to elderly recipients of National Livelihood Security at reduced rate to poor older persons. Others pay regular rates.

TABLE 3.19
Contents of Home Care Services by Facility

Type	Contents
Home-help Service centre	Domestic support service: preparing meals, dish washing, shopping, cleaning etc. Personal care service: assistance in feeding, bathing, walking, toilet using etc. Social service: giving phone calls and visits, writing letters Counselling and education service Facilities: 228
Adult day Care centre	Rehabilitative services Food services and bathing services Leisure activities Education for the families with the disabled elderly Facilities: 211
Short stay Care centre	Food services Rehabilitative services Others Facilities: 66

Source: Based on the Welfare Law for Older Persons.

Policies for a Meaningful and Comfortable Life

Vitalization of Community Senior Centres

The community senior centre (*Kyungrodang*), a representative type of leisure facility for older persons in Korea, is supported with 44,000 won a month for operational expenses, and 250,000 won a year for heating expenses, both of which come from the state government budget. There are 48,800 community senior centres now. Moreover, to vitalize the activity of these centres, various programmes are being developed and distributed. Also, assistance in daily living, such as cleaning services and meal delivery services, will be provided in cooperation with women's associations and the young in the community.

Establishment of Multi-purpose Senior Centres

To offer comprehensive welfare services such as health counselling, culture, and recreation to older persons, 145 multi-purpose senior centres are currently in operation and more will be established, focusing on metropolitan areas.

Expansion of Opportunities for Volunteer and Social Activities

The rate of volunteer activity participation among older persons in Korea is very low due to the country's social environment, although some do participate in voluntary activities such as environmental protection and traffic regulation. Volunteer activity can boost both the physical and mental health of older persons and make their lives more productive and meaningful. In this regard, there is a plan to induce more elderly people to participate in volunteer activities by increasing the number of community volunteer programs and providing commuting expenses.

Boosting Respect for the Elderly

Celebration of Elderly Week and Day of the Elderly

The government celebrates "Elderly Week" and "Day of the Elderly" on October 2 to boost the spirit of respect for the elderly. In addition, the government selects and gives rewards to family members who have demonstrated exemplary filial acts and to citizens who have contributed to the welfare of the elderly. The government also organizes sports events for the elderly and seminars on ageing.

Expansion of Senior Concession System

The senior concession system, which is aimed at promoting respect for the elderly, is applied to a total of 13 items, including public transport fares and free entrance to national parks or public places, for older persons aged 65 or above. It will be expanded with the cooperation of other ministries concerned.

CONCLUSION

Ageing is progressing rapidly in Korea. Korea is already an ageing society and will become an aged society in 2019. Rapid ageing, of course, is a result of rapid decreases in fertility and mortality. Consequently, ageing is one of the major demographic problems we have to solve. As the number of older persons increases, the general public, the government, and specialists become much more concerned with the problem of ageing.

As we have seen in section 2, older persons are not a homogeneous group. They consist of various subgroups according to their demographic and socioeconomic characteristics. For example, some older persons are older than others, some live in rural areas, some live alone, some suffer from economic hardships, and some are unhealthy. To formulate policies on ageing, it is important to recognize that these subgroups have different welfare needs.

Ageing is much more than a family affair, and it requires government intervention. Despite the strenuous efforts of the government, however, welfare policies for older persons are not enough in terms of budget, scope, and institutional support. Also, welfare policies and programmes for older persons are not yet specific enough to meet the different needs of the various subgroups of older persons. There are still considerable gaps between welfare needs of older persons and the government policy. More effort from the government is needed to solve the problems of ageing.

Notes

[1]   This chapter draws heavily on the authors' previous work: "Population Aging in the Republic of Korea" by Ahn (1997) and "Living Profiles of Older Persons and Social Policies on Aging in Korea" by Chung (1999).

[2]   Ageing index = (population 65 years and above/population under 14 years old)*100.

[3]   The survey "Living Profile and Welfare Service Needs of Older Persons in Korea" was conducted in 1998. 9,355 households and 2,535 persons aged 65 or above were interviewed. Of 9,355 households interviewed, 21 per cent were households with older persons.

References

Ahn, K.C. *Population Aging in the Republic of Korea*. Yonsei Journal of Educational Research, 1997.

———— et al. *A Study on the Characteristics of the Elderly, Report on Population*, National Statistical Office, Republic of Korea, 1995.

Bumagin, V. and K. Him. *Aging is A Family Affair*. Thomas Y. Corwell, Publisher, 1979.

Chung, K.H. et al. "Report of the Survey 'Living Profile and Welfare Service Needs of Older Persons' ", Korean Institute of Health and Social Affairs, 1998.

Chung, K.H., ed. *Living Profiles of Older Persons and Social Policies on Aging in Korea*, KIHASA, 1999.

Hermalin, A. "Aging in Asia: Setting the Research Foundation", Asia-Pacific Population Research Reports, East-West Center, 1995.

Kim, D.S. et al., ed. Population of Korea, I, II, National Statistical Office, 2002.

Kim, H.J. "Poor Elderly and Social Policy". In *Korean Journal of Sociology* 14, 1980.

Korea National Statistical Office (KNSO). Population and Housing Census Reports, 1960–2000.

————. Population Projection, 2001.

————. Social Indicators in Korea, 2003.

Ministry of Health and Welfare. White Chapter of Health and Welfare, 2004 (in Korean).

————. Guidebook for Programs and Policies for the Elderly, 2004 (in Korean).

————. Annual Report on Welfare Facilities, 2004 (in Korean).

Pifer, A. and L. Bronte. *The Aging: A Guide of Public Policy*. University of Pittsburgh, 1984.

Rhee, K.O. et al. *Status of the Elderly in Korea and Policy Implications*, KIHASA, 1994.

Yoon, J.J. "A Socio-demographic Study on the *Korea Elderly*", *Korean Journal of Gerontology*, "Study on the Social Caring of the Elderly", in *Korean Journal of Sociology* 16, 1982.

4

SINGAPORE'S RESPONSE TO AN AGEING POPULATION[1]

Yap Mui Teng

INTRODUCTION: SINGAPORE'S AGED POPULATION IN COMPARATIVE PERSPECTIVE

Of the ten ASEAN countries, Singapore has the highest proportion of the population that is elderly or aged[2] (defined as those aged 60 years and older) although Indonesia has the largest number by far (Figure 4.1). According to the United Nations, Singapore's elderly made up nearly 11 per cent of the population in 2002, compared with about 8 per cent for the next "oldest" countries — Indonesia and Thailand — and only 4 per cent for Cambodia, the "youngest" of the 10 countries (UN Population Ageing 2002 wallchart). In numerical terms, however, Singapore has among the smallest number of the old, at about 460,000, compared with over 17 million in Indonesia.

Concern over the ageing of the population, however, is not only about the growing number and proportion of the old. It is also about the changing age structure of the population as encapsulated in the "dependency ratio". The latter is the ratio of persons in the "dependent" age groups, typically below age 15 (the "young dependents") and age 60 or 65 and older (the "old dependents"), relative to the remaining "working age" population 15–59 or 64 years. While there is not necessarily a one-to-one correspondence between age and dependency at the individual level (a criticism often levelled at the usefulness of the dependency ratio), the concept remains a simple and easy to use measure of age structure changes which have tremendous potential

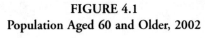

FIGURE 4.1
Population Aged 60 and Older, 2002

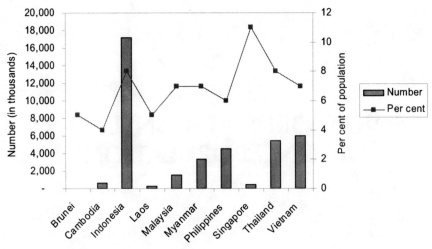

Source: World Population Ageing: 1950–2050, United Nations.

consequences for the population. The rising old dependency ratio, the ratio of the old to working age population, experienced or to be experienced by many countries is generally acknowledged to impact its health care and social security systems, and even its future economic prosperity and political development, besides entailing the need for, and availability of, support (see, for example, Nizamuddin 1999; Schulz, in the same volume, however cautions against turning demographic ratios into social predictions [p. 135]).

As Figure 4.2 shows, Singapore currently has the lowest proportion of the young and highest proportion of the old compared with the other ASEAN countries. This difference is due to differences in the timing of fertility declines among the various countries. Singapore's demographic transition began earlier, with sharp fertility declines in the late 1960s and early 1970s, compared with the other ASEAN countries. The Total Fertility Rate (TFR) fell from more than four children per woman in 1965 to replacement level just 10 years later, and has remained below replacement since.

Figure 4.3 shows the projected age composition of populations in the ASEAN countries in 2050, based on projections made by the United Nations (United Nations 2002). According to this projection, the proportion aged 60 and above in Singapore will likely rise to 35 per cent, or about one in three persons. In comparison, the other ASEAN countries, except Cambodia and Laos, would have about 20–25 per cent in this age group. More importantly

FIGURE 4.2
Age Composition of Population, 2000

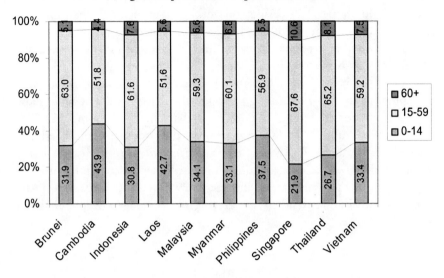

Source: World Population Ageing: 1950–2050, United Nations.

FIGURE 4.3
Age Composition of Population, 2050

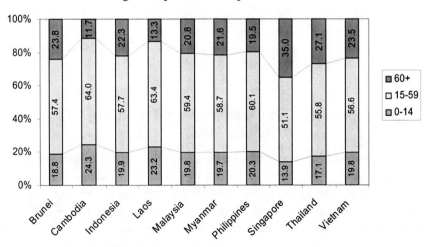

Source: World Population Ageing: 1950–2050, United Nations.

for Singapore, the proportion in the working ages is projected to decline from about 67 per cent in 2000 to about 50 per cent in 2050. Thus, whereas there were ten elderly per 100 persons of working ages in 2000, the number is projected to rise to nearly 50 per 100 in 2050. The other ASEAN countries are all projected to experience a rise in the old dependency but not nearly to the extent that is likely to be experienced by Singapore.

Table 4.1 below shows Singapore's official projections on the number and proportion of the old, using age 65 as the cut-off age. The table shows that the number of elderly will grow more than threefold, from 235,000 in 1999 to 796,000 in 2030. As a proportion of the population, the elderly will increase from about 7 per cent to 18.9 per cent over the same period. Similarly there will be a threefold rise in the old dependency ratio, from 10 elderly per 100 persons of working age to 29.5 per 100. Regardless of the projection used, the trend in the greying of the Singapore population is evident.

TABLE 4.1
Size of Elderly Population and Dependency Ratios, Official Projections

	1999	2010	2020	2030
Number of elderly aged 65+ (000s)	235	312	529	796
Proportion of elderly aged 65+[a]	7.3	8.4	13.1	18.9
Old dependency ratio (65+ years)[b]	10.4	11.6	19.0	29.5

Notes: a) Of citizens/permanent residents
  b) Citizens/permanent residents aged 65 and above per 100 of those aged 15-64.
Source: MCD 1999, p. 29, table 1-1.

CONCERNS AND DEVELOPMENT OF A POLICY ON THE AGED IN SINGAPORE

In Singapore, concerns over the growing population of the elderly and its implications were raised since the early 1980s. A high level Committee on the Problems of the Aged, headed by then Health Minister Howe Yoon Chong, was appointed in 1982 to study "the problems of the increasing number of people aged 60 or more in our society and their consequences to our society and to recommend measures to prevent, ameliorate or deal with the problems" (Ministry of Health 1984, p. 1). In 1988, when the government appointed a number of advisory councils to flesh out a national plan to bring Singapore to developed country status by the end of the 20th century, the "aged" was again among the subjects. The Advisory Council on the Aged, headed by then Minister for Law and for Home Affairs, S. Jayakumar, endorsed most of the recommendations of the 1982 Committee. A National Advisory Council on Family and the Aged (NACFA) was also set up in 1989 under the purview of the then Ministry of Community Development. NACFA incorporated two working committees, the Committee on the Family (COF) and the Committee on the Aged (COA). In 1998, the COA winded up as the Inter-ministerial Committee (IMC) on the Ageing Population,[3] was set up "to lead a co-ordinated national response to address the challenges and maximise the opportunities that an ageing population bring" (http://app.mcys.gov.sg/web/indv_abtageing.asp). The IMC is now in its second term with a new group of members appointed in 2003. The recommendations of the Advisory Councils and IMC (so far) have been translated into Eldercare Master Plans — a 7-year Eldercare Master Plan (FY1994–2000) and a 5-year Eldercare Master Plan (FY2001–2005). These serve as blueprints for services including strategies and plans designed to achieve the desired outcomes formulated (MCDS n.d. Eldercare Master Plan (FY2001 to FY2005), reprinted in 2002).

In 1997 as well, an IMC on the Health Care of the Elderly (IMCHE) was set up by the Ministry of Health to review health care needs and identify measures to be put in place "over the next 5–10 years to ensure health care needs would be met and health care remains affordable" (Ministry of Health 1999, Executive Summary, para. 1). On the employment front, the government also established a Tripartite Committee in 1995 to study the implications of extending the retirement age beyond age 60 and "ensure that the higher retirement age would not undermine workers' employability and job security as well as employers' cost competitiveness" in view of the "ageing population, increasing life expectancy and the heavy reliance on foreign workers" (Ministry of Labour 1997, pp. 9–10).

Reflecting the importance of the issue in the minds of Singapore's leaders, various government reviews of the state of Singapore's economy and society have discussed the ageing population issue. The Singapore 21 Committee (1997), the Economic Review Committee (2001–2002) and the Remaking Singapore Committee (2002–2003) have included the topic in their discussions. The section below reviews the state of the elderly population in Singapore and looks at some future challenges. This will be followed by a review of developments to date with regard to policy measures recommended and implemented.

State of the Elderly in Singapore

The 1995 Survey of Senior Citizens, the latest national survey available, showed that the health status among respondents aged 60 and older was generally good (Table 4.2). Although more than 30 per cent received treatment for some chronic illness, more than 95 per cent could live independently. About 87–97 per cent could perform essential household tasks such as cleaning, laundry, meal preparation (Ministry of Health et al. 1996).

The study also showed, however, that the majority of those aged 60 and older had little or no formal education — 67 per cent reported no qualifications and another 23 per cent had only primary school qualifications. About 25 per cent of the men and 69 per cent of the women had either never married or were widowed, divorced or separated. Together, these findings suggest that the current generation of elderly must rely on others for support. About nine out of 10 of the 60 and older studied did not make any provision for their own old age financial security and about two-thirds did not have any CPF savings. Even among those with CPF savings, 62 per cent were of the opinion that this was inadequate.

TABLE 4.2
Health Status of Senior Citizens Aged 60 and Over

	Good	Not too Good	Poor	Total
Self assessment of health	83.4	15.7	0.9	100.0

	Male	Female	Total
Hospitalised in the past year (%)	7.4	7.9	7.7

	Male	Female	Total
Receiving treatment for longstanding illness (%)	31.4	32.9	32.2

	<= 3	>= 4	Total
Katz Index (higher = more dependent)	96.2	3.8	100.0

Source: Adapted from Ministry of Health et al. 1996, various tables.

On a brighter note, co-residence or living in close proximity to children remains the norm in Singapore. Only 9.3 per cent of the sixty-plus lived alone or in other arrangements, and 5.8 per cent lived with their spouses only. About 85 per cent lived in multigenerational households, which presumably included financial and other support. Even among those who lived alone or with their spouses only, the majority (56 per cent and 80 per cent) received financial and/or in-kind support from their children, if these were present. For 73 per cent of the elderly aged 60 and above, their children were their most important source of financial support (MOH et al. 1996 Table 5.3). Women were more likely than men to rely on their children. The proportion that reported "children" as the most important source of financial support declined with age, however — from 86 per cent among those aged 75 and older, to about 57 per cent among those aged 60–64 years.

Policy Concerns

Going forward, the future elderly are expected to be better educated, given the advances in educational attainment among baby boomers who will reach retirement age around 2010 (Tables 4.3 and 4.4). The proportion with upper secondary and higher qualifications is likely to rise as is the proportion with a history of better paid jobs and higher incomes. Thus they are also likely to be wealthier and perhaps less dependent on others for financial support. However, the IMC also cautioned that "(t)he senior citizens of the future will clearly be different from their counterparts of today — they will have different

TABLE 4.3
Socio-economic Characteristics of the Baby Boomers, 1999

	Late Baby Boomers	Early Baby Boomers	Pre-War/ War-time Cohorts
Per cent with upper secondary or higher qualifications	25.8	17.0	11.8
Per cent in professional, managerial and technical jobs	43.3	37.0	31.7
Average monthly income from work	$3,310	$3,380	$2,890

Source: "Baby Boomers", http://www.singstat.gov.sg/chapters/snippets/baby.html.

TABLE 4.4
Educational Attainment of Senior Citizens, 1995–2030

	1995		2010		2030	
	No. (000)	%	No. (000)	%	No. (000)	%
Total	130.5	100.0	196.0	100.0	506.4	100.0
Primary and below	116.4	89.2	139.6	71.2	191.2	37.8
Secondary	9.0	6.9	32.1	16.4	161.1	31.8
Upper secondary	3.3	2.5	16.7	8.5	87.6	17.3
University	1.8	1.4	7.6	3.9	66.5	13.1

Source: MCDS 1999 (IMC report Table 1-2: Education Profile of Persons aged 65–74, p. 31).

values, aspirations and needs" (MCDS 1999, p. 34 para. 20), and being "articulate and used to high living standards, older Singaporeans could be a significant lobby group" (p. 33 para. 14) that could sway policies in their own narrow interest rather than that of the wider society.

The Singaporean elderly of the future are also expected to live longer, although neither the IMC nor the IMCHE made specific projections on the likely age. Be that as it may, the IMC's Workgroup on Health Care estimated on the basis of the 1995 Survey of Senior Citizens that there would be 12,000 with poor ADL among senior citizens aged 65 and above in 2000, increasing to 37,000 in 2030. However, it also added that the disability rate could fall and the number with poor ADL decrease "if preventive measures and healthy lifestyle are promoted" (MCDS 1999, p. 100). If the experiences of the more developed countries can be used as gauge, it is likely that the future elderly of Singapore will both live longer and have longer disability-free years (see Table 4.5).

However, the elderly are also acknowledged to use disproportionately more health care than the general population as "they are more prone to disease and disability and their complications" and "they are more likely to need continuous long-term care" (Ministry of Health 1999, chapter 1 para. 4). According to the IMCHE, the elderly is projected to make up a growing proportion of public hospital admissions — from 20 per cent in 1995 to 23 per cent in 2000, 32 per cent in 2010 and 43 per cent in 2030 (chapter 5 para. 3). It also acknowledged that "despite healthy living, health will deteriorate with age" (chapter 5 para. 1) and "the future will see more 'very old' elderly,

TABLE 4.5
Life and Health Expectancies at Birth, Singapore and Selected Countries, 1999

Rank	Country	Life expectancy (yrs)		Health Expectancy (yrs)		% of lifespan lived with disability	
		Male	Female	Male	Female	Male	Female
1	Japan	77.6	84.3	71.9	77.2	7.3	8.4
2	Australia	76.8	82.2	70.8	75.5	7.8	8.1
3	France	74.9	83.6	69.3	76.9	7.5	8.0
8	Switzerland	75.6	83.0	69.5	75.5	8.1	9.1
24	USA	73.8	79.7	67.5	72.6	8.6	8.8
28	Denmark	72.9	78.1	67.2	71.5	7.9	8.4
30	Singapore	75.1	80.8	67.4	71.2	10.2	11.8

Source: Adapted from Koh Eng Chuan, "Measuring Old Age Health Expectancy in Singapore", *Statistics Singapore Newsletter,* July 2000, pp. 5–9 (based on World Health Report 2000, WHO).

with a different socio-economic profile and possibly different patterns of use" (para. 9). Thus, even if most health care expenditures are incurred only in the last few years of life, "the rapidly ageing population and the elderly's growing health care needs are of increasing national concern" (MOH 1999). One reason for concern would be the financing of these growing health care needs, besides ensuring that appropriate and sustainable health care services are available. As the IMC's Workgroup on Landuse has noted, "(w)hilst senior citizens are able to live longer lives, their health care may be deferred but cannot be avoided" (MCDS 1999, p. 148).

As life expectancy increases as well, the elderly can be expected to spend more years in retirement. Thus, unless the retirement age is raised in tandem and/or human resource practices are changed so that everyone who is able could continue working, ensuring adequate financial resources for old age is another vital aspect of the challenges posed by the ageing of the population (MCDS 1999, p. 125). A further potential challenge is the projected change in family size and structure that could impact on the willingness and ability to care for the elderly. This arises from recent trends in marriage delay and non-marriage, reductions in family sizes, divorce and widowhood, and preference for independent living (the latter, according to the IMC Workgroup on Landuse, citing the Ministry of Health, could be 25 per cent in the long term). Another trend is female labour force participation, which affects the availability of these traditional caregivers. The result could be an escalation of expenditure on the care of the elderly (since family care is purportedly cheaper than institutional care), and possibly taxation, to provide for the old. The potential for intergenerational conflict, as apparent in some of the more developed countries currently, also figured in the IMC's deliberations (see IMC Report 1999). According to the IMC, "(t)he next ten years before 2010 present a window of opportunity for us to introduce policies, plans, services and infrastructure to meet the needs of an ageing population. The implementation of the IMC's recommendations will require a coordinated national effort on the part of all sectors and levels of society. We must continue to monitor changing trends and ensure that our policies remain relevant so that we can ensure "Successful Ageing for Singapore" (p. 27, short report).

Policy Response

Throughout these reviews, the basic principles recommended by the Howe Committee continued to underpin the government's approach towards the elderly. These are: physical and financial independence in old age, integration of the elderly in the family and community, and family and community care over institutionalisation. Moreover, the solutions chosen should be "affordable", "sustainable", and conducive to social cohesion in the long run. Thus, the desired outcomes identified by the IMC, and accepted by the government, are:

1. At the individual level, older Singaporeans should be healthy, active and secure. They should be able to age with respect and dignity, and should lead independent and fulfilling lives as integral members of their families and communities

2. At the family level, we would like to see strong, extended, caring families. Family relationships of interdependence should complement the older person's independence. For the frail or ill, the family should continue to be the first line of support.

3. At the community level, we would like to see a strong network of community services, opportunities for engagement and integrated communities. We want to foster a deep sense of community ownership and a high degree of participation in securing the well-being of the older person and the family.

4. At the national level, we want a high level of national preparedness, a competitive and vibrant economy as well as social cohesion and rootedness. We would like the State to provide the leadership necessary to drive a coordinated national approach to the challenges of an ageing population. (www.mcds.gov.sg/imc/html/abt_imc.html, downloaded 5 October 2004).

The vision of the IMC is to "achieve '**Successful Ageing for Singapore**', that is, to ensure that all levels of society are well prepared for the challenges and opportunities of an ageing Singapore". In the event, the government has accepted the recommendations of the IMC made in 1999. In addition to the desired outcomes above, the Ministry of Community Development, Youth and Sports (MCYS), as the lead government agency on ageing issues, also adopts the following three key principles:

a) Social integration of our Elder
    a. Our senior citizens should be valued as contributing members of society,
    b. Our policies must enable them to remain with their families, and in the community for as long as possible,
    c. Our policies should cater to all groups of the elderly — the frail, the ill, as well as those who are well and healthy

b) Collective responsibility from all sectors (Many Helping Hands approach)
    a. Every individual has a personal responsibility to plan and prepare for his or her old age.
    b. The role of the family and the community is to provide the first and second line of support respectively for those who need care and support.
    c. The role of the state is to set out the policy framework, provide the infrastructure and resources necessary for the other sectors to play their part.

c) Long term sustainability
    a. The financial impact of long-term aged care can be severe. We have to implement policies and programmes in a cost-effective manner and ensure their financial sustainability (http://app.mcys.gov.sg/web/indv_policy.asp)

SPECIFIC POLICIES AND PROGRAMMES

In the following sections, specific policies and programmes will be examined under three broad headings: health care, financial security, and social integration.

Health Care

The policy on health care for the elderly, as it has developed over the years, can be summarized as follows:

a) Health promotion and disease prevention to enable the elderly to remain healthy and active in the community

b) Early detection and treatment of diseases to avoid disability and complications

c) When disease and disability set in, the focus of care should be on retraining the elderly to care for themselves or with the help of their family

d) The elderly sick should be cared for in the community for as long as possible and institutionalisation should be a last resort.

e) Healthy and independent elderly should be encouraged to help the sick and dependent elderly.

f) The government will continue to be the main provider of acute hospital care, complemented by a variety of community-based services ("stepdown care"), including acute hospitals, nursing homes, day care and day rehabilitation centres, home medical care and home nursing, and so on, run by voluntary welfare organizations.

g) Private sector general practitioners and dentists have also been drawn in to provide care to low-income elderly in their neighbourhood at subsidized public sector rates. This enables eligible elderly to have access to care near their homes instead of travelling to a government polyclinic. The private practitioners are reimbursed by the Ministry of Health.

h) In terms of health care financing, Singapore has, since the 1980s, moved away from a purely tax-financed health care system to one based on saving for one's own medical needs through the Medisave (a component of the Central Provident Fund), co-payment to prevent over-consumption, and an endowment fund, Medifund, which provides a safety net for those who are unable to pay their hospital bills.

i) While initially wary of over-consumption and escalation of health care costs due to third party payment, the government has over the years increased the role of insurance in health care financing. A catastrophic insurance scheme, Medishield, was introduced under the CPF with premiums payable with Medisave savings. The government has also allowed a limited number of private insurers to provide similar schemes, and with premiums similarly payable with Medisave. It is currently reviewing the effectiveness of the Medishield scheme in helping to pay for large hospital bills. To improve participation of the elderly in the Medishield scheme, the government also introduced a Medishield for the Elderly scheme which, when budget surpluses permit, pays the premium for elderly who have been accepted by Medishield or other Medisave-approved insurance schemes. Those who do not qualify due to pre-existing conditions receive a top-up equivalent to the amount of the premium. The elderly already in the scheme can receive the equivalent premium rebate "in recognition of their prudence and personal responsibility in taking up catastrophic insurance coverage" (IMC website, http://www.mcds.gov.sg/imc/html/IMCInitiatives.html).

j) A long-term care insurance, Eldershield, has also been introduced. The scheme provides cash benefits to the insured who cannot perform three or more activities of daily living (ADLs) to purchase services as needed. An Interim Disability Assistance Programme for the Elderly (IDAPE) was introduced at the same time to help Singaporeans who were either too old to join the Eldershield scheme, and those aged 40–69 who had pre-existing disabilities at the launch of Eldershield. IDAPE is fully funded by the government and eligible Singaporeans need not pay any premium. However, the benefits are also reduced and subject to a means test.

k) In view of the potential escalation in public health care expenditure, the government has also taken various steps to keep this in check. For example, the Casemix method has been introduced in determining the amount of subsidy to be provided to public hospitals. This method takes into account the type of treatment delivered compared with the earlier method of relying on patient days of stay. According to MOH, the introduction of Casemix is to ensure a better allocation of resources (http://www.moh.gov.sg/corp/systems/casemix/overview.do, downloaded 26 October 2004).

Another factor which can contribute to raising health care cost is technology, and in this regard, the MOH has indicated that while the government would ensure that "good and affordable" basic medical care will be available to all Singaporeans and "(t)he basic medical package will reflect good, up-to-date medical practice, which is cost-effective and of proven value", it "will not provide the latest and best of everything" (http://www.moh.gov.sg/corp/systems/our/deliverysys.do, downloaded 26 October 2004).

l) An Eldercare Fund was set up in April 2000, as an endowment fund, to finance the operating subsidies of eldercare facilities and services run by voluntary welfare organizations. These include community hospitals, nursing homes, rehabilitation centres and so on. Since July 2003, subsidies to users of step-down care have also been revised to provide the bottom 10th percentile by household income with 75 per cent subsidy, while the $10–30^{th}$ percentile drew 50 per cent subsidy and the $30–50^{th}$ percentile 25 per cent subsidy. Per capita, rather than total, household income is used as the criterion.

Financial Security

Financial security in old age is seen as comprising life-long employability, prudent financial planning with a "basic needs" Central Provident Fund system as the main formal pillar, and mutual support among family members. In line with the "many helping hands" approach adopted in its overall welfare policy, the government and community will step in and provide the safety net when individuals and families are not able to help themselves.

Employment and employability

Employment is seen as a way for the elderly to remain healthy and integrated, besides being a source of income. In this regard, and in view of the slowing work force growth, and longer and healthier lifespans enjoyed by more Singaporeans, the government has taken steps to promote employment and employability of older workers.

a) In 1993, the government extended the retirement age from 55 to 60 years through the introduction of the Retirement Age Act (after failing to get employers to do so voluntarily). It further announced its intention to extend the retirement age gradually to 67 by 2003. In the event, the retirement age was extended to 62 in 1999 and has not been raised further since. The raising of the retirement age from 55 to 60 years enabled some 63,000 Singaporeans, who would otherwise have retired, to remain in the work force, raising the labour force participation rate of this group from 47 per cent in 1993 to nearly 53 per cent in 1996

(Ministry of Labour 1997). The labour force participation rate of the 55–59 age group was 56.8 per cent in 2003, having fallen slightly from 58.2 per cent recorded in 2002 (Department of Statistics 2004 Table 4.2). The labour force participation rate for the 60–64 age group has not changed significantly since 1999, however, fluctuating between 32 per cent and 35 per cent over the past five years. While calls have also been made for the removal of the retirement age, this has not been accepted by the government.

b) The government has also reduced the rates of employer contribution to their older workers' provident fund as the higher cost of employing such workers is seen as an obstacle to their continued employment (or re-employment if retrenched). Thus the employer contribution rate was reduced to 7.5 per cent for workers aged 55–65 and 5 per cent for workers aged 65 and above with effect from 1 July 1993. From October 2005, moreover, employer contribution for workers aged 50–55 will also be reduced below that for workers below age 50 (though not as low as for workers aged 55 and above).

c) The medical benefits scheme for civil servants was also adjusted to put greater responsibility on the individual and reduce the burden of employer-provided medical benefits. New employees are given an additional 1 per cent contribution to their Medisave account, which they could use to purchase medical insurance, but they would also have to be responsible for their entire hospitalization bill. Employers' co-payment for outpatient care is also capped.

d) Lifelong employability is the current mantra, with the government providing the bulk of the funds for training and skills redevelopment for older workers who generally have low educational attainment. Financial support is also given to participating employers and employees. A People-for-Jobs Traineeship Programme (PJTP) was launched in 2001 to help older job seekers who are prepared to switch sectors. The government also provides financial support to companies that put in place traineeship programmes aimed at helping older workers prepare better for new job requirements, and in 2004, the programme was expanded to help displaced executives and professionals, besides lower skilled workers. Currently, for every PJTP worker aged 40–49 years, the monthly wage support is 50 per cent of monthly gross salary or $2,000 per month, whichever is the lower, for a period of up to 6 months. For those workers who are 50 and over, there is an additional three months of wage support (i.e. from 7th to 9th month) at 25 per cent of gross salary or $1,000 per month, whichever is the lower. As of end-February 2004, there were more than 5,000 companies registered under the programme, and in total, more than 16,000 older workers have been placed in employment. In addition, there is also the Skills Training and Employability Enhancement for the Retrenched and unemployed workers programme (STEER), which is an extension of the Skills Redevelopment Programme for retrenched and unemployed workers, and it links full-time training to job placement.

e) In 1996, the Back to Work programme was introduced to encourage housewives and retirees to return to the workforce. Employers were also encouraged to employ older workers and to promote friendly human resource practices and redesign jobs (Ministry of Manpower 1999). The IMC's Workgroup on Employment and Employability also recommended that Golden Manpower Centres be set up at Community Development Councils to "provide information, training, and job placement of older workers" (p. 18). Since that time, and with rising unemployment due to economic cycles and restructuring, such roles have become even more important.

Financial planning and saving for old age

The Central Provident Fund has been, and will continue to be, the main formal institution for financial security in old age. However, it has also evolved from a scheme conceived simply as a source of cash income in old age to include provision for home ownership and health care. Liberal use of CPF savings, particularly with regard to housing, has resulted in what has been dubbed the "asset-rich, cash-poor" phenomenon with many members having only small cash balances on their accounts which are unlikely to be adequate to last them through their retirement. There has also been concern that the coverage of the CPF scheme is inadequate as only non-employees are not covered. The rate of return on CPF savings has also been generally acknowledged to be low (MCDS 1999). More recently, there has been concern that the CPF is a statutory cost contributing to the high cost of doing business in Singapore, thus affecting Singapore companies' competitiveness in an increasingly globalized environment (Ministry of Trade and Industry 2003). For these reasons, the government has recently introduced some major changes to the CPF system in what is seen as the slaughtering of one of its sacred cows.

The most important of these changes is probably the reduction of employer contribution for all workers, announced in October 2003. Unlike in the past when the government had maintained that it would keep total CPF contribution at 40 per cent of gross monthly salary (comprising 20 per cent each from employer and employee), this will be reduced to 30 per cent–36 per cent (comprising 20 per cent from employee and 10 per cent–16 per cent from employer), depending on economic conditions. The salary ceiling for contribution is also lowered. These changes, *ceteris paribus*, would effectively reduce the quantum of CPF savings employees are able to accumulate for retirement. At the same time, however, the government also increased the amount (known as the "Minimum Sum") that CPF members must retain in their account for old age, the Special Account, which can only be withdrawn at age 55. The interest rate paid by the CPF Board on monies saved in the SA is higher than that for the Ordinary Account which can be drawn upon for housing and other investments.

Following the recommendation of the IMC, the government has also introduced the Supplementary Retirement Scheme (SRS), which is a private-sector operated (by the three major local banks) scheme that hopes to encourage Singaporeans to save more for their old age beyond their CPF contributions. Participation is voluntary; however, the government grants tax exemption on the amount saved in SRS and when withdrawn at retirement, only 50 per cent of the sum withdrawn is taxable. There is, however, a penalty for early withdrawal, defined by the retirement age at the time of joining the scheme. Participants can contribute varying amounts, subject to a cap based on the SRS contribution rate (15 per cent for citizens and PRs, and 35 per cent for foreigners who are not included in the CPF scheme) and the preceding year's income. SRS was introduced in April 2001.

To enhance returns on CPF savings, members have been allowed to invest in CPF-approved, privately managed, fund schemes. The number of private fund managers approved has also been increased. However, this could be a double-edged sword until such time when investors become more financially savvy with better education on the subject, as recommended by the IMC. CPF members are also encouraged to purchase annuities with their CPF monies upon reaching withdrawal age, rather than keeping them in their CPF accounts.

Limits have been placed on the amount of CPF savings that can be used for investment in housing. This would hopefully stem over-investment in residential properties, the main reason that CPF balances at retirement have been low.

Family support

Schemes introduced to encourage Singaporeans to maintain their parents include the following:

a) Parent (and grandparent) relief: Taxpayers who maintain their parents or grandparents in Singapore are given income tax relief, but these not meant to cover all expenses incurred. First introduced in the 1960s, the amount of relief has been raised over the years, and the current relief is $5,000 for each parent living in the same household, and $3,500 for each parent not living in the same household. An additional $3,000 relief is provided for each handicapped parent/grandparent. The parent/grandparent must not have an income of more than $2,000 and must be at least 55 years old, unless handicapped or infirmed. The claimant must have incurred at least $2,000 a year in maintaining the elderly.

b) Singaporeans who contribute to their parents' (or grandparents') Minimum Sum account are also given income tax relief.

c) Those with Medisave accounts may also use their savings to pay for the hospitalization bills of their parents and grandparents, among other family members.

In addition, the Maintenance of Parents Act was passed, and the Tribunal for the Maintenance of Parents set up, in 1996, to enable elderly parents who have no other support to claim financial support from their children.

Government and community-based financial assistance

Like other segments of the population, the needy elderly qualify for financial assistance provided by the state if they are unable to work and have no other means of support. Although the quantum of assistance is small (about S$230–$850, depending on family size), such individuals and households may also receive financial assistance with housing, health care and utilities. In-kind assistance is also provided by community-based voluntary welfare organizations. Private sector corporations are also included in the network of "helping hands" for those in need. Donations to charitable causes draw a tax relief equal to twice the amount of the donation.

Social Integration

As mentioned, the elderly should remain in the community and with their family for as long as possible and institutionalization should only be a last resort. Measures to promote "ageing in place" include gradual refurbishment of public housing blocks to provide lift-landings on every floor (rather than every two or three floors), review of the building code to provide for elder- and disabled-friendly public spaces, and refurbishment of rental flats occupied by low-income elderly to include elder friendly features. The lift upgrading programme, however, also requires residents to share the cost (albeit a small proportion) with the government and this has occasionally resulted in the upgrading scheme being rejected (upgrading can proceed only if at least 75 per cent of the residents agrees to it).

While the government promotes the extended family as an ideal (as recommended by the IMC), it has also accepted that "intimacy at a distance" may be preferred to co-residence. Thus, the Housing and Development Board (HDB) has introduced studio apartments for the elderly to live on their own, and first-time purchasers of resale HDB flats who choose to live within 2 km of their parents'/children's home receive a higher grant than those who do not. To prevent isolation of the elderly, the studio apartments will be integrated with flats of other sizes in the HDB blocks.

To enable the elderly to move about easily, low floor public buses are being introduced gradually to replace existing buses, and train (MRT/LRT) stations are also being upgraded to provide barrier-free access. The Land Transport Authority has embarked on a major exercise to retrofit existing MRT stations built before 1995 to enhance accessibility. The project is to benefit not just the elderly, but also people with physical/vision impairment or disabilities, families with young children, and commuters with bulky bags. Lifts will be installed at all existing MRT stations. Other initiatives include ramps, toilets for the handicapped, wider fare gates, tactile guidance system. The expected completion date of this exercise was 2005. A sticking point that has yet to be resolved, however, is the request by the public and the IMC for concessionary fares on public transport to be extended to a full day, instead of only for off-peak periods, as at present. To date, this has yet to receive a favourable response from Singapore's major public transport operators (which are run as public companies) on the grounds that it could raise the costs of public transportation to other users.

To enable the elderly to remain in the community, a variety of community-based services have already been implemented over the years. These services are for the well elderly as well as the frail. Examples of the former include Senior Citizens' and Retirees' clubs, Seniors Activities centres and befriender services for the isolated and lonely elderly. For the frail, there are day care centres for the frail elderly who need supervised care during the day, day rehabilitation centres, and dementia day care centres. Home care (medical, nursing and home help) and counselling services are also available. With the exception of the People's Association, which is a statutory board, the services are mainly provided by volunteer welfare organizations. Under the Eldercare Masterplan (FY2001–2005), multi-service centres and "neighbourhood links" will form a network for the delivery of community-based services to the public. The former are one-stop centres where both young and young can turn to for assistance. The type of services in these MSCs will vary depending on local needs, but will include childcare, eldercare, and family related services. The objective is to put all community-based services under one roof so that residents need not go to different locations for different services. Neighbourhood links are information and referral points as well as centres where the elderly (and other age groups) can be mobilized to form local support networks and organize social and recreational activities. These work in tandem with local grassroots organizations such as the block-level Residents' Committees and Citizens' Consultative Committees. MSCs will be built progressively to coincide with the community centres and community clubs building plans. Twenty neighbourhood links were slated for FY2001–2005, and 11 are in operation as of January 2004. About 1000 volunteers, including 93 elderly volunteers, have been recruited through these neighbourhood links.

Caregiver Kits have also been developed to provide information to families caring for a loved one at home; help families organize and provide the best possible care, and in doing so, relieve the stresses of the caregiving, and increase satisfaction. The kits are also to facilitate a new caregiver's understanding of the abilities and needs of the person being cared for, thus enhancing the care provided. The kit is given free as a form of support for family caregivers. A caregiver centre was also launched in October 2002, by Touch Community Service, and was supported by MCDS and NCSS. The Centre provides information, professional advice, and support to caregivers. It is a one-stop community resource facility for all ages and disabilities. The Centre also conducts training, provides support groups and offers consultative help on creating disabled/elder-friendly environments. It also showcases mock-up flats with disabled/elder-friendly fittings, furniture and appliances.

A healthy attitude towards ageing and the aged among older persons and the community is also an essential aspect of Singapore's policies on and programmes for the aged. An "Active Seniors Programme (ASP)" has been launched to provide an avenue for older persons to contribute to the community by sharing their talents, experiences, and wisdom with others. Any locally-based organization could propose innovative projects that promote active participation of older persons in the community for funding on a cost-sharing basis. ASP was launched in September 2001. Since its launch, ASP has benefitted some 20,000 people, comprising both seniors and children. As of December 2003, there were 11 projects costing about $1.04 million, involving 2,600 seniors. Activities include drama;

intergenerational table tennis games; retired professionals providing management advice and consultancy to new, small and medium-sized enterprises, and voluntary welfare organizations; senior caring for rehab patients at home; and recycling projects.

In terms of public education, the IMC also proposed a year-round programme be established, in addition to the annual senior citizens' week. To promote positive attitudes towards the elderly and ageing among children and youths, a CD-ROM has been developed as resource material for Civics and Moral Education lessons in schools. Talks are also conducted for secondary and junior college students. Media campaigns and a video on the golden years have been launched to promote active ageing and encourage healthy older people to remain active and engaged. The role of grandparents are also being recognized with a Grandparents' Day, which is normally held at the end of Senior Citizens Week. Seniors are also being recognized through the model Grandparent and Active Senior Citizen awards.

To enhance intergenerational ties, the IMC has also urged the government to review all existing policies and programmes and extend those that cater to the two-generation family to the three-generation family. The revision of the income tax relief policy to include grandparents is an instance where this recommendation has been accepted and implemented. The IMC also proposed giving elderly persons CPF top-up grants during the years of budget surplus for use in activities that promote lifelong planning and healthy lifestyles. This is "intended to give our senior citizens a stake in the long-term health of the economy". The IMC also recommended that the government promote a culture of renewal within organizations while elderly leaders should be able to step down "gracefully and honourably" and given opportunities to contribute.

CONCLUDING REMARKS

The implications of an ageing population have been recognized early in Singapore. This issue has been revisited many times over and policies and programmes have been developed over the years. However, these remain works-in-progress and will continue to be developed in the years to come. Some issues that are likely to require constant review will be the adequacy of financial provisions for old age and health care costs. The effectiveness of policies and programmes should also be evaluated regularly, and in-depth studies carried out to provide better understanding of changing needs and requirements.

Notes

[1] Chapter prepared for the ISEAS Workshop on Ageing and the Status of the Older Population in Southeast Asia, 22–23 November 2004, Seminar Rooms I and II, Institute of Southeast Asian Studies, Singapore. Comments made are her own and do not reflect the views of the Institute of Policy Studies.

[2] These two terms will be used interchangeably with another term, the old, in this chapter.

[3] Hereafter referred to as the IMC, in contrast to the Interministerial Committee on the Health Care of the Elderly which will be abbreviated as the IMCHE.

References

Department of Statistics. *Yearbook of Statistics Singapore 2004*.

Ministry of Community Development. "Report of the Inter-Ministerial Committee on the Ageing Population", 1999.

Ministry of Health. "Report of the Committee on the Problems of the Aged", 1984.

———. "Report of the Inter-Ministerial Committee on Health Care for the Elderly", 1999. Source: <www.moh.gov.sg>.

——— et al. (1996). The National Survey of Senior Citizens in Singapore 1995.

Ministry of Labour. "Report of the Tripartite Committee on the Extension of the Retirement Age", 1997.

Ministry of Manpower. "Older Workers". Paper No. 3/99, 15 July 1999. <http://www.mom.gov.sg/MOM/MRSD/Publications/869_op_08.pdf>.

Ministry of Trade and Industry. *New Challenges, Fresh Goals — Towards a Dynamic Global City*, Report of the Economic Review Committee, 2003.

Nizamuddin, Mohammed. "Population Ageing: An Overview". In *Population Ageing: Challenges for Policies and Programmes in Developed and Developing Countries*, Robert Cliquet and Mohammed Nizamuddin, eds., UNFPA and CBGS. Brussels, 1999.

Schulz, James H. "Population Ageing: Economic Growth and Generational Transfers (Labour, Productivity and Saving Issues)". In *Population Ageing: Challenges for Policies and Programmes in Developed and Developing Countries*, Robert Cliquet and Mohammed Nizamuddin, eds., UNFPA and CBGS. Brussels, 1999.

United Nations. *World Population Ageing: 1950–2050*. New York, 2002.

5

PUBLIC POLICY TOWARDS THE ELDERLY IN INDONESIA

Alex Arifianto

INTRODUCTION

In the past, old age policy has not been a major priority for the Indonesian Government, due to the fact that the number of elderly Indonesians (those who are 60 years of age or older) only formed a small percentage of Indonesia's population. The government focused most of its priorities on younger Indonesians of working age in order to assist them in gaining employment. Responsibility for the care of the elderly largely fell to their families, since it was assumed that productive citizens would take care of their aged and infirm parents. Very few government resources were allocated to assist elderly Indonesians, especially those who are poor and/or have no immediate family members to assist them.

Since the late 1990s however, changes have begun to occur in the way the Indonesian Government views the problem of ageing and old age security. This is due to the fact that demographic projections have predicted that the number of elderly Indonesians will increase significantly in the next few decades. In addition, due to the changes in family structure and economic conditions, it becomes increasingly difficult for families to care for elderly relatives by themselves, leaving many elderly Indonesians vulnerable to poverty or at risk of falling below the poverty line.

Thus, ageing increasingly becomes a policy issue that needs to be addressed by the government. Several new laws were passed which aim to ensure that elderly Indonesians receive adequate support for their livelihood in their old age. Questions remain, however, on whether the approaches undertaken by this legislation are the best way to address the ageing problem in Indonesia and its policy implications.

This chapter will describe the problem of ageing in Indonesia and the development of ageing policy in the country, looking at both past and current legislation. Part I will describe the demographic trends on ageing in Indonesia, while Part II will outline their possible policy implications. Part III will describe current developments in Indonesia's ageing policy, primarily by looking at past and current legislation enacted by the Indonesian Government related to ageing. The analysis will focus on the newly enacted national social security law that is aimed at protecting elderly Indonesians from old age insecurity. Finally, Part IV will suggest some future directions for the ageing policy in Indonesia and review possible policy alternatives directed at addressing this problem.

DEMOGRAPHIC AGEING TRENDS IN INDONESIA

For more than three decades, Indonesia has made significant progress in its economic and human development. This has resulted in better health conditions for Indonesians and longer life expectancy. The country's life expectancy has increased dramatically during the last three decades, from 45 in 1970 to 66 in 2004 (UNDP 2003). Consequently, the number of Indonesians aged 60 years and older has increased from 4.48 per cent of the population in 1971 to 7.97 per cent of the population in 2000 (ADB 2004, p. 47).

During the past three decades, Indonesia has also successfully implemented the family planning (*keluarga berencana*) programme, which has reduced the number of children born into typical Indonesian families. While in the early 1950s the average Indonesian family consisted of six children and their parents, in the 1990s the typical Indonesian family consisted of approximately 2.5 children and their parents (United Nations 1999). While family planning has been credited with helping to reduce poverty among Indonesian families (by reducing the cost for parents in raising their children), it also creates adverse consequences for them when those parents grow older, as will be outlined in the next section.

At the same time that the birthrate has declined, the number of older Indonesians has increased at a rapid rate. It is estimated that by the year 2020, elderly Indonesians over 60 years old will account for about 11.34 per cent of the population (ADB 2004, p. 47). This trend will continue for the forseeable future. It is estimated that in the year 2050, about one-third of all Indonesians will be aged 55 years or older and about 20 per cent will be aged 65 years or older (ILO 2003).

Currently most of Indonesia's elderly population lives in rural rather than in urban areas (9.97 million vs. 7.79 million) (ADB 2004, p. 47). Thus, rural districts tend to age faster compared with urban districts. However estimates show that, due to the urbanization process, most elderly Indonesians will eventually live in urban areas (Arifin and Ananta 2004, pp. 5–7). While in 2005, the ratio of rural vs. urban elderly was 2.3 times, in 2003 the ratio was reduced to 1.7, and by 2020, the number of urban elderly will surpass the rural elderly (ADB 2004, pp. 47–48). At the same time, the number of elderly women aged 65 years and older is about 4.7 million, while the number of elderly men is about 4.1 million (Arifin and Ananta 2004, p. 8).

If we look at the elderly population at the provincial level, the oldest provinces are Yogyakarta, Central Java, East Java, Bali, and West Sumatra (ibid., pp. 4–5). The province with the largest elderly population is Yogyakarta, with 8.48 per cent of its population aged 65 years and older in 2000. This could be attibuted to the combination of a relatively low fertility rate and a high rate of out-migration from this province (ibid., p. 5). The district of Gunung Kidul in Yogyakarta has the largest elderly population among the more than 400 districts/cities in Indonesia, in 2000 10.49 per cent of its population was 65 years of age or older (ibid., p. 5).

It is estimated that about half of all Indonesia's elderly are still active in the labour force, mostly in the informal sector/agriculture (Koesobjono and Sarwono 2003, p. 391). Unfortunately, most of these elderly have difficulties in supporting themselves, with an average income of Rp 500,000 (about USD 55) per annum in 1999 (Hatmadji et al. 1999, p. 48). Because of their lack of earnings, a large number of them (about 45 per cent) have to rely on family support, while 31.5 per cent are self-employed. Their only asset is often their house or land (Hatmadji and Pardede 1999).

IMPLICATIONS OF POPULATION AGEING IN INDONESIA

The rapid ageing of Indonesia's population within the next two to three decades will no doubt create various public policy implications for the country. First of all, there will be a greater demand for old age income support schemes as more Indonesians get older, and eventually, as their health deteriorates, they will have to leave the labour force. To receive an adequate income after retirement, the elderly will have to accumulate enough savings during their time in the labour force, or receive income support from external sources (their family, the government or private foundations/charities). As suggested earlier, since the income of many elderly Indonesians is not sufficient to support themselves after retirement, many of them will have to rely on these secondary income sources.

The increased number of the elderly in the country's population will also result in an increased demand for medical care and services for this sector of the population. The experience of other countries with populations that are already aged shows that while people are living longer, health expenditures tend to increase at the same time, since as they grow older, they will spend more on various health-related services such as medicine, hospitalization, and nursing home care. As a result, health expenditures as a percentage of the Gross National Product (GNP) could be expected to increase as well. In developed countries (such as Western Europe and North America), where the ageing phenomenon is currently most prevalent, health expenditures accounted for 9.2 per cent of GNP in 1990, compared with 4.7 per cent in developing countries and 8.1 per cent for the whole world (World Bank 1993, p. 52).

In the past, elderly Indonesians could rely on the extended support of their families, both as caregivers at the time they experience health problems, and also as providers of supplemental financial support. Unfortunately, the rapid ageing of Indonesia's population is occurring at the same time as the country is undergoing rapid modernization as well as recovering from the impact of the 1997/98 Asian financial crisis.

Modernization has brought many changes that impact on the family support system in Indonesia. A national family planning programme has succeeded in significantly reducing Indonesia's birthrate. While this policy has resulted in reduced family expenditures for the support of children, it also means that elderly Indonesians will be supported by fewer children when they are entering old age. This, of course, could reduce the amount of support they will receive from their children in old age.

Among other changes in the family brought about by modernization is the likelihood that younger family members who are still in the labour force will migrate to bigger cities, where most jobs are perceived to be located, or even to other countries. While they might be able to earn better wages in the city/another country, younger family members will be living further from their elderly parents. As a result, there is less likelihood that the children will be able to fulfil the role as their parents' caregivers in times of need (Hugo 1996, p. 17).

Consequently, support for elderly Indonesians is increasingly shifting from personal care, in which the elderly receive direct emotional and physical care from their own family members, to a more impersonal and financially-oriented system of care, in which assistance is given in the form of cash or through hired assistants (nurses, domestic help, etc.) (Koesbijono and Sarwono 2003, p. 394). Thus, while some elderly Indonesians might enjoy adequate financial support, they might lack the personal care and attention that can only be provided by their families.

Even when their families are caring for them, the elderly often do not get the care that they need. Families of the elderly often do not get professional training or consultation on how to care for the elderly appropriately. Very often, they have to take on this responsibility suddenly without any warning (i.e. when the elderly suffer from serious illnesses that render them disabled or incapacitated). As a result, the quality of care the elderly receive from their family members is often poor. In order to assist family members to care for aged relatives they need information on a number of matters, including nutritional and dietary matters, hygienic and sanitary measures, use of rehabilitation tools, and appropriate medication (van Eeuwijk 2004, p. 11).

As a result of these shortcomings, the Indonesian elderly increasingly have to turn to third-party institutions for care. These services could come from the government or the private sector, whether they be for-profit and not-for-profit organizations (e.g. nursing homes and hospitals/clinics). Unfortunately, resources provided for the elderly by these institutions are also limited. Only about 10 per cent of all Indonesians (both workers and their spouses) have some form of pension coverage,[1] while only 15 per cent of Indonesians are currently covered by some form of health insurance scheme provided by either the public or the private sector[2] (ILO 2003). Additionally, it is virtually impossible for those aged 65 years and above to receive health insurance coverage, even though this age group is more vulnerable to more serious medical problems (ibid., p. 193). Finally, social welfare spending for elderly Indonesians still receives a low priority in the government's budget. In the 2004 state budget, the government only allocated 21.5 billion Rupiahs (US$236,000) for such services (ADB 2004, p. 99), an amount which is far from sufficient in meeting the needs of elderly Indonesians.

Elderly Indonesians also have more difficulty accessing charities that offer assistance to people in need, since these charities often prefer to allocate their scarce resources to help orphaned and poor children (Hugo 1996, p. 17). In addition, most elderly Indonesians are still unwilling to enroll themselves in nursing homes. A study found that while half of the elderly believe that a nursing home could be an important facility for their old age needs, only 15 per cent of them indicated that they would be willing to live in such an institution (ibid., p. 18). However, those who choose to live in one find that their economic situation and their happiness improved after moving into a nursing home, and they generally feel satisfied about their welfare (Niehof 1995, p. 432).

In conclusion, the state of Indonesia's elderly population is clearly at a crossroad. Since their number is increasing rapidly, there will be greater demands from this group for both old age income support schemes and health care. Unfortunately, the traditional family support systems that these elderly tend to rely on are increasingly becoming strained due to the fact that the Indonesian family size continues to decline and also due to other changes resulting from modernization (e.g. out-migration to cities/other countries and more formalized family relations based on financial rather than personal needs). At the same time, third-party infrastructure available to support elderly Indonesians is still underdeveloped, given the lack of available schemes provided by both the government and the private sector to support the needs of the elderly population.

It is clear that a comprehensive ageing policy is needed in Indonesia. Exactly how this policy should be framed will be explored in the next two sections.

PAST AND CURRENT AGEING POLICY IN INDONESIA

To review past and current ageing policy in Indonesia, a search on each piece of legislation (*Undang-Undang*) passed by the Indonesian Government and Indonesian Parliament (DPR) related to social policy towards elderly Indonesians and social welfare in general were scrutinized and analysed.[3] Several pieces of legislation were included in this analysis, including The Social Assistance for the Elderly Law of 1965, The Social Welfare Law of 1974, The Workers' Social Security Law of 1992, The Old Age Welfare Law of 1998, and the National Social Security System Law of 2004. The details of this legislation is as follows:

The Social Assistance for the Elderly Law of 1965 (Law No. 4/1965)

This legislation was the first attempt by the Indonesian Government to provide some form of public assistance for elderly Indonesians. It defines the elderly as: "each individual who, due to their old age, is unable to work and does not have adequate resources to support their livelihood" (GOI 1965, section 1). The type of assistance authorized by this law was cash subsidies and health/long-term care assistance given to the elderly, which could be channelled through government institutions, private institutions, and individuals (ibid., sections 2 and 3). The Ministry of Social Affairs is authorized to regulate and enforce this law (ibid., section 4). Private institutions and individuals interested in providing assistance to the elderly must register themselves with the Ministry of Social Affairs and provide updates to the Ministry if there are changes in their legal status (ibid., sections 7 and 11). The Ministry has the right to revoke government assistance given to a private institution/individual if it finds that they do not comply with relevant regulations set up by the Ministry (ibid., section 10).

This law was quite progressive in offering old age assistance to the elderly, especially given that it was written in the 1960s when a smaller portion of Indonesia's population was classified as elderly. Due to the change of administration from President Sukarno to General Suharto in March 1966, less than a year after its enactment, the law was never fully enforced and carried out by the New Order government. It remained on the statute books however, until it was repealed more than three decades later by The Old Age Welfare Law of 1998.

The Social Welfare Law of 1974 (Law No. 6/1974) and The Workers' Social Security Law of 1992 (Law No. 3/1992)

This law stipulates that each Indonesian citizen has the right to a decent standard of social welfare and the responsibility to participate in various social welfare activities (GOI 1974, section 1). It further stipulates that the Indonesian Government has the right to create and operate the following programmes: 1) social assistance programmes; 2) social security system; 3) guidance, mentoring, and social rehabilitation activities for disadvantaged citizens; and 4) social education and development activities (ibid., section 4, subsection 1). It then states that the government would establish a national social security system, which would be detailed in separate legislation (ibid., section 5). In addition, community members are authorized to engage in social welfare activities in the form of establishing foundations or other not-for-profit legal entities, which would be regulated by separate legislation (ibid., sections 8 and 9).

It would not be until almost two decades later however, that the government started to issue separate legislation that would spell out in more detail the various social welfare activities stipulated by this legislation. These included the Law No. 3/1992 on workers' Social Security (*UU Jamsostek*), which created several social security benefits for workers: 1) worker injury benefits; 2) death benefits; 3) retirement benefits; and 4) health care benefits. To participate, each employer has to make a contribution of between 7.24

and 11.24 per cent of the total wages paid to their workers. This amount is equal to about one month of a worker's annual salary. In addition, workers have to contribute 2 per cent of their wages to the retirement benefits programme (Arifianto 2004, p. 7). Workers' retirement funds are invested in a provident fund managed entirely by a state-owned company, PT Jamsostek.

While, theoretically, this law applies to all Indonesian workers, regardless of whether they work in the formal or informal sector; in practice only some formal sector workers were covered by this scheme, specifically, those who work in medium and large-sized enterprises (those that employed more than 10 employees). This means that the vast majority of Indonesian workers (80 per cent of the total workforce) are not covered by this scheme (ibid., p. 8). In addition, it is also estimated that only about half of the employers required by the Indonesian Social Security Law to make contributions to the scheme are actually making contributions (ILO 2003, p. 63). Thus, the number of workers who are actually covered by the *Jamsostek* programme is much lower than what was stipulated by the law.

Additionally, *Jamsostek* does not create adequate incentives for its members to save for retirement because the benefits received by those who make contributions to *Jamsostek* are very small. A World Bank study done by Leechor (1996) estimated that the total pension payments received by a *Jamsostek* recipient at retirement is only valued at about 7 per cent of their final basic salary after 35 years of active work, while another study conducted by the International Labor Organization (ILO) found that the average value of a *Jamsostek* pension only amounts to five-and-a-half months of their basic salary, or eight-and-a-half months of the current minimum wage (UMR) (ILO 2003, p. 90). It has been concluded that these workers would earn a better rate of return on their investments if they put their retirement savings into a bank account rather than the *Jamsostek* scheme.

In addition, the rate of return on investments in the *Jamsostek* fund is also very low. The ILO found that income from such investments is valued cumulatively at 38 per cent below the level of inflation and 63 per cent less than the average market rate (ILO 2003, p. 94). This is caused by the fact that the *Jamsostek* fund is invested mostly in banks — 80 per cent in 1997 and 86 per cent in June 1999 (Perwira et al. 2003). While such an investment is considered relatively safe, in the long run, it earns less than other investment schemes, such as those invested in stocks, bonds, and mutual funds.

Finally, critics have argued that the management of the *Jamsostek* fund has not been open and transparent. For instance, it has been found that PT *Jamsostek* as the sole provider of publicly-funded retirement benefits in Indonesia has failed to provide financial statements and regular progress reports that can be accessed by workers participating in the scheme and the general public (Leechor 1996, p. 39).

We can conclude that due to the above weaknesses, the 1974 and 1992 social welfare legislation were not successful in their aims to provide social security protection for Indonesians, specifically the elderly. Recognizing this flaw, the Indonesian Government has decided to develop a more comprehensive social security law and the legislation was debated and enacted during the 2003/2004 legislative year. An analysis of this law would be detailed later in this section.

The Old Age Welfare Law of 1998 (Law No. 13/1998)

In 1998, when the Suharto Government collapsed in the aftermath of the 1997/98 Asian financial crisis, the caretaker government of President B.J. Habibie decided to revise and rewrite various laws that had been enacted by his predecessors. Among the laws that were subjected to this revision was The Social Assistance for the Elderly Law of 1965. It was repealed and replaced by The Old Age Welfare Law of 1998.

This law stipulates that elderly Indonesians have the same rights as any other citizens (GOI 1998, section 5, subsection 1). They are entitled to various public services, including: 1) religion/spiritual service; 2) health care service; 3) employment service; 4) education and training service; 5) special privileges when using public utilities and legal services; and 6) access to social protection (for "infirm" elderly) and social assistance (for "able-bodied" elderly) schemes (ibid., section 5, subsection 2). Unlike earlier laws, the law also stipulates that the responsibility for the improvement of the elderly citizens' welfare should be shared by the government, the community and the families of elderly citizens themselves (ibid., section 8). Finally, community members are authorized to engage in activities to improve the welfare of the elderly (ibid., sections 22 and 23).

The new law seems to have broadened the number of public services available for the elderly significantly, not just the provision of social assistance schemes as the 1965 law stipulates, but also other services listed above. It also categorized the elderly into two groups: 1) able-bodied elderly, who are defined as those who are still able to work or produce goods and services, and 2) infirm elderly, who are defined as those who are no longer able to work and are entirely dependent on assistance from another person/ institution (ibid., section 1, subsections 3 and 4). Thus, this law seems to recognize that the elderly are not a homogeneous group, some are more likely to have an active and healthy life than others. The bill, however, lacks the specific programmes and services that are geared towards improving the welfare of the elderly, stating that they would be defined in separate legislation. Thus, the exact programmes available to improve the welfare of elderly Indonesians remain in doubt.

To complement this bill, the government has created a five-year *National Strategy to Improve the Welfare of the Elderly*, starting in the year 2003. The strategy was created by the Office of the Coordinating Ministry of Social Welfare (*Menko Kesra*) and is aimed at enhancing coordination between various governmental institutions, community, private sector, civil society organizations, and organizations representing elderly Indonesians, in order to create a national strategy that would incorporate the role of elderly Indonesians in the country's development and to build the support of the family and society for improving the welfare of the elderly (The Yogyakarta Special Province 2003).

To support this national strategy, President Megawati Soekarnoputri issued Presidential Decree (*Keppres*) No. 52/2004 on the Creation of the National Committee on Ageing. This committee is mandated to assist the President to coordinate the implementation of the *National Strategy to Improve the Welfare of the Elderly* and to provide professional advice to the President on the creation of the government's social policy towards the elderly (GOI 2004*a*, section 3, subsection 1). It specifies that the committee will consist of twenty-five members, with representatives from various government agencies, civil society organizations working on the issue of old age welfare, universities, and the private sector (ibid., sections 4 to 7). In addition to the National Committee on Ageing, provincial and district/city governments in Indonesia can also create their own committee on ageing, which would coordinate with the national committee in their respective duties (ibid., sections 20 and 21).

It is hoped that these new initiatives will encourage the development of a comprehensive policy towards the aged in Indonesia. Since these initiatives are still in the early stages however, it remains to be seen whether these initiatives would be successful in their aim to create such a policy.

The National Social Security System Law of 2004 (UU SJSN/Jamsosnas)

The most recent legislation related to public policy towards the elderly in Indonesia is The National Social Security System Law of 2004, which was enacted on September 28, 2004. Among key features of the new law is that it mandates the creation of several social security schemes for citizens: old age pension, old age savings, national health insurance, work-injury insurance, and death benefits (GOI 2004*b*, section 18).

The law also mandates that, within the next decade or so, social security coverage should be expanded to cover all citizens, including the informal sector, the unemployed, and the poor (Arifianto 2004, p. 16). The schemes above would be largely financed by payroll taxes imposed on employers and workers, mostly in the formal sector. In addition, the government will subsidize the contributions of the poorest citizens (ibid., p. 20).

Specifically related to the old age income security issues are two programmes that were created by the new law: the old age pension programme and the old age savings programme. The old age pension programme is a defined-benefit social insurance programme,[4] and it will presumably operate as a partially funded pay-as-you-go scheme.[5] As stipulated in the draft law, this programme will only accumulate social security contributions for the first 15 years, and will only start paying pension benefits to retirees after this (GOI 2004b, section 41).

This old age pension scheme has similar features to the publicly-run pension programmes established in most developed countries in Western Europe and North America. The programme will be further divided into four components: old age pensions, disability pensions, widow/widower pensions, and child pensions, (ibid., section 41).

The defined benefit of the old age pension should normally be a percentage of the average income from the previous year. The fixed minimum pension under the proposed plan has been set at 70 per cent of the minimum wage. The same benefit level also applies to the disability pension programme. Widows/widowers and children will receive a minimum pension of between 40 per cent and 60 per cent of the local minimum wage (GOI 2003, pp. 59–60). Widows/widowers will continue to receive pension benefits until they die, remarry, or start working full-time. Children will continue to receive pension benefits until they marry, start working full-time, or reach 23 years of age, whichever comes first (GOI 2004*b*, section 41).

The retirement age is currently set at 55, and a worker who has contributed to the scheme for at least fifteen years will be entitled to receive full pension benefits from the programme. These workers, or heirs if a worker dies before reaching retirement age, will receive monthly pension payments. Workers who retire before reaching the fifteen years' contribution requirement above, will be entitled to receive the accumulated amount of their pension contributions, plus the investment returns, in a lump sum. They will not, however, be eligible to receive a monthly pension (ibid., section 41).

On the other hand, the old age savings programme is a retirement programme in which participants will be entitled to receive benefits before or upon reaching retirement age and, in the event of the death of a participant, his or her spouse, children, or official heirs will be entitled to receive benefits. It will be a compulsory savings programme. Thus, it will be similar to the compulsory savings scheme created by the Workers' Social Security Law of 1992. It is a fully-funded, defined contribution pension programme.

The benefits of this pension plan will be provided as a lump-sum payment if a worker dies, becomes permanently disabled, or retires. If a worker dies or becomes permanently disabled, benefits will go to their heirs (spouses and children under the age of 23). The total amount of programme benefits received by members is the entire amount of their contribution accumulated over the years plus the investment returns on their contribution. At the earliest, workers may start withdrawing money from their account five years before they reach retirement age. They may even use a portion of the money saved in their account as a loan after they have made contributions for a given period of time, the details of which will be stipulated in a future government regulation (ibid., section 37).

For both of the above programmes, each member must contribute either a percentage of their income (formal workers) or a flat-rate amount (informal and self-employed workers) to this savings programme. Contributions from formal workers will be split equally between themselves and their employers. The National Social Security Provider Agency will be required to provide an annual report to each worker on his or her accumulated contributions and investment returns. Exactly how the government plans to invest the funds collected by this scheme will be stipulated in a future government regulation (ibid., sections 38 and 42).

Despite the government's best intention to create the above schemes, many stakeholders, including employers' associations, labour unions, insurance companies, and independent experts have raised a number of issues about the social security schemes created by this new law.

First, there is a high probability of the programme running into deficit because it will offer very generous pension benefits, with a minimum benefit of 70 per cent of the local minimum wage. Since many Indonesian workers, especially those who work in the informal sector, have earnings below the local minimum wage, many of them will receive this guaranteed benefit. Due to the substantial liability, the possibility of serious financial problems in this pension scheme in the future is quite high.

Secondly, the government's plan to subsidize the coverage of low-income persons is also questionable. According to the draft law, Indonesians whose income falls below the regional minimum wage (UMR)[6] will be considered as "low-income" earners and, therefore, will be eligible to receive a government subsidy to help cover their pension contributions. There are however, a substantial number of Indonesians who earn less than the UMR, especially those who work in the informal sector or are not permanently employed. This could put significant financial strain on the government budget. If this issue is not addressed, it could become another factor that could endanger the long-term sustainability of this programme.

Thirdly the combination of a relatively young retirement age (55 years), low number of working years to qualify for pensions (15 years) and a rapidly ageing population, is a recipe for disaster for any public pension programme, and it seems that this proposed scheme will suffer from such a fate and become financially unsustainable. Attempts to correct the problem such as raising contributions and cutting pension benefits are only temporary fixes that will make the programme less attractive to participants. Eventually, the pension scheme could suffer from a default, which would place significant financial liabilities on the government and employers as well as result in a significant loss of retirement income for workers.

Fourthly, it is estimated that the impact of the proposed *Jamsosnas* old age pension scheme on the current Indonesian elderly population would be minimal. Since the system is a partially funded pay-as-you-go scheme, unless they make contributions, the current retirees will not benefit at all. Although it is the current poor retirees that need the *Jamsosnas* old age pension scheme the most, they do not have the financial resources to contribute to the scheme.

People who retire between when the *Jamsosnas* pension scheme takes effect and when it starts paying pensions (about fifteen years after its establishment according to the draft law) also will not benefit from the *Jamsosnas* pension scheme. As stipulated in the draft law, they will not be eligible to receive a pension. They will only receive the money accumulated in their old age savings accounts (contribution plus investment earnings).[7] In general however, only those who retire fifteen years after the *Jamsosnas* pension scheme has been in place and have made regular contributions to the scheme will receive pension benefits.

Thus, unlike what has been claimed by the proponents of the *Jamsosnas* bill, the *Jamsosnas* pension scheme will not be very helpful for current retirees who do not have the resources to contribute to the scheme. This group is however, still vulnerable to old age poverty, if not more so compared with future retirees who will have participated in the *Jamsosnas* pension scheme. Consequently, the government might have to establish a separate pension or income support scheme for this group.

Finally, the government's proposal disregards the role of competition in providing social security benefits to Indonesians, as, according to the bill, the government will be solely responsible for social security provision, in spite of the fact that most formal sector workers already obtain adequate health and retirement benefits from their employers. The government alone will continue to make decisions on how the fund is managed, invested, and distributed among beneficiaries, while workers themselves will not be allowed to participate in the decision-making related to the trust fund, even though it is actually their own money, and most Indonesians workers have little confidence in publicly-run social security schemes. These facts indicate that it is not a good idea for the government to regulate as well as operate the national social security scheme. These functions need to be separated in order to have a truly functional social security system that is beneficial for workers.

To conclude, while the new social security law is the first step in providing adequate social security benefits for all Indonesians (especially the elderly), it needs to be amended further, so that the schemes proposed by the law are more transparent and financially sustainable. If this law is revised, the views of all stakeholders involved should be heard and incorporated into the amended law, including their demands for a more accountable, affordable, sustainable, and competitive social security system.

FUTURE POLICY DIRECTIONS FOR AGEING POLICY IN INDONESIA

From our analysis of the raft of legislation related to ageing and old age security in Indonesia, we can make the following observations. First, as the number of elderly Indonesians grows, an ageing policy increasingly becomes more important in the country's policy and legislative agenda. Second, there is an increasing recognition on the government's part that caring for the elderly should not be the sole responsibility of the government, but also of the community, the private sector, and most importantly, the elderly and their families themselves. Indonesia's ongoing transition that commenced in 1998 from an authoritarian to a democratic state also means that voices from civil society organizations (including those representing the elderly) can no longer be ignored by the government and their views need to be incorporated into the government's policy agenda.

Unfortunately, the new social security law reverses this approach of shared responsibility somewhat, by putting the government in charge of the proposed social security programmes and treating everybody else simply as contributors to the social security scheme or as beneficiaries when it is time for them to start collecting benefits. This state-centred approach not only excludes other stakeholders from playing important roles in providing social security for the elderly, but is also questionable in light of the Indonesian government's weak capacity to implement its programmes due to serious governance problems. These are evident from its implementation of the *Jamsostek* scheme and other social security programmes in the past.

In light of these facts, what then is an appropriate ageing policy for Indonesia? While this will continue to be a subject of debate, this report presents a number of possible options to be considered in the development of the country's ageing policy.

First of all, it has to be recognized that an ageing policy should be dynamic and easily adaptable to new conditions, such as changing demographics, improvements in medical care, the availability of resources to fund old age security provisions, and so forth. No policy should be set in stone, doing so would be a mistake since it could lead to possible long-term repercussions for the country. We should learn as much as possible from other countries that have already encountered a changing age demographic.

Secondly, we have also recognized that most of the care and resources provided for the elderly in Indonesia primarily comes from their own families and most Indonesian elderly prefer to receive care from their own family members. Thus, there should be incentives to ensure the long-term sustainability of these arrangements as the country continues its modernization. This might include efforts to create new employment for Indonesian workers, preferably in better-paying sectors, combined with efforts to attract new investors to the country that would generate such jobs. The country might also consider introducing tax incentives to induce families to care for their aged relatives and lessen some of the financial burden of these families. Finally, training should be provided for families of sick and infirm elderly, who suddenly have to bear the burden of caring for them, so that they are able to provide appropriate and humane caring for their elderly relatives.

Thirdly, with regard to the creation of a national social security system that would largely benefit elderly Indonesians, it should be recognized that in most developing countries, a government monopoly in delivering social security programmes and essential public services to poor and vulnerable citizens is no longer a workable model, and in many cases, such monopolistic provisions have failed to achieve their goals. Instead, social security programme design and implementation should be a partnership between the government, the private sector, NGOs/civil society groups, and service customers (poor and vulnerable citizens). Different arrangements could be created to implement such partnerships (privatization, contracting out, and schemes to increase clients/service customers' voices in decision-making processes).

For instance, this could be done by adopting a three-pillar approach[8] in providing for pension/retirement benefits for the poor, in which the government sponsors the first pillar in the form of a social safety net, providing a social safety net for the old, particularly the old whose lifetime income was low. The second pillar is a fully privately managed funded pillar that handles peoples' mandatory retirement schemes and insurance — it links pension benefits to worker's contributions as in a defined contribution plan. The third is a voluntary pillar for people who want a higher standard of living in old age. The three-pillar approach in pension provision has been adopted by more than 30 countries, from both the developed and developing world, and at least 20 other countries are considering adopting it at this time (James 2004). Thus, such an approach might be worth considering in Indonesia as it develops a more comprehensive old age security strategy for its poor elderly.

Fourthly, with regard to elderly health care, the government could use incentives to induce more citizens to purchase private health insurance. This could include a tax credit to help pay health insurance premiums or a medical savings account plan set up by private financial firms in which workers could save a portion of their salaries; any withdrawals made from this account for health care needs would not be subject to any taxes or fees.

The use of partnerships such as these in implementing social protection schemes would improve the effectiveness and outcomes of these programmes, enhancing the service delivery of the programmes to their constituents, and would increase citizen's support for, and confidence in, those programmes. More such partnerships need to be built into the social protection policy in this country.

It is, however, recognized that private individual retirement accounts by themselves would not be useful for those elderly people who are already reaching retirement age and have no means to contribute to the individual account schemes.[9] For this group, the government should pursue a special pension programme to assist them in meeting their retirement expenses. The amount of assistance provided by this programme would meet the basic expenses of these poor elderly (e.g. food, utility bills, etc.) and also would provide emergency assistance when the elderly face chronic health problems. Such programmes should ideally be financed through general tax revenues so that it would not create an additional burden for business and current workers (or for the elderly population themselves) through new taxes or fees. These special pension benefits for the poor could be given either as a means-tested pension scheme or as a universal flat benefits scheme.[10]

It should also be noted that the successful implementation of any social security scheme, including those that support the elderly, requires active cooperation between the government and all non-governmental stakeholders involved in efforts to reduce poverty in Indonesia (civil society, NGOs, the private sector, and the poor themselves). With a continuing partnership between the government and the private sector, civil society groups and representatives of poor citizens, it is hoped that social protection efforts can accomplish their intended goals optimally.

Finally, there needs to be capacity and financial building activities among the private sector organizations (both for-profit and not-for-profit) and NGOs to increase their attention to and support for elderly Indonesians. Resources to support the elderly in need, both in cash and in kind, need to be increased and better training is needed for the staff of these institutions so that their attention to the special needs of the elderly will be increased. The government could support this endeavour by granting tax exemptions and deductions for groups that receive charitable donations to support poor elderly persons who are unable to care for themselves.

CONCLUDING THOUGHTS

With a real partnership among all stakeholders, along with a firm political will to improve living standards of all elderly Indonesians, and a credible mechanism to ensure that all stakeholders follow through with the above commitments, it is hoped that Indonesia can successfully develop a comprehensive ageing policy that is able to improve the welfare of all elderly Indonesians effectively and sustainably, both now and in the future.

Notes

[1] Workers who have pension coverage tend to be civil servants (covered by the Taspen scheme) or those working with state-owned enterprises and large companies (ILO, 2003). In addition, some private sector workers also contribute to the compulsory old age savings scheme (*Jamsostek*).

[2] Specifically, 10 per cent are covered by a public health insurance scheme (*Askes* for civil servants, *Jamsostek* for private formal sector workers, and community health maintenance schemes (JPKM). About 5 per cent have private health insurance coverage (ILO, 2003).

³   In this analysis, we only look at the legislation in the form of laws that have been enacted by the government. Other legislation, such as government regulation (*Peraturan Pemerintah*), Presidential Decree (*Keputusan Presiden*), and Ministerial Decree (*Keputusan Menteri*) were not included in this analysis.

⁴   *A defined benefit scheme* is a retirement plan in which workers are guaranteed a benefit upon retirement, usually based on years of service, age, and final or lifetime earnings. The government/employers are responsible for funding the plan's promised benefits and are liable for the risks associated with the scheme. An alternative is the *defined contribution scheme*, that is a retirement plan in which benefit is a direct product of the contributions paid to the investment accounts, plus the return on investments from these accounts. The risks, though not the control, of this pension scheme rest with the workers (ILO 2003, p. xxii, Weller 2002, pp. 3–4).

⁵   A *pay-as-you-go* system is a social security system in which no funds are set aside in advance and benefits for current retirees plus administrative costs are paid out of the current workers' contributions (ILO 2003, p. xxii). A *partially funded pay-as-you-go* scheme means that the system is partially financed in advance to create a reserve fund for future use by retirees but does not pay contributions at the present. After the system matures, it would start paying out pension obligations to retirees and then it could continue as a full pay-as-you-go scheme.

⁶   The minimum wage in Indonesia is decided not at the national level, but at provincial, and sometimes at district/city level. The minimum wage is commonly called the Regional Minimum Wage (Upah Minimum Regional-UMR).

⁷   The only exception is when a worker dies before reaching retirement age or has contributed to the Jamsosnas pension scheme for 15 years. In these cases, their heirs (surviving spouse and children) will continue to receive their pension benefits until they die or start working full-time (or for the children, when they reach 23 years of age) (GOI 2004*b*, section 41, subsections (4) and (6)).

⁸   For additional background on the three-pillar approach on pension reform, see World Bank (1994).

⁹   For a recent comprehensive study on this topic, see Gill et al. (2005).

¹⁰ For various case studies of countries that have adopted this pension scheme, see Help Age International (2004) and James (2004).

References

Arifianto, A. *Social Security Reform in Indonesia: An Analysis of the National Social Security Bill (RUU Jamsosnas).* Working Paper, The SMERU Research Institute, Jakarta, Indonesia, September 2004.

Arifin, E.N., and A. Ananta. *Aging at Provinces and Districts in Indonesia.* Paper presented at the International Workshop on Old-age Vulnerabilities: Asian and European Perspective, Brawijaya University, Malang, Indonesia, 8–10 July 2004.

Asian Development Bank. *Sustainable Social Protection and Providing for the Vulnerable in the Informal Sector.* Mid-term Report of the Sustainable Social Protection Technical Assistance Team, Vol. 1. Jakarta, Indonesia, August, 2004.

Gill, I., T. Packard, J. Yermo and T. Pugatch. *Keeping the Promise of Social Security in Latin America*, Latin American Development Forum, The World Bank. Stanford, CA: Stanford University Press, 2005.

GOI (Government of Indonesia) (1965). *The Social Assistance for the Elderly Law of 1965. Jakarta.* Available at <http://kambing.vlsm.org/bebas/v01/RI/uu/1965/uu-1965-004.txt> (accessed 9 October 2004).

GOI (Government of Indonesia) (1974). *The Social Welfare Law of 1974.* Jakarta. Available at <http://kambing.vlsm.org/bebas/v01/RI/uu/1974/uu-1974-006.txt> (accessed 9 October 2004).

GOI (Government of Indonesia) (1998). *The Old age Welfare Law of 1998.* Jakarta. Available at <http://kambing.vlsm.org/bebas/v01/RI/uu/1998/uu-1998-013.txt> (accessed 7 October 2004).

GOI (Government of Indonesia) (2004). Presidential Decree No 52/2004 on the Creation of the National Committee on Aging. Jakarta. Available at <http://www.ri.go.id/produk_uu/produk2004/kp2004/kp52'04.htm> (accessed 7 October 2004).

GOI (Government of Indonesia). *Draft of The National Social Security System Law of 2004.* Jakarta. Version of 28 September 2004.

Hatmadji, S.H. and E.L. Pardede. *Demographic Structure and Socio-economic Conditions of the Elderly Population in Indonesia.* Paper presented at a seminar on The Household Structure of the Elderly Population in Indonesia, Jakarta, 6 March 1999.

Hatmadji, S.H., Mundiharno and E.L. Pardede. *Elderly Population in Indonesia: A General Overview and Case Study in the District of Bogor and Cirebon, West Java.* Paper presented at IPADI National Seminar: Institutionalizing National Development Approach through Population Vision. Jakarta, 23 March 1999.

Help Age International. *Age and Security: How Social Pensions Can Deliver Effective Aid to Poor Older People and Their Families*, Help Age International Report. London, UK. October 2004.

Hugo, G. *Intergenerational Wealth Flows and the Elderly in Indonesia.* Paper presented at the Continuing Demographic Transition Seminar. Canberra, Australia, 14–17 August 1996.

International Labor Organization. *Social Security and Coverage for All: Restructuring the Social Security Scheme in Indonesia — Issues and Options.* Jakarta: ILO, 2003.

James, E. *Reforming Social Security: What Can Indonesia Learn from Other Countries?* Paper presented at the Bappenas/GIAT Workshop on Options for Establishing a Viable Social Security System, Jakarta, 24 June 2004.

Koesoebijono, S. and S. Sarwono. "Managing the Elderly in a Crisis Situation". In *The Indonesian Crisis: A Human Development Perspective*, Aris Ananta, ed., pp. 283–416. Singapore: Institute of Southeast Asian Studies, 2003.

Leechor, C. *Reforming Indonesia's Pension System*, Policy Research Working Paper No. 1677. World Bank, Washington, D.C., October 1996.

Niehof, A. "Aging and the Elderly in Indonesia: Identifying Key Issues". *Bijdragen tot de Taap, Land, en Volkenkunde*. Leiden: KITLV Press, 1995.

Perwira, D., A. Arifianto, A. Suryahadi, and S. Sumarto (2003). *Workers' Protection Through Formal Social Security System: The Indonesian Experience*. Working Paper (in Indonesian), The SMERU Research Institute, Jakarta, Indonesia. June.

United Nations. *World Population Prospects: The 1998 Revision*. Vol. 1 & 2. New York: UN, 1999.

United Nations Development Programme. *Human Development* Report: Millennium Development Goals: A Compact Among Nations *to End Human Poverty (sic)*, Annual Edition. Oxford, England: Oxford University Press, July 2003.

Van Eeuwijk, P. *The Burden Behind Long-term Care in Urban Indonesia.* Paper presented at the International Workshop on Old-age Vulnerabilities: Asian and European Perspective, Brawijaya University, Malang, Indonesia, 8–10 July 2004.

Weller, C. (2002). *PURE: A Proposal for More Retirement Income Security*. Economic Policy Institute, Washington, D.C. Available at <http://www.cepr.net/pages/ progressive_agenda/pages/retirement_Income.htm> (accessed 27 August 2004).

The World Bank. *World Development Report 1993: Investing in Health*. New York: Oxford University Press, 1993.

———. *Averting the Old Age Crisis: Policies to Protect the Poor and Promote Growth.* Oxford, England: Oxford University Press, 1994.

The Yogyakarta Special Province (2003). *Socialization of the Government's 2003– 2008 National Action Plan to Improve the Quality of the Elderly*. December 11. Available at <http://www.pemda-diy.go.id/berita/mod.php?mod=userpage& page_id=558&menu=> (accessed 9 October 2004).

6

NATIONAL POLICY FOR THE ELDERLY IN MALAYSIA: ACHIEVEMENTS AND CHALLENGES

Tengku Aizan Hamid and Nurizan Yahaya

INTRODUCTION

The global population grew from one billion to six billion between 1804 and 1999, with the highest rate of growth (2 per cent) occurring as late as the 1960s. The world's most recent billion took only 12 years to accomplish and life expectancy at birth grew from about 30 years two centuries ago to a global average of 66 years today (United Nations 1999, 2001; Riley 2001). The remarkable human population growth for the past 200 years can be, in part, attributed to the fact that more and more people survive to older ages. The demographic transition of human societies, beginning in the 19th and 20th centuries, is continuing well into the new millennium (United Nations, 2002). With the confluence of lowered fertility and mortality rates in most countries around the world, the global population is ageing at an extraordinary scale.

All societies throughout the world, be it the more developed or the less developed, are no exception to this trend. In the past, the growth of the older population was exclusively a problem faced by the more developed countries. That is no longer true today. The structural change in the global population is further complicated by the accelerated rate of ageing in the less developed societies that are taking a shorter and shorter time to make the demographic transition. In fact, since 1955, the rate of ageing in the less developed regions grew to almost three times that of the more developed regions. Many third world countries are ageing faster at lower development levels and there is less time for developing nations to adjust and react to the rapid demographic transition in their population. In the *World Population Ageing: 1950–2050*, published by the Population Division of the United Nations, it was concluded that:

> *The developing countries will also reach that stage (same percentage of persons aged 60 years and over as the more developed regions did in 2000) over a much shorter period of time than that required by the more developed regions. In many cases, rapid population aging will be taking place in countries where the level of economic development is still low.*
>
> — United Nations 2002, p. 34

POPULATION AGEING IN ASEAN COUNTRIES

It has often been said that the world population ageing is unprecedented, pervasive, profound, and enduring (UN 2002), and there is no better example to this than the rapid demographic transition achieved by Southeast Asian countries in the past two decades (Concepcion 1996; ESCAP 2002; Westley & Mason 2002). ASEAN country members such as Indonesia, Malaysia, Singapore, and Thailand have been undergoing significant changes due to rapid modernization, urbanization and industrialization. The rapid ascension to economic prominence and aggressive wealth creation by the Tigers of the Southeast Asian region has resulted in better public health care services and facilities, higher quality of life, easier access to education, and development of other public infrastructure — factors that have been conducive towards greater quality of life, longevity, and successful ageing.

As early as 1989 itself, Chen and Jones predicted that:

> *Irrespective of what will happen to the proportion of elderly people in the population, the absolute numbers of old people will grow very rapidly in ASEAN countries over the remainder of this century.*
>
> — Chen & Jones 1989, p. 15

The absolute number of older persons in South-Eastern Asia has grown by almost 250 per cent since 1950, charting a rise from 10.7 million to 37.3 million in 2000. The absolute number of older persons aged 60 and above, for example, doubled in Indonesia, Malaysia, Philippines, Singapore, and Thailand over a short period of 20 years from 13.95 million to 27.42 million in the year 2000. The Southeast Asia region is projected to record a 15 per cent hike in its proportion of older persons from 7 per cent in 2002 to 22 per cent in 2050 (UN 2002). Come 2050, the figure is expected to reach a new high of 176 million, making a further 370 per cent increase in the number of older persons in the region. Southeast Asian countries, like many other developing nations around the world, are experiencing rapid population ageing with the convergence of lowered fertility and mortality rates.

MALAYSIA: NATION IN TRANSITION

Malaysia has been using the "60 years and over" demarcation "as the cut-off point in deliberating aging trends" since the United Nations World Assembly on Ageing in 1982 at Vienna (Pala 1998). At present, the Malaysian mid-year population stands at 23.27 million persons (Department of Statistics 2001). The 2000 Census recorded a total of 1,451,665 older persons in the country, which means that 1 out of every 16 persons in Malaysia today is 60 years old or older. The proportion of older persons in Malaysia has risen from 4.8 per cent in 1960 to 6.1 per cent in 2000. When compared with the number of older persons in the 1980 and 1991 Censuses, the elderly population has clearly shown a significant percentage increase. Since three decades ago, the absolute number of older persons in Malaysia has almost tripled from 546,100 to the 1.45 million today. Figure 6.1 charts the rise of the aged population in Malaysia since 1960. Consistent with UN medium variant projections, Malaysia will actually achieve full "aged" nation status in 2035, when the proportion of persons aged 60 years and above reaches the 15 per cent mark.

Like many other countries around the world, Malaysia is experiencing population ageing characterized by lower fertility and mortality rates (United Nations 1999; Pala 1998). The Total Fertility Rate (TFR) in Peninsular Malaysia dipped from 6.2 in 1960 to 3.3 in 1996 (Ministry of National Unity and Social Development [MNUSD], 1999). Life expectancy in the country has risen significantly since independence (Table 6.2). In 1957, life expectancy at birth for the male and female population was 55.8 and 58.2 years respectively. In less than half a century, life expectancy at birth in the year 2000 increased to 70.5 years for males and 75 years for females (Department of Statistics 2001). Women live longer than men and they form the fastest growing segment in the old-old category. The sex ratio (number of males for every 100 females) shifts noticeably in women's favour as they get older (Table 6.3). In the 2000 Census, Perak, Selangor, and Johor recorded the highest absolute number of older persons, combining to form 38 per cent of the total elderly population in the country. However, the states of Perak,

FIGURE 6.1
Malaysia Population and Percentage Aged 60 Years and Above, 1960–2000

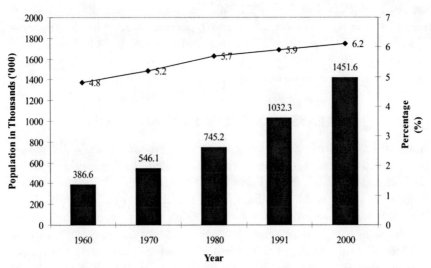

Source: Pala, 1998; Department of Statistics, 2001.

Perlis, Melaka, and Pulau Pinang are ageing more rapidly than others (Table 6.4). As Pala (1998) noted, states with a high percentage of older persons are either senders of migrants or had low rates of natural increases, which explains some variance for the rate of ageing in these states.

The ageing effect is also more pronounced in rural areas than urban locations due to migration. The rural areas are aging more rapidly due to the loss of the younger population to the cities. The quick growth of the urban areas slows down the rate of ageing although the absolute number of older persons residing in the location has more than tripled in the past two decades (Table 6.5). The proportion of the population aged 60 years and above in a given community is influenced by the local fertility and mortality changes, which are derived from the external flows of in-migrants and out-migrants of different ages. The selective migration population means that an area that pushes out population would have a higher aged population and an area that takes in population will have a lower aged population. Therefore demographic ageing must also take into consideration the geographical and spatial issues of population distribution. Communities with a growing and vibrant local economy are particularly attractive to younger migrants while those with few employment opportunities are likely to experience a departure of youth to

TABLE 6.1
Malaysian Population by Age Group (1980, 1991* and 2000)

Age Group	1980 ('000)	1980 Per cent (%)	1991* ('000)	1991* Per cent (%)	2000 ('000)	2000 Per cent (%)
0–4	1,779.6	13.5	2,344.6	12.8	2,612.7	11.2
5–9	1,782.8	13.6	2,333.3	12.7	2,646.5	11.4
10–14	1,633.5	12.4	2,030.9	11.0	2,491.8	10.7
15–19	1,493.5	11.4	1,832.9	10.0	2,367.0	10.2
20–24	1,265.1	9.6	1,682.8	9.2	2,087.2	9.0
25–29	1,058.4	8.1	1,627.7	8.9	1,921.1	8.3
30–34	874.7	6.7	1,469.1	8.0	1,800.2	7.7
35–39	671.3	5.1	1,217.7	6.6	1,705.0	7.3
40–44	624.0	4.8	969.4	5.3	1,487.5	6.4
45–49	473.3	3.6	699.7	3.8	1,168.5	5.0
50–54	414.8	3.2	635.3	3.5	918.9	3.9
55–59	319.8	2.4	467.8	2.5	616.6	2.6
60–64	269.7	2.1	388.9	2.1	551.0	2.4
65–69	188.2	1.4	252.9	1.4	346.7	1.5
70–74	146.6	1.1	203.2	1.1	264.1	1.1
75+	140.6	1.0	223.6	1.2	286.5	1.2
Total	13,136.1	100.0	18,379.7	100.0	23,274.7	100.0

Note: * adjusted figures (past enumeration survey estimate)
Source: Department of Statistics (2001, 1995, 1983).

TABLE 6.2
Life Expectancy at Birth of Malaysians by Gender (1957–2000)

Year	Malay Male	Malay Female	Chinese Male	Chinese Female	Indian Male	Indian Female	National Average Male	National Average Female
1957	50.2	53.4	59.5	66.7	57.5	54.6	55.8	58.2
1966	61.3	62.5	66.2	71.2	62.5	61.9	63.1	66.0
1970	63.8	65.5	65.1	73.4	60.2	63.9	61.6	65.6
1980	66.5	68.9	68.0	74.0	62.1	67.0	66.4	70.5
1990	69.0	72.4	70.6	76.3	64.4	70.4	68.9	73.5
1996	68.8	72.7	71.9	77.6	65.0	72.8	69.3	74.0

Source: MNUSD (1999).

TABLE 6.3

Sex Ratio for Older Persons by Age Group from 1970 to 2000

Age Group	Sex Ratio			
	1970	1980	1991	2000
60 – 74	112.4	98.2	91.7	94.7
75 +	89.5	93.4	82.2	79.2
Total (60+)	108.4	97.2	89.6	91.4

Source: Pala, 1998.

TABLE 6.4

Distribution of the Elderly Population by State and Race (2000)

State	Number of Older Persons	Percentage (%) within States	Percentage (%) of Total	Malay	Chinese	Indian/ Others*
Johor	172,390	6.3	11.9	88,661	70,393	7,931
Kedah	130,900	7.9	9.0	96,863	23,939	6,690
Kelantan	94,857	7.2	6.5	87,706	4,944	249
Melaka	51,115	8.0	3.5	28,117	19,314	2,407
N. Sembilan	63,378	7.4	4.4	31,955	22,387	7,306
Pahang	71,385	5.5	4.9	46,273	20,616	2,731
Perak	189,763	9.3	13.1	24,184	64,617	12,623
Perlis	18,767	9.2	1.3	15,564	2,447	197
Pulau Pinang	103,605	7.9	7.1	30,734	61,366	8,114
Sabah	100,168	3.8	6.9	63,657	21,677	3,929
Sarawak	133,541	6.4	9.2	89,915	41,256	402
Selangor	189,644	4.5	13.0	71,615	80,865	30,309
Terengganu	54,856	6.1	3.8	52,037	2,307	100
F. T. K. L.	74,962	5.4	5.2	14,298	46,028	9,440
F. T. Labuan	2,334	3.1	0.2	1,323	700	84
Total	1,451,665	6.2	100.0	804,166	501,007	93,861

Note: * for Sabah, Sarawak & F. T. Labuan
Source: Department of Statistics (2001).

TABLE 6.5
Distribution of Older Persons by Stratum from 1970 to 2000

Year	Urban			Rural		
	('000)	%	% in stratum	('000)	%	% in stratum
1970	146.9	26.9	5.2	399.2	73.1	5.2
1980	245.2	32.9	5.5	500.0	67.1	5.8
1991	470.7	45.6	5.3	561.6	54.4	6.5
2000	785.3	54.1	5.4	666.4	45.9	7.5

Source: Pala (1998); Department of Statistics (2001).

cities. If this situation continues for a long period, there will be a significant shift in the age structure of the local communities. The structure and process of population ageing are intimately linked to the economic landscape of the country. Furthermore, differences in ethnic dimensions in the Malaysian population can be traced back to colonial times where the occupational segregation of the population by economic functions and roles resulted in differing socio-economic outcomes. This partially explains the difference in the population growth and distribution of the country.

EARLY ADMINISTRATIVE RESPONSES TO POPULATION AGEING

The challenges of population ageing come in many forms, are highly diversified, and vary with commonalities as well as unique features, which reflect the complex history of the countries in the region. As the age-sex structure of the population changes, new challenges arise. Population ageing at lower levels of development assuages the government's ability to engage effectively the multiple challenges of the demographic transition due to limitations in resources and the rapidity of the ageing process. The Malaysian government has in fact taken active measures in addressing ageing issues in the country since the early 1980s. At that time, the well-being of older Malaysians was mostly the responsibility of the then Ministry of Social Welfare, an arrangement which reflected the colonial structure which the country inherited. On 27 October 1990, a cabinet reform resulted in the establishment of a new Ministry of National Unity and Social Development (MNUSD). The Department of Social Welfare under the new ministry, acting through the Destitute Persons Act 1977 (Act 183), Rules for the Older Persons' Homes 1983, and Rules of the Welfare Homes for the Poor 1981, functions as a safety net for homeless older persons who are unable to support themselves or who have no next-of-kin willing to support them. A Care Centres Act 1993 (Act 506 for West Malaysia only) was also passed to regulate private home operators who provide similar elderly care services. Federal schemes have been set up to provide assistance to the elderly by means of income supplement. The Department of Social Welfare still maintains and partially supports well over 130 old folks homes, including the 11 state-run *Rumah Sri Kenangans*, that provide shelter to the destitute elderly, but there is no mistaking the government's preference for filial commitments. A tax relief in 1992 for adult offspring covers the medical expenses incurred by ageing parents (maximum of RM5,000) and the medical benefits enjoyed by civil servants are now extended to include their parents. These moves reflected the government's position in encouraging the family to share caring responsibilities for the elderly in the society.

It was clear that before the mid-1990s, the Malaysian government had the administrative bodies in place to undertake possible issues that might arise from changes in population demographics. The direct uptake of the matter in the public sphere began in 1992 with the declaration of a National Day for the Elderly, which is celebrated annually on 1 October. By 1995, the need for a national policy was imminent.

NATIONAL POLICY FOR THE ELDERLY (NPE)

The Cabinet agreed to a National Policy for the Elderly (NPE) on 25 October 1995 that serves as a preparatory measure by the administration in facing the prospect and challenges of population ageing. The National Policy for the Elderly was created:

> To Ensure the Social Status, Dignity and Well-Being of the Elderly as Members of the Family, Society and Nation by Enabling them to Optimize their Self-Potential, have Access to all Opportunities and have Provision for their Care and Protection.
>
> — National Policy for the Elderly, 1998

The NPE has three principal objectives, namely:
a. To enhance the respect and dignity of the elderly in their family, society and nation.
b. To improve the potential of the elderly so that they continue to be active and productive in national development, and to create opportunities to assist them to continue to be self-reliant.

c. Encourage the establishment and availability of specific facilities to ensure the care and protection of the elderly towards enhancing their well-being.

Prior to the National Policy for the Elderly (NPE), issues concerning the elderly were handled on an ad-hoc basis due to the lack of a definitive guiding principle and overall strategy. For that reason, the NPE was hailed as an important step in not only coordinating efforts to tackle ageing issues, but also liberating the administration from a welfare-based approach to the "problem".

Historically, the National Policy for the Elderly (NPE) can trace its origins to the 1982 United Nations World Assembly on Ageing in Vienna where the International Plan of Action on Ageing (IPAA) was formulated. In 1990, a Declaration of Rights and Responsibilities of Older Persons by the International Federation on Ageing (IFA) was made. This consequently led to the formation of the 18 United Nations Principles for Older Persons on 16 December 1991. In many ways, the U.N. Principles for Older Persons, or more commonly known as Resolution 46/91, was a catalyst for the present NPE. Ideas of independence, care, participation, self-fulfillment, and dignity are evident throughout both documents and are considered universal themes of importance and relevance to older persons. From the document, it is clear that the NPE is meant to serve as a guideline to aid related planning at the lower levels of administration. The Department of Social Welfare continues to play a major role in the execution of the NPE as a general Plan of Action was adopted to facilitate NPE's implementation, with the cooperation of other related agencies.

PLAN OF ACTION FOR THE NATIONAL POLICY FOR THE ELDERLY

To achieve the objectives of the NPE, a strategy based on 1) Respect and Dignity, 2) Self reliance, 3) Participation, 4) Care and Protection, and 5) Research and Development were incorporated into an action plan. These five principles were similar to that of the World Assembly on Ageing in 1982, Vienna. The formal Plan of Action for NPE was adopted and launched in 1998 by the then Minister of National Unity and Social Development, Datin Paduka Zaleha Ismail in conjunction with the 7th National Day of Older Persons celebrations.

A Technical Committee was established in July 1996 under the Department of Social Welfare of the then Ministry of National Unity and

Social Development (now Ministry of Women, Family and Social Development). In line with bureaucratic tradition, the Department of Social Welfare has been identified as the agency responsible for coordinating the implementation of the action plan. To better implement the programmes and activities for the elderly, six sub-committees were established and headed by their respective lead agencies as below:

1. Social and Recreation Sub-Committee
   Chaired by the Department of Social Welfare
2. Health Sub-Committee
   Chaired by the Ministry of Health
3. Education, Religion and Training Sub-Committee
   Chaired by the Ministry of Education
4. Housing Sub-Committee
   Chaired by the Ministry of Housing and Local Government
5. Research Sub-Committee
   Chaired by the National Population and Family Development Board
6. Liaison Sub-Committee
   Chaired by the Ministry of Information

The Plan of Action (Department of Social Welfare, 1999) was formed by listing the various activities and programmes under the respective sub-committees. The Plan of Action consists of 74 types of existing and soon-to-be-implemented activities and programmes. Early planning for activities was made for the period from 1997 to 2005, to be implemented "by governmental agencies, the private sector, non-governmental organizations, civil society and older individuals" in areas such as a) education, b) employment, c) social participation, d) recreation, e) transportation, f) housing, g) family support system, h) geriatric health, i) social security, j) media portrayal, as well as k) research and development of older persons, p. 50.

NATIONAL ADVISORY AND CONSULTATIVE COUNCIL FOR THE ELDERLY

A National Advisory and Consultative Council for the Elderly (NACCE) was established on 22 May, 1996 to assist the government in formulating proper responses to the advent of population ageing. Current council members (2002–05) include the Minister of Women, Family and Social Development, Chief Secretaries from eight government ministries, Directors from four government departments, representatives from various Corporate/Statutory

Bodies, non-governmental organizations (NGO), and individuals from different professional backgrounds. The NACCE meets on a regular basis, but plays a largely perfunctory role as the council is not invested with any direct grant-making ability and institutional or political capacity. The NACCE reviews suggestions forwarded through the Technical Committee and its members are appointed by the Ministry of National Unity and Social Development (now Ministry of Women, Family and Social Development). As the successful conclusion of any activity or programme is dependent on the respective lead agencies, the NACCE has little real control over the actual events on the ground.

ACHIEVEMENTS

It would be difficult to describe every single achievement of the respective sub-committees (Social and Recreation, Health, Education, Religion and Training, Housing and Research) as some activities and programmes are not directly attributable to the mechanisms of the NPE. Rather, it is much preferable to highlight new developments in the different areas over the years and note their significance for the older population, then proceed to determine the amount of influence that the policy has had on its conception, planning, and implementation.

Financial Incentives

Apart from the long-standing tax relief for medical costs incurred by ageing parents, few new measures have been introduced by the government that directly benefit the elderly. The Merdeka Bonds, issued quarterly by Bank Negara with a maturity period of two years as well as a guaranteed tax-free return of 5 per cent per annum for retired persons (aged 55 and above), started on 4 February 2004. Up to August 2004, RM1.5 billion worth of bonds have been fully subscribed. An additional RM1.75 billion was issued up to the end of 2005.

The 2004 Budget speech also included other minor extensions such as a proposed income tax exemption on retirement benefits for those aged between 50 and 55 years old (previously only for those 55 years and above), and tax relief on contributions to EPF, Takaful and premiums for life insurance to be increased from RM5,000 to RM6,000. A sum of RM129.5 million was allocated under the family development programme, which includes moral rehabilitation and day care centres for the elderly, and daily expenditure on food in shelter institutions for the elderly was increased from RM3.90 to RM8.00 per person.

Social Security, Welfare and Old Age Income Support

The Employees Provident Fund (EPF) is the most important social security scheme in Malaysia made mandatory by law under the Employees Provident Fund Act 1991 (Act 452). EPF is the most important retirement scheme for private sector retirees in Malaysia with 9,965,947 contributor accounts total RM180,127.6 million in contributions in 2001 Compared with the 8,050,738 members (4.18 million active) with RM113,491.7 million worth of contributions in 1996 (Ong 2002; Department of Statistics 2001), the EPF has grown at a steady rate of 4.7 per cent per annum in size. The EPF is the largest component of the provident and pension funds system in the country, followed by pension funds and then SOCSO (Social Security Organization) (Holzmann, MacArthur & Sin 2000). When the Malaysian EPF was developed over fifty years ago, it was not indexed to inflation. Hence, the essential question remains whether EPF savings are adequate for old age income support (Kumar 1997; Ong 2002). Moreover, the lump sum withdrawal tends to have high exposure to the risks of improper personal finance management or unsound investments in late life. In December 2003, a suggestion to introduce EPF-like measures to retain a minimum percentage/sum in the contributor's account was prematurely abandoned as it was met with hostile public reaction due to the lack of confidence in the EPF's investment earning abilities in light of the disappointing returns in recent years.

Civil servants are a unique group that receives life-long pension upon retirement, a facility which less than 1 per cent of the Malaysian population enjoys (Ong 2002). The Congress of Unions of Employees in the Public and Civil Services (CUEPACS) estimated that there were about 900,000 civil servants (including the army and the police) in the country with a population of 23 million (CUEPACS 2004; Department of Statistics 2000). Total current expenditure for pension in 2000 amounted to RM4,187 million and made up 7.4 per cent of the Federal Government Expenditure (Department of Statistics 2001). As a non-contributory social security scheme, optional retirement is made available to women at the age of 45 years and men at the age of 50 years (with exceptions of some civil servants in the police force, prison or fire department and psychiatric ward nurses). The pension, upon the death of the civil servant, can be transferred to his/her immediate next-of-kin (e.g. spouse) or dependents. The pension amounts to about half of the last-drawn basic salary and slightly over one-third of the actual take-home pay. A recent reinterpretation of the mandatory age of retirement from 55 to 56 years for the public servants was made via amendments to the Pensions Act 1980 (Act 227) and Statutory and Local Authorities Pensions Act 1980 (Act 239) in 2002 and 2001 respectively.

The total number of elderly aid recipients under the *Skim Bantuan Warga Tua* in 1995 was 10,049 persons receiving RM8,697,630 (Ong 2002). According to the 2002 Annual Report by the Department of Social Welfare, MNUSD, the amount of aid has increased more than threefold to RM30,808,272 and is disbursed to 31,978 older persons. The number of recipients under the scheme represents only a small fraction of the elderly poor in the country, in particular the rural areas, where many live below the poverty line.

Leisure and Recreation

Every year, the National Day of Older Persons is celebrated throughout the month of October and the Social and Recreation Sub-Committee has been responsible for its planning and organization. The sub-committee also arranges for institutional visits to old folks' homes during festive periods throughout the year and encourages the establishment of senior citizens clubs and other elderly-related recreational associations (e.g. tai-chi). In this instance, it works closely with the National Council of Senior Citizens Organizations Malaysia (NACSCOM), a federation of 34 senior citizen associations with about 12,000 members in Malaysia.

The Day Centre for Senior Citizens (*Pusat Harian Warga Tua*) is one of the major programmes under the Plan of Action and the concept revolves around the set-up and maintenance of a place for social gatherings and activities for older Malaysians. The government has approved the construction of 19 Day Centres at an estimated cost of half a million ringgit each. By 2000, eight centres had been completed and are now in operation at a) Tanjung Malim, Perak; b) Kg. Cheras Baru, Kuala Lumpur; c) Kg. Seri Sikamat, Seremban, Negeri Sembilan; d) Raub, Pahang; e) Bentong, Pahang; f) Pekan, Pahang; g) Bukit Payong, Terengganu; and h) Kg. Raja, Terengganu. All the Day Centres are managed by the Central Welfare Council of Peninsular Malaysia. There are also many day centres operated by NGOs in states such as Sarawak, Malacca, Pulau Pinang and Setapak, Federal Territory of Kuala Lumpur.

USIAMAS, or the Golden Age Foundation, is an organization that has registered members who are older persons. Together with associations such as the Malaysian Government Pensioners' Association (Persatuan Pesara Kerajaan Malaysia) and NACSCOM, the three represent grass roots organizations with elderly members. A professional organization, the Gerontological Association of Malaysian (GEM) was founded in 1992 and it is made up of academicians, doctors, nurses, and members of other professions from a variety of disciplines and background who work together towards the betterment of the elderly in the country. Some of the NGOs receive funding for different projects (e.g. DAGS or Demonstrator Application Grant Scheme) and they work closely with the administration in conducting programmes and activities for older persons.

Elderly Abuse, Neglect and Maltreatment

In 2000, the Central Welfare Council of Peninsular Malaysia, Federal Territory Kuala Lumpur, introduced a telephone service programme called TeleCare which began operating on 8 July. The programme, jointly handled by an NGO with the cooperation of Telekom Malaysia, aims to provide referral services and assistance to older persons. The smart partnership reflects the tripartite approach of government funding, private sector support and non-governmental organization management to ageing issues. No age-specific legislation has been introduced and cases are heard under the usual legal avenues for general abuse, neglect, and maltreatment.

Concessionaries and Special Treatments

A 50 per cent concession is made available to senior citizens travelling by air (Malaysian Airline System, Air Asia, Pelangi Air & Berjaya Air) or land (KTM Berhad). Many other private transportation companies offer a special rate for older persons and special seats are offered to the elderly and the disabled. In most service counters (both public and private), special waiting lines and seats are provided to minimize their waiting time, and maximize their comfort.

Health

The Ministry of Health formed a National Council of Health for the Elderly on 17 July 1997 with the mission to "improve awareness, knowledge, skill and cooperation among the different agencies towards preparing a comprehensive health care service for the elderly".

To this end, the Ministry of Health receives an allocation of RM52 million to carry out its Elderly Health Care Programme which includes training of manpower, development of physical infrastructure, and research in medical and health requirements of older Malaysians. However, due to the economic crisis, the allocation between 1995 and 1999 was reduced to RM3.2 million and RM3.5 million was to be paid for the year 2000. Currently, four hospitals have individual units or geriatric wards to cater to the medical needs of the elderly, namely;

1. Hospital Tengku Ampuan Rahimah, Klang, Selangor;
2. Hospital Seremban, Negeri Sembilan;
3. Hospital Kuala Lumpur; and
4. University Malaya Medical Center (UMMC), Federal Territory of Kuala Lumpur

Altogether, there are five geriatricians and five psycho-geriatricians in the Ministry of Health and local university hospitals. By June 2003, about 55 per cent of the rural health clinics had implemented health care services for older persons, and 11,600 health personnels received in-service training for handling elderly patients. About 176 health centres all over the country have formed Senior Citizen Clubs (*Kelab Warga Emas*) that conduct recreational, social, and health activities for members. The Ministry of Health has also published numerous education materials related to healthy old age living and age-related diseases for distribution to the general public. Health awareness campaigns have been organized, including recent ones with a focus on mental health. All older Malaysians who use the public health care system pay minimum fees and most of them receive medication and treatment at subsidized rates.

Education and Training

In 2005, a new elective course was made available to upper secondary level students. The new subject, entitled Basic Gerontology and Geriatric Services (*Gerontologi Asas dan Perkhidmatan Geriatrik*), offers a practical and hands-on approach to the component of care that provides skills-based training to future health aid (Tengku Aizan Hamid, Rodhiah Mohd. Yassin & Suriah Abdul Rahman 2005). Apart from the inculcation of values through Moral Education, elements of respect and care for the elderly are integrated in all school subjects. At the tertiary level, a new post-graduate programme on Gerontology (Masters & Ph.D) is offered by the Institute of Gerontology, Universiti Putra Malaysia. The Institute was established on 1 April 2002 and is a research-based entity with two laboratories, the 1. Biosocial, Cognitive and Functional Laboratory, and 2. Gerontechnology Laboratory. Units of courses are also available in Universiti Malaya and Universiti Kebangsaan Malaysia providing training on aspects of gerontology and geriatrics.

In preparation for their impending retirement, pre-retirement courses are organized by the respective government agencies and some private corporations. The Employee Provident Fund Group and the Public Service Department conduct similar programmes for civil servants who are approaching the mandatory retirement age.

The Manpower Department (*Jabatan Tenaga Rakyat*) conducts registration and placement for retirees. From its launch in August 1996 till June 1998, 1,801 older Malaysians have signed up and 230 of them found jobs through the JTR. In 1999, the Manpower Department successfully registered 199 retirees and returned eight of them into the workforce. In 2000, the department registered 108 retirees and placed 24 of them back into the job market. The government also provides incentives for employers who hire public sector retirees by bearing the full cost of retraining for them. A directory of senior citizens is published regularly to register older persons with potential to contribute their services and expertise to the community.

Religion

The Tabung Haji, a private organization, encourages its contributors to donate to a charity programme that helps older Malaysian Muslims to perform the Fardhu Haj in Mecca. Other church-group and faith-based initiatives also have their own programmes and home visits that reach out to older persons in the community, offering services and assistance through their own initiatives.

Housing

The Uniform Building By-Laws (UBBL) 1991 specifically addressed the need for disabled-friendly designs to enable greater access by the handicapped. The amendments have been gazetted and the Local Authorities have been tasked to enforce the UBBL 1984 on building requirements for disabled persons. This includes the building of ramps, railings, elevators, and lifts or other extensions necessary for the access of people with handicaps. It is part of creating an enabling environment to meet the needs of the disabled and the elderly in the community.

Research

There are currently several researches being conducted at academic institutions which touch on mental health, quality of life, perception of needs and problems, ergonomics, finance, and intergenerational relationships of older persons. The establishment of the Institute of Gerontology provided a focal point for elderly research in the country and together with the other government agencies (e.g. National Population and Family Development Board or NPFDB), many studies are being conducted for a variety of purposes. Documentation attempts and bibliographic efforts are underway to record the various local studies to avoid duplication and enable easy referencing.

POLICY ANALYSIS: NPE AND OLDER MALAYSIANS

The assessment of any public policy begins with the identification of assessment criteria and dimensions. Discussing the successes or failures of a social/public policy is dependent on the original intention of the policy itself. Criticisms of the policy could stem from reasons ranging from the poor execution of its plans to the inadequacy of the policy itself in addressing the situation, despite being implemented successfully.

Thomas and Robertson (1990) developed "a model described as 'the cycle of social policy' for understanding, analysis, and assessment of social policies" (p. 196). They proposed an idealized model for policy analysis and evaluation, outlining the various factors for consideration in determining the relative degree of success through case study of two social policies. The six stages of the cycle are a) Problem Identification, b) Policy Formulation and Adoption, c) Policy Implementation, d) Policy Outcome, e) Policy Evaluation, and f) Dissemination of Policy Information, as illustrated in Figure 6.2.

The role of researchers, in this cyclical nature of policy-making, is to monitor the implementation of the policies, assessing the adequacy of resource allocation, its impact on the intended target beneficiaries, the structure and mechanism of executing agencies, as well as the fulfillment of the original objectives. As pointed out by Thomas and Robertson (1990), some of the stages and activities might not be present and a social policy might not have a formally established evaluation or assessment strategy. When this happens, informal information gathering or feedback from policy-makers and

FIGURE 6.2
The Cycle of Social Policy (Thomas & Robertson, 1990, p. 196)

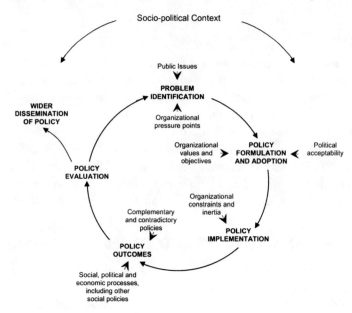

implementers can help shed some light on the overall impact of the programmes and activities.

Likewise, the fundamental problem with the NPE is the absence of clear performance indicators in its action plan. Although there is a proposed monitoring mechanism in the Plan of Action, there are no standardized ways of measuring achievement. The actualization of policy objectives will remain a slow work-in-progress if no systematic effort is made to evaluate the effectiveness of the various programmes. It is often difficult to distinguish whether a programme exists at the behest of the policy, or the programme is merely part of a routine departmental activity. In addition, previously existing schemes (of pre-NPE days) are reassigned under the respective sub-committees and there is little inter-ministerial cooperation. Most of the programmes and activities are carried out in isolation and the usual departmental boundaries are highly visible.

As it is, wholesale adoption of Resolution 46/91 did not fundamentally change the welfare-oriented approach of the administration. Older persons, despite the NPE, are still regarded as passive recipients of social work rather than subjects of empowerment or understanding. In its ninth year of implementation, the NPE has achieved some form of success in terms of bringing ageing issues to the fore and has organized as well as banded together various agencies to work on the matter. More Malaysians are now aware of the need for proper planning towards a good old age lifestyle and public interest on senior citizens is on the rise. The leading English daily in the country, the *Star*, dedicates a regular column on ageing issues.

Nevertheless, limitations in resources mean that the NPE is best served through a broad-based approach where the more common and more urgent needs of the elderly are given priority. Thus, the principal concern of the existing Plan of Action is still how best to position government agencies in facilitating aid, assistance, and relief to as many older Malaysians as possible. At this stage, the NPE is still focused on inter-department cooperation and integrated monitoring of activities.

CHALLENGES

In his review of European ageing policies, Walker (2002) highlighted five main challenges faced by the older populations of the EU:

1. Ensuring economic security in old age;
2. Maintaining intergenerational solidarity;
3. Combating social exclusion caused by age discrimination;
4. Providing long-term care in the context of changes in the family and residence patterns; and
5. Enabling older people to participate as full citizens.

Walker 2002, p. 759

Each country has its own unique context — e.g. level of development, culture, and socio-political environment, which requires different policy approaches and emphasis. There is a dire need to appreciate the "tremendous diversity in the situation of older persons, not only between countries but within countries and between individuals, which requires a variety of policy responses" (U.N. 1991). As the principal author previously noted:

> The older population is not a homogenous [sic] group. They are different based on gender, experiences, social economic background, social class, ethnicity, religion and in spatial and geographical location. The diversity of the older population may affect the provision and accessibility of care. In a plural society like Malaysia these differences are reinforced by the

different rate of ageing amongst the major ethnic groups. The diversity also influence[s] the kind of planning that should be made to cater for their current and future needs.

— Tengku Aizan 2001, p. 41

In many ways, the challenges faced by older Malaysians are not wholly dissimilar to that of other societies. Income security in old age is important for maintaining a healthy, independent, and comfortable lifestyle. There is always a need for quality long-term care and greater access to medical services. We have to involve older persons in the community and promote better intergenerational relationships and solidarity. But what are the challenges that lie ahead with all these expectations?

Firstly, the changing demographic and socio-economic characteristics of the older population will result in new expectations and needs for different services and goods. The successive cohorts of older Malaysians will be more affluent, more educated and better informed on the available options for retirement living. They will live longer and have greater demands on health care; they will gradually get themselves organized and perhaps learn to find a strong platform for advocacy to voice their opinions and rights.

The various bodies, government, private or non-government, will have to address the structural efficiency of their organizations and strive to be more accountable and transparent in their dealings with older Malaysians as the audience will no longer be satisfied with one-off or gloss-over efforts to appease their demands. If the public loses confidence in the state's ability to provide for the security of their old age, the government will have failed in discharging its responsibilities to protect the welfare and interest of its people. While the government's emphasis on the family is to be applauded, there must be equally attractive options available to those who do not have a family to turn to in late life. Government policies, programmes and initiatives must ensure the optimal utilization of the elderly workforce and move beyond the welfare-oriented approach towards older persons.

Without proper research, without proper planning, and without proper evaluative strategies, the NPE will remain a hollow exercise that is unsystematic and erratically implemented. There has to be a more aggressive approach towards the issue of old age and ageing, and there has to be some form of funding agency or formal political platform *vis-à-vis* the Women Affairs Department (HAWA) in promoting the cause of older persons. Without a clear focal point to snowball the efforts on population ageing, the programmes and activities remain in isolation. The National Advisory and Consultative

Council for the Elderly has to take up the challenge and create a greater cooperative spirit between the respective stakeholders, and channel available resources to make this a reality.

CONCLUSION

The rapid increase in the size and growth of the older population in Malaysia is concordant to the changes in national fertility and mortality rates elsewhere in the world. In recognition of the challenges of a greying population, a National Policy for the Elderly (NPE) was introduced and a National Advisory and Consultative Council for the Elderly (NACCE) was established. Appearing at the turn of the one-decade mark of the NPE, this chapter aims to provide an overview of the achievements and challenges, while offering some suggestions for a systematic review of the policy's successes and failures, strengths and weaknesses, as well as areas for further improvement. As the data are mostly secondary in nature, limited by the incidental reporting and documentation by the respective stakeholders in related areas such as health, finance, welfare, social security, housing and others, the authors do not profess to being exhaustive in this attempt to fashion an overall picture of the NPE and elderly-related developments in the country. From the activities and programmes implemented so far, however, some policy objectives have been met, but a more coordinated mechanism is needed for proper evaluation of the outcomes. As it is, the NPE is a loose, non-interventionist and low impact entity with a broad focus that is largely undirected. The effective implementation of the NPE is not the sole responsibility of the government, but a joint effort by all parties. Here, the National Advisory and Consultative Council for the Elderly (NACCE) has an important role to play in ensuring the active participation, continued involvement, and long-term commitment of the various organizations and individuals to issues on old age and ageing.

References

Atchley, R.C. *Social Forces and Aging: An Introduction to Social Gerontology.* Wadsworth: Belmont, CA., 2000.

Asher, M.G. *Social Security in Malaysia and Singapore: Practices, Issues and Reform Directions.* Institute of Strategic and International Studies. Malaysia: Kuala Lumpur, 1994.

Association of Southeast Asian Nations. *ASEAN Statistical Yearbook 2003.* ASEAN Secretariat: Jakarta, 2003.

Bengtson, V.L. and J. Kuypers. "The Family Support Cycle: Psychosocial Issues in the Aging Family". In *Life-span and Change in a Gerontological Perspective*, J.M.A. Munnichs, P. Mussen, E. Olbrich, & P.G. Coleman, eds., pp. 257–73. Orlando, FL: Academic Press, 1985.

Bengston, V.L. and Roberts R.E.L. "Intergenerational Solidarity in Aging Families: An Example of Formal Theory Construction". *Journal of Marriage and the Family*, 53 (1991): 856–70.

Cavanaugh, J.C. and F. Blanchard-Fields. *Adult Development and Aging*, 4th edition. Wadsworth: Belmont, CA., 2002.

Chan, A. "Singapore's Changing Age Structure and the Policy: Implications for Financial Security, Employment, Living Arrangements and Health Care". *Asian MetaCentre Research Chapter Series*, No. 3, 2001.

––––––. "The Social and Economic Consequences of Ageing in Asia: An Introduction". *Southeast Asian Journal of Social Sciences* 27, no. 2 (1999): 1–8.

Chen, A.J. and G. Jones. *Ageing in ASEAN: Its Socio-Economic Consequences*. Singapore: Institute of South-east Asian Studies, 1989.

Cohen, J.E. "Population Problems: Recent Developments and their Impact". *Asia-Pacific Review* 7, no. 2 (2000): 86–98.

Concepcion, M.B. "The Greying of Asia: Demographic Dimensions". In *Added Years of Life in Asia: Current situation and Future Challenges. Asian Population Studies Series, No. 141*. Singapore: Institute of Southeast Asian Studies. United Nations Economic and Social Commission for Asia and the Pacific (UNESCAP). Bangkok, Thailand, 1996.

DaVanzo, J. and A. Chan. "Living Arrangements of Older Malaysians: Who Co-resides with their Adult Children?". *Demography* 3, no. 1 (1994): 95–114.

Debavalya, N. *Ageing Population among ASEAN Countries: A Case of Thailand*. Chapter presented at the Seminar on Ageing Population among ASEAN Countries, AFPPD, Kuala Lumpur, 19 July 2003.

Department of Statistics Malaysia. *Population Distribution and Basic Demographic Characteristics. Population and Housing Census of Malaysia 2000*. Department of Statistics, Malaysia: Kuala Lumpur, 2001.

––––––. *Education and Social Characteristics of the Population. Population and Housing Census of Malaysia 2000*. Department of Statistics. Malaysia: Kuala Lumpur, 2002.

Department of Social Welfare. *National Policy for the Elderly (NPE)*. Ministry of National Unity and Social Development, Kuala Lumpur, 1994.

––––––. *Plan of Action for the National Policy for the Elderly (NPE)*. Ministry of National Unity and Social Development, Kuala Lumpur, 1999.

Economic and Social Commission for Asia and the Pacific. "National Policies and Programmes on Ageing in Asia and the Pacific: An Overview and Lessons Learned". *Social Policy Chapter No. 9*. United Nations, New York, 2002.

Haaga, J., C. Peterson, J. DaVanzo and S.M. Lee. *Health Status and Family Support of Older Malaysians. Labor and Population Program.* Working Chapter Series 93–17, DRU-378-NIA. RAND, United States, 1993.

Hermalin, A.I. *Ageing in Asia: Facing the Crossroads.* Comparative Study of the Elderly in Asia. Research Reports. Report No. 00-55, August 2000. Population Studies Center, University of Michigan; Michigan, 2000.

Hooyman, N. and H.A. Kiyak. *Social Gerontology: A Multidisciplinary Perspective.* 5th edition. Boston: Allyn and Bacon, 1999.

Hoskins, D.D. "Thinking about Ageing Issues". *International Social Security Review* (Special Issue) Volume 55 – No. 1/2002: The Challenge of Ageing for Social Security

Holzmann, R., I.W. Mac Arthur and Y. Sin. *Pension Systems in East Asia and the Pacific: Challenges and Opportunities.* Social Protection Discussion Chapter No. 0014, 2000.

ILO-OECD. *Adequacy and Social Security Principles in Pension Reform*, Chapter commissioned for Joint ILO-OECD Workshop: Development and Reform of Pension Schemes, Paris, December 1997.

International Law Book Services (ILBS). *Pension Laws of Malaysia.* Kuala Lumpur: Legal Research Board, 2000.

Japanese Organisation for International Cooperation in Family Planning. *Population Aging in Asia.* Tokyo: JOICFP, 1989.

Jitapunkul, S., N. Chayovan and J. Kespichayawattana. "National Policies on Ageing and Long-term Care Provision for Older Persons in Thailand". In *Ageing and Long-Term Care: National Policies in the Asia-Pacific*, D.R. Phillips, and A.C.M. Chan, eds. Singapore: Institute of Southeast Asian Studies; Canada: International Development Research Centre, 2002.

Kaufman, G. and P. Uhlenberg. "Effects of Life Course Transitions on the Quality of Relationships between Adult Children and Their Parents", *Journal of Marriage and the Family* 60 (1998): 924–38.

Keasberry, I.N. *Elder Care, Old Age Security and Social Change in Rural Yogyakarta, Indonesia.* PhD Thesis, Wageningen University, Wageningen, 2002.

Kinsella, K. and Velkoff, V.A. An Aging World: 2001, *POPULATION-PARIS*-VOL 57 2002; PART 6: 928–29.

Knodel, J. and N. Debavalya. "Living Arrangements and Support among the Elderly in South-East Asia: An Introduction". *Asia-Pacific Population Journal* 12, no. 4 (1997).

Knodel, J., N. Chayovan and S. Siriboon. "The Impact of Fertility Decline on Familial Support for the Elderly: An Illustration from Thailand". *Population and Development Review* 18, no. 1 (1992): 19–102.

Lee, G.R., J.K. Netzer and R.T. Coward. "Filial Responsibility Expectations and Patterns of Intergenerational Relations", *Journal of Marriage and the Family* 51 (1994): 559–65.

Leete, R. *Malaysia's Demographic Transition: Rapid Development, Culture, and Politics.* Kuala Lumpur, Oxford University Press, 1996.

Mason, K.O. "Family Change and Support of the Elderly in Asia: What Do We Know?". *Asia-Pacific Population Journal* 7, no. 3 (1992): 13–32.

Mehta, K.K. (2002). "National Policies on Ageing and Long-term Care in Singapore: A Case of Cautious Wisdom?". In *Ageing and Long-Term Care: National Policies in the Asia-Pacific*, Phillips, D.R. and Chan, A.C.M., eds. Singapore: Institute of Southeast Asian Studies; Canada: International Development Research Centre.

National Commission on the Elderly, Thailand. *Ageing in Thailand: 2001 — Key Issues and New Challenges.* The Preparatory Committee for the Second World Assembly on Ageing, The National Commission on the Elderly, Thailand, 2002.

National Population and Family Development Board Malaysian. *The Malaysian Population Profile.* Kuala Lumpur: Ministry of National Unity and Social Development, 1999.

―――. *The Malaysian Family Profile*, Kuala Lumpur, Ministry of National Unity and Social Development, 1999.

NPFDB, Malaysia and Rand Corporation, USA. Report of the Malaysian Family Life Survey — *II, 1988*, Kuala Lumpur, Ministry of National Unity and Social Development, 1992.

Ofstedal, M.B., J. Knodel and N. Chayovan. "Intergenerational Support and Gender: A Comparison of Four Asian Countries". In *Comparative Study of the Elderly in Asia. Research Reports.* Report No. 99–54, March 1999. Michigan: Population Studies Center, University of Michigan, 1999.

Ong, F.S. "Ageing in Malaysia: A Review of National Policies and Programmes". In *Ageing and Long-Term Care: National Policies in the Asia-Pacific*, D.R. Phillips, and A.C.M. Chan, eds. Singapore: Institute of Southeast Asian Studies; Canada: International Development Research Centre, 2002.

Pala, J. *Senior Citizens and Population Ageing in Malaysia.* Population Census Monograph Series, No. 4, Kuala Lumpur: Department of Statistics Malaysia, 1998.

Phillips, D.R. and A.C.M. Chan, eds. *Ageing and Long-Term Care: National Policies in the Asia-Pacific.* Singapore: Institute of Southeast Asian Studies; Canada: International Development Research Centre, 2002.

Pillemer, K. and K. McCartney, eds. *Parent-Child Relations Throughout Life.* New Jersey: Lawrence Erlbaum Associate, 1991.

Ramesh, M. "Privatization of Social Security in Southeast Asia". *The Review of Policy Research* 19, no. 3 (2002): 142–60.

Riley, J.C. *Rising Life Expectancy: A Global History.* New York: Cambridge University Press, 2001.

Rossi, A.S. and P.H. Rossi. *Of Human Bonding: Parent-Child Relations across the Life Course.* New York: Aldine de Gruyter, 1990.

Social Security Administration. *Social Security Programs Throughout the World: Asia and the Pacific 2002.* SSA, Office of Policy, USA, 2003.

Stark, O. *Altruism and Beyond: An Economic Analysis of Transfers and Exchanges in Families and Groups.* Cambridge: Cambridge University Press, 1995.

Stockwell, E.G. *The Methods and Materials of Demography,* condensed edition. California: Academic Press, 1976.

Tengku Aizan Hamid, Jariah Masud and Chai Sen Tyng. "Socioeconomic Status of Older Malaysians: A Gender Comparison", *Malaysian Journal of Family Studies* (2004, in the press).

United Nations. *United Nations Principles for Older Persons*; [On-line]. Abstract: <http://www.un.org/esa/socdev/iyoppop.htm>. Division for Social Policy and Development [DESA], United Nations, New York, 1998.

———. *The World at Six Billion.* Population Division, Department of Economic and Social Affairs [DESA], United Nations, New York, 1999.

———. *World Population Prospects: The 2000 Revision*; Population Division, Department of Economic and Social Affairs [DESA], United Nations, New York, 2001.

———. *World Population Ageing: 1950–2050*; Population Division, Department of Economic and Social Affairs [DESA], United Nations, New York, 2002.

———. *Population Ageing 2002 (Wall Chart).* Population Division, Department of Economic and Social Affairs [DESA], United Nations, New York, 2002.

——— (n.d.). *World Population Prospects: The 2002 Revision Population Database.* Retrieved July 30, 2003, from Population Division, Department of Economic and Social Affairs [DESA], United Nations Web site: <http://esa.un.org/unpp/>.

United Nations Population Fund. *State of World Population 1999. Six Billion: A Time for Choices.* New York: United Nations Population Fund [UNFPA], 1999.

———. *Asia and the Pacific: A Region in Transition.* New York: United Nations Population Fund [UNFPA], 2002.

United Nations Economic and Social Commission for Asia and the Pacific. *2004 ESCAP Population Data Sheet.* Bangkok, Thailand: UNESCAP, 2004.

———. *Report and Plan of Action of Population and Poverty 2000. Asian Population Studies Series No. 159.* Bangkok, Thailand: UNESCAP, 2000.

———. *Policies and Programmes for Older Persons in Asia and the Pacific: Selected Studies. Social Policy Paper No. 1.* Bangkok, Thailand: UNESCAP, 2001.

———. *Ageing in Asia and the Pacific: Emerging Issues and Successful Practices. Social Policy Paper No. 10.* Bangkok, Thailand: UNESCAP, 2002.

Westley, S.B. and A. Mason. "Asia's Aging Population". In *The Future of Population in Asia*, pp. 83–95. Honolulu: East-West Center, 2002.

Public Service Department Website: <http://www.jpa.gov.my>.

CEUPACS Website: <http://cuepacs.redirectme.net/main.htm>.

7

AGEING POLICIES AND PROGRAMMES IN THAILAND

Nibhon Debavalya

INTRODUCTION

It is now widely recognized that the demographic trends of the past decades in many developing countries, including Thailand, are leading to unprecedented increases not only in the absolute numbers of older persons, but also in their relative proportion to the population. At the same time, rapid social and economic changes are underway that are widely assumed to have profound implications for the circumstances under which the future elderly will live. These changes include the decline in the number of children couples have, greater longevity, increased involvement of women (the predominant providers of care) in economic activities outside the home, physical separation of parents and adult children associated with urbanization and age-selective, rural-to-urban migration, and ideational changes, especially the spread of western-style individualism through the mass media and public education. The present chapter is intended as an overview of the situation of ageing population in Thailand, with detailed analyses of ageing policies and programmes.

AGEING SITUATION IN THAILAND

The Asian region has experienced a rapid decline in fertility over the past several decades. The decline has been more rapid in East and Southeast Asia compared with the other regions in the world. The sustained decline in mortality has resulted in a gradual rise in life expectancy at birth with female life expectancy in general showing a higher and faster improvement than that of males.

As we know, fertility transition first took place in East Asia. Most East Asian countries have completed or are nearing completion of the transition from high to low fertility. Japan was the forerunner with fertility already having fallen below replacement level. Japan thus completed its fertility transition well before most other Asian countries had begun their transition. It is very interesting to contrast the different factors that resulted in the fertility transition in the predominantly rural populations of China and the Republic of Korea (Concepcion 1993). Although a family planning programme played a supporting role in the fertility reduction in the Republic of Korea, their reproductive revolution came about as a result of individual family decisions to restrict fertility. That is, even after family planning programme activities were lessened, fertility continued to fall sharply and has been below replacement since the mid-1980s. In China, government intervention in individual decisions to marry and to have children characterized the country's birth control programme. The family planning achievements resulted in the total fertility rate (TFR) falling to fewer than two children per woman from 1990–95.

While some ASEAN countries have intermediate levels of fertility, others are seeing below-replacement fertility rate levels. Singapore was the first country to reach replacement level in the second half of the 1970s. In Thailand, starting in the late 1960s, fertility declined substantially and continuously through the next two decades, and reached replacement level at the beginning of the 1990s. According to Knodel, Chamratrithirong and Debavalya (1987), the reproduction revolution in Thailand was due to (i) rapid and fundamental social change; (ii) a cultural setting conducive to fertility regulation; (iii) "latent demand" for family planning, and (iv) the efforts of the official family planning programme.

As shown in Table 7.1, the population of older persons, aged 60 and above, of Thailand was 5.87 million or 9.4 per cent of the total population in 2000. This compares with 5.4 per cent in 1980. This proportion is expected to reach 12.0 per cent in 2010, and one-fifth of the population by 2025. Whilst the number of older persons in Thailand is expected to rise dramatically over the next decades as seen in Table 7.1, a more important issue for Thailand is the speed of population ageing.

Whilst they are imperfect measurements, dependency ratios can give an indication of the potential burden of support on the working-age population.

TABLE 7.1
Population by Age Groups, Thailand 2000–2025

Age	2000	2005	2010	2015	2020	2025
0–14	15,324	14,868	14,245	13,920	13,455	12,977
15–59	41,045	43,202	44,754	45,601	45,478	44,857
60+	5,867	6,693	8,042	9,539	11,888	14,452
Total	64,236	64,763	67,041	69,060	70,821	72,286

Source: National Economic and Social Development Board (2003), Population Projections for Thailand 2000–2025, Bangkok.

These ratios include the child dependency ratio (number of young people aged 10–14 years relative to working-age individuals aged 15–59), or the old-age dependency ratio (persons aged 60 and above relative to working-age individuals). The old-age ratio is clearly rising now. In 1960, for example, the total dependency ratio was 92 per 100 working population, and almost all of the dependent population were children (Jitapunkul, Chayovan and Kespichayawattana, 2002). As birth rates declined, the child dependency ratio declined, resulting in an initial reduction of the total dependency ratio. Conversely, because of the process of population ageing, the old-age dependency ratio increased. According to the National Economic and Social Development Board (NESDB) population projection, after 2023, the old-age dependency ratio in Thailand would be higher than the child dependency ratio. This implies that the burden of support for the older persons would become more onerous.

Inequalities and the feminization of ageing exist in Thai society. Poor older people, particularly those living in rural areas, have suffered from the inequities and feminization of ageing by being further excluded from accessibility to health services, credit schemes, income generating activities, and decision-making (Table 7.2).

Patterns and Trends in Living Arrangements

Knodel and Debavalya pointed out the central role co-residence between elderly family members and younger generation adults, especially their own adult children, has traditionally played in the familial support systems in the Asian region (Knodel and Debavalya 1997). The majority of older persons in Asia co-reside with at least one adult child (ESCAP 2002b). Indeed, in

TABLE 7.2

Characteristics of Elderly Women and Men Indicating a Vulnerable Situation for Elderly Women, Thailand (percentages)

	Male			Female		
	Total	Urban	Rural	Total	Urban	Rural
Marital status						
Single	1.10	1.30	1.10	3.00	5.20	2.40
Married	83.30	85.60	82.70	48.90	42.80	50.40
Widowed-divorced-separated	15.50	12.80	16.20	48.00	52.00	47.10
Unknown	0.10	0.30	–	0.10	–	0.10
Education						
None	19.40	14.40	20.60	40.90	33.00	42.70
Lower than grade 4	9.60	6.50	10.20	10.60	6.60	11.60
Grade 4	59.50	47.30	62.30	44.30	45.20	44.10
Higher than grade 4	10.70	30.90	6.10	3.80	14.50	1.30
Others	0.80	0.90	0.80	0.40	0.70	0.30
Working status						
Yes	41.80	29.40	44.50	23.80	16.60	25.60
Adequacy of income						
Inadequate	37.00	21.30	40.50	34.10	18.60	37.80
Index of working opportunity (IWO)[a]						
Ratio between "% working status as yes" and "inadequacy of income"	112.90	138.00	109.90	69.80	89.20	67.70

Note: [a] A population with a high IWO means that the population has a high opporunity to work. This index is useful for comparing the opportunity to work or inequality of finding work among various populations.

Source: Sutthichai Jitapunkul, Napaporn Chayovan and Jiraporn Kespichayawattana (2002). "National Policies on Ageing and Long-term Care Provision in Thailand", in David R. Phillips and Alfred C.M. Chan, eds., *Ageing and Long-term Care: National Policies in the Asia-Pacific* (Singapore/Canada: ISEAS/IDRC Canada/TRF/ISEAS.

Thailand the most prominent feature of the living arrangements of the Thai elderly population, which is the most crucial aspect of the familial system of support and assistance, is co-residence with an adult child. Traditionally, the elderly continue to live in the residence they have occupied since early in marriage and at least one child remains co-resident. During much of the period of co-residence, an interdependent relationship is likely to exist with forms of support and assistance going in both directions between parents and children. Eventually, however, as the health and physical ability of the elderly deteriorate with age the balance of services presumably flows increasingly from the younger to the older generation.

Using various national surveys data from 1986 to 1995 and data from recent Thai censuses, Knodel and Chayovan found out that all sources through the 1990s show close to, or above, 80 per cent of the elderly with a living child as co-resident. Data also indicate that very few Thai elderly live alone and this has not changed over the period covered. In contrast, there are substantially more elderly living with spouses. This could reflect an increased tendency for adult children to establish separate, but possibly nearby households, as long as elderly parents have each other to live with. The finding that living alone has not increased, however, suggests that once one of the parents dies, co-residence often resumes.

Overall, almost half of the Thai elderly live in a three-generation household. There is little difference in this respect between urban and rural elderly. Almost all the elderly who live with a child live with an adult child. Thus, the percentage who live with at least one child aged 18 or older is only slightly lower (69 vs. 71 per cent) than the percentage who live with any child. Elderly persons are considerably more likely to live with an ever married child than a single child, although this is far more so for the older than the younger elderly, reflecting the greater likelihood that the elderly's children are married as the elderly themselves grow older (Knodel, Chayovan and Siriboon 1996).

The elderly who live with single children are about as likely to live with a son as a daughter (about 20 per cent in each case). In contrast, far more Thai elderly persons live with an ever married daughter than an ever married son (34 vs. 20 per cent). This tendency is strong among both men and women, and younger and older elderly; however, it is largely a rural phenomenon. Among the urban elderly, there is little difference in the proportion who live with an ever married son or daughter. The rural-urban differences in this respect undoubtedly reflect the far greater influence of Chinese ethnicity (and the associated preference for residing with a married son) among urban Thais compared with their rural counterparts (Knodel and Chayovan 1997).

In addition, survey and census data on the living arrangements of the elderly and their linkages with related aspects of material exchanges and contact with their children indicate that a widespread and functioning familial system of support and care for the older population has been maintained in Thailand despite rapid social and demographic changes over recent decades. Although differences in samples and data collection methods preclude arriving at firm conclusions, there is some suggestion in the available data that co-residence of elderly parents with at least one child, literally defined as living in the same dwelling unit, is declining. However, this does not appear to represent an erosion of the support system, judging from the fact that increased daily contact between older parents and non-co-resident children almost fully compensates for this decline. Rather, it may reflect a tendency to "buy more privacy" for both generations by establishing nearby households, a possibility made more affordable by rising incomes, while retaining sufficient proximity to permit maintaining essential aspects of traditional intergenerational obligations of care and support.

National Policy and Development for the Elderly Population

The first provision for older persons in Thailand was the Government Welfare Institution for the Elderly, which was established in 1953. However, there were no formal national policies on ageing until 1986. After the First World Assembly on Ageing held in Vienna in 1982, the International Plan of Action on Ageing was disseminated to member states. The Thai government responded to this by setting up the National Committee for the Elderly. In 1986, the National Committee for the Elderly developed the National Long-term Plan of Action for the Elderly (1986–2001).

The First National Long-term Plan of Action for the Elderly (1986–2001)

The plan supported the implementation of government policies on care for older people and was used as a framework and guideline for activities initiated by authorized organizations such as the National Committee on Ageing of Thailand, 1986. However, data were very limited on older people in Thailand at the time the plan was being developed. Therefore, the main features of this plan were based on recommendations of the International Plan of Action on Ageing, a report by the First World Assembly on Ageing. Public and Non-governmental organizations' participation in the plan's development was also limited.

The First National Long-term Plan of Action for the Elderly mainly targeted older persons. Its objectives were:

1. To provide older people with general knowledge on the changes of age and necessary environment adjustments, including health care
2. To provide older persons with the protection and support of families and communities, including other welfare services as deemed necessary
3. To support the role of older people in participation in family and other activities
4. To emphasize the responsibility of the society for older people.

Measures to be taken in the plan were confined to four aspects of life in old age, including health, education, income and employment, and social and cultural aspects. The major measures were:

1. To disseminate knowledge to older persons on self-adjustment, self-health care, prevention of disease, nutrition, and proper exercise
2. To extend social welfare services for older persons, particularly for those without income or with insufficient income, and with no support.
3. To provide education, training or occupational counselling for the capable elderly to equip them with knowledge and skills for employment
4. To organize recreational activities for older persons to facilitate the transfer of their knowledge and experience to younger generations
5. To campaign for recognition of the importance of the extended family system and the social values of respecting and paying gratitude to ancestors and older persons
6. To cooperate with religious institutions in disseminating morals for the spiritual help of older persons, including the development of moral teaching using diverse and appropriate methods
7. To promote and support the role of communities and the private sector in providing welfare services for older persons and providing the opportunity for them to participate in various activities
8. To train personnel in caring and providing services for older persons
9. To collect basic data and to encourage study, research, monitoring, and evaluation of the issues concerning older persons' children (Jitapunkul, Chayovan and Kespichayawattana 2002).

Implementation of the First National Long-term Plan

As previously mentioned, measures in the plan are confined to 4 aspects of life in old age including health, education, income and employment, and social and cultural aspects. The major measures include extending social welfare services to those without income or with insufficient income and with no support, and promoting and supporting the role of communities and the private sector in providing welfare services.

After the First Long-term Plan for Older Persons was announced in 1986, many major programmes related to older adults have been implemented. The Department of Social Welfare, Ministry of Labour and Social Welfare[1] is the principal organization responsible for social service provision, including both institutional and community care. However, like in many countries, the formal social services especially for long-term care in Thailand, have begun with institutional services. The first institutional service for older person was established in 1956 and called "Home for Older Persons". It provides services for the low-income elderly who cannot stay with their families or have no relatives to stay with. The elderly who are eligible for staying in "Home for Older Persons" have to be independent in personal care and have no need for nursing care. At present, there are twenty residential homes in sixteen provinces with some eligibility qualifications revised. However, when these elderly people get older, they turn frail and need personal or nursing care. Unfortunately, public nursing homes for older persons are not yet available in Thailand. Inevitably, the elderly living in residential homes who need special care have to be taken care of by staff of the residential homes.

The Department of Social Welfare has developed Social Service Centres for Older Persons since 1979. At present, there are 18 Social Service Centre for Older Persons, which provide mainly day care and rehabilitation services. Apart from the day care and basic rehabilitation programmes, these centres also provide medical screening and treatment, counselling, recreation activities, and mobile clinics. However, the provision of those services is on a small scale and serves only several thousand users. Moreover, other well established home/community services for long-term care are not available at present. Most of the available community services for the elderly and disable persons cannot be regarded as long-term provisions and are provided only on request or in an emergency situation.

In spite of the activities previously mentioned, it should be pointed out that in general, there was little progress in state activities related to elderly organizations between 1986–91.

Later in 1992 the Government of Thailand developed "The Essence of the Long-term Policies and Measures for the Elderly (1992–2001)". These measures helped accelerate actions, particularly welfare driven by state organizations. They also influenced the Eighth National Economic and Social Development Plan (1997–2001), which for the first time, included a section providing social welfare benefits to older persons. These welfare benefits included a living allowance to indigent elderly people, universal free health services, and discounted fares for public transport.

In 1993, the Department of Social Welfare set up a welfare fund, which provided 200 Baht per month to poor older persons. Since 1999, the monthly allowance has been increased to 300 Baht per month. About 400,000 older persons receive this payment. In 1999, 200 "Community Service Centre for the Elderly" (place in temples) were set up. These community centres, operated by communities' leaders, are able to provide only recreation activities and health promoting programmes, but not community/home care.

Many non-government organizations, such as the Thai Red Cross Society, HelpAge International, the Duangprateep Foundation, some religious organizations and several non-profit organizations, provide community care for older persons, especially those in poor and remote areas. HelpAge International has several projects, which aim to support income-generating programmes in rural areas. It also funds many projects on community services, including social and health services in several areas. Some non-government organizations also run institutional care programmes including homes for the elderly and nursing homes. At present there are seven residential homes, organized by non-government organizations, most of which are located in Bangkok and nearby provinces. Non-profit and for-profit private sector organizations have been major contributors for nursing home services in the last decade. The major contributors are private hospitals and religion-linked non-government organizations. From the currently available data collected by Department of Social Welfare, there are ten nursing homes (with a total of approximately 500 beds) that provide care and rehabilitation for the frail elderly whose families could afford. And there are over fifty private hospitals providing the hospital-based care for the elderly and disabled which can be considered nursing homes. Most of the nursing homes also provide short-to-medium-term admission for rehabilitation (Jitapunkul, Chayovan, Yodpet and Kespichayawattana 2002).

In 1994, there were 3,487 registered senior citizen clubs in Thailand. However, the actual number may be higher since many clubs are not officially registered. Most of the senior citizen clubs are located in state hospitals. The Senior Citizen Council of Thailand, established in 1988, supervises all registered senior citizen clubs. The Thai Government supports activities of senior citizen clubs via the Ministry of Public Health and the Ministry of Labour and Social Welfare.

In 1992, the Ministry of Public Health started a free health care programme for Thai older persons. Since then, older persons are entitled to receive medical services free of charge in all state hospitals and health centres under the supervision of the Ministry of Public Health and the Bangkok Metropolitan Administration. Although there is no special inpatient service, all state-run hospitals, which have 60 beds or more, have set up geriatric clinics. These clinics are concerned with health promotion, disease prevention, and acute general medical problems. They give little support for rehabilitation and do not offer home visits or social services. At present, there is no long-stay care service for older persons provided by state health care providers.

The Thai government has promoted seniority and family values by creating an "elderly day" and a "family's day" during the Songkran festival, a traditional Thai New Year day. Several programmes have also been established for promoting this event including television programmes, radio programmes and community ceremonies in several areas throughout the country.

Public transportation support for older persons is only available on trains operated by the Royal Thai Railway Authority, which is a state enterprise. Older persons can receive a 50 per cent fare reduction from June to September.

Education and training for health personnel, caregivers, and older persons are available across the country. Education and training for health and social professionals, family members and caregivers are provided by many government and non-government organizations. The Thai government is fully supportive of these activities, which are essential for providing future services for older persons.

The non-formal educational programmes for older persons provided by the Department of Non-formal Education, Ministry of Education, give older Thai persons a chance to be educated, and to continue being physically, intellectually, and mentally active. Many educational courses or sessions for older persons are arranged regularly throughout the year by various organizations and senior citizen clubs. Many government and private organizations also provide pre-retirement programmes for their employees.

A "Declaration on Thailand's Older Persons" was announced during the United Nations' International Year of Older Persons in 1999. The declaration covers issues of dignity, worthiness, and the right protection of older persons. It was also stressed that the older persons should be viewed as consistently active members of the society (Jitapunkul, Chayovan, Yodpet and Kespichayawattana 2002).

A new development regarding the state's response to the ageing of the Thai population can be seen in the new Constitution in 1997, which explicitly states the rights of the elderly (who do not have subsistence income) to seek assistance from the state (Section 3 Article 54) and says that the state must provide welfare for the elderly in order to improve their quality of life and enable them to support themselves (Section 5, Article 80). The current Constitution appears to assume the state's responsibility for its elderly population without considering the readiness of its social and economic situation.

In summary, the development of the First National Long-term Plan 1986–2001 had been mainly influenced and driven by the United Nations recommendations. Although there is increased recognition of the importance of population ageing and the need for policies and programmes to address the rapidly growing population in the older age groups, issues of ageing have thus far been considered to be of low priority, and by and large, have received less attention from the government compared with other problems.

For the Plan itself, a prominent criticism of the First National Long-term Plan was that it did not have a policy on preparing people for old age, which is essential in order to ensure that individuals enter old age with an acceptable quality of life. This should be a lifelong learning programme, which will help current and future elderly to have more knowledge to help themselves in terms of economic security and health care. Another issue not covered is the long-term care provision for older persons. In addition, strengthening family values and sustaining family support for older persons should be included. However, the role of the government in providing basic care services cannot be neglected. An important consideration in Thailand is how social security schemes, which currently cover only a fraction of the population, can take hold without duplicating the problems experienced by developed countries, particularly the problems of draining financial resources. Another weak point of the First National Long-term Plan is that there was no mechanism for monitoring and evaluation of the Plan. These and other criticisms have been seriously considered for the drafting of the Second National Plan for Older Persons (2002–21).

The Second National Plan for Older Persons (2002–21)

In 2000, the Thai government set up a national committee called "the National Commission of the Elderly". A priority task of the Commission was to develop a new national long-term plan for older persons. The Second National Plan for Older Persons was drafted and conceptualized mainly on the motivation and movement of local institutions and individuals concerned with, and interested in, issues of ageing. It was endorsed by the government before the Second World Assembly on Ageing in Madrid in 2002.

The Plan developed with core concepts that the primary responsibility for preparing for quality of life in old age should rest with the individual as a member of society. The "family" should be the next unit responsible for preparing a person as a member of society to live well in the retirement years. The next players accountable in terms of creating quality of life in old age are the "community" and "local administrations". Lastly, the government will also have to bear the responsibility of designing appropriate social schemes for older citizens.

The Second National Plan for Older Persons was developed as a set of integrated strategies and action covering five sections as follows (Drafting Committee of the Second National Plan for Older Persons, National Commission on the Elderly 2001).

Section 1:   Strategies in the preparation of quality ageing

Measure 1   Income security for old ages
  1.1.   Extend across-the-board income security for old age
  1.2.   Encourage savings at early age
  1.3.   Introduce tax incentive measures to promote savings for old age

Measure 2   Integrating life-long education for all
  2.1.   Encourage desirable childhood good health behaviours in school curriculum
  2.2.   Provide, on a life span and continuous basis, formal and informal education to prepare the public for ageing
  2.3.   Promote public awareness of the importance of quality ageing
  2.4.   Offer pre-retirement schemes as incentives for the transition to old age

Measure 3   Public education initiatives to promote the dignity of life in old age
  3.1.   Utilize education as a mechanism to engage and assist people in society to embrace responsibility in taking care of their families, especially older persons in the community
  3.2.   Offer formal and informal educational programmes on older persons and life in old-age
  3.3.   Promote understanding of the multigenerational society and strengthen the solidarity between generations through education, religion, culture, and sports activities
  3.4.   Raise social awareness of the contribution of older persons to society for the purpose of promoting harmony in the multigenerational society

Section 2:   **Strategies for promoting the well-being of older persons**

Measure 1   *Health promotion, disease prevention and self-care for older persons*

1.1.   Provide appropriate training programmes for diversified groups of older persons according to their needs

1.2.   Make counselling services for older persons available in government and community health centres

1.3.   Continually and systematically disseminate useful information to older persons to improve their lives

Measure 2   *Supporting and strengthening co-operation amongst organizations and networks supporting older persons*

2.1.   Promote linkages between NGOs and Government networks to form senior citizen networks

2.2.   Support the activities of organizations working with ageing and older persons

Measure 3   *Promoting income security and employment for older persons*

3.1.   Promote employment for older persons

3.2.   Provide job training and job opportunities

3.3.   Promote income generating projects in the community for older persons

Measure 4   *Raising awareness of older persons as mentors of society and capitalizing on their past contributions*

4.1.   Honour older persons who have made outstanding contributions to society and the nation

4.2.   Encourage and promote the participation of older persons in social activities

Measure 5   *Employing various means of communication to disseminate information about the activities of older persons to the public. Access to a wide range of information must be provided for older persons*

5.1.   Encourage the mass media to broadcast programmes/ information for older persons

5.2.   Support programme productions based on older persons

5.3.   Ensure availability of, and accessibility, to information for older persons

Measure 6   *Providing accommodation and a suitable living environment*
              for older persons
6.1.   Set standards for the accommodation and living environment
              of older persons
6.2.   Arrange for both the government and the private sector to play
              a part in providing and coordinating accommodation for older
              persons
6.3.   Provide incentives to older persons to acquire low-interest
              loans to buy or renovate their accommodation/houses

Section 3:   **Strategies of social security for older persons**

Measure 1   *Income security*
1.1.   Provide welfare support for poor and incapacitated older persons
1.2.   Promote the establishment of a community fund which can be
              used to support older persons in the community

Measure 2   *Health security*
2.1.   Improve the quality of health care systems and health security
              for older persons

Measure 3   *Family, caregivers, and protection of the rights of older persons*
3.1.   Provide tax deductive incentives for caregivers who look after
              their disabled and dependent parents or elderly relatives
3.2.   Pass laws on older persons' rights, to protect older persons who
              might be subjected to abusive on unfair treatment, or negligence
3.3.   Encourage and promote the multigenerational family in society
              so that older persons may live with other members of the
              family throughout their lives

Measure 4   *Service systems and support networks for older persons*
4.1.   Improve public service systems to facilitate older persons'
              mobility
              4.1.1.   Reduce fares for mass transit systems
              4.1.2.   Improve the mass transit systems to accommodate
                       older persons' needs
              4.1.3.   Improve public facilities such as roads, walkways,
                       buildings, and toilets to accommodate the needs
                       of older persons, including older persons with
                       disabilities

4.1.4. Provide appropriate facilities for older persons in public areas such as roads, walkways, buildings, and toilets

4.1.5. Set standards for the facilities in parks and places where older persons can exercise and relax

4.1.6. Provide parks and places where older persons can exercise and relax

4.2. Develop health and social services in the community, focusing on home visits. The services should include:

4.2.1. multipurpose senior citizen centres

4.2.2. day care centres

4.2.3. home visits

4.2.4. home care

4.2.5. home health care

4.2.6. mobile services units, particularly, for remote areas

4.2.7. surveillance systems in the community

4.2.8. volunteer systems

4.2.9. education and training for caregivers and volunteers

4.3. Encourage local authorities and religious institutions/ community religious centres to contribute and participate in the welfare and services for older persons by:

4.3.1. Making available funds for improving older persons' quality of life

4.3.2. Supporting the community in providing services and welfare for older persons

4.3.3. Supporting older persons in counselling services

4.4. Encourage the private sector in providing standardized health care and social services for older persons

4.5. Provide alternative medical care for older persons such as traditional Thai medical care

4.6. Set up geriatric clinics, geriatric wards, and long-stay care facilities to meet the needs of older persons

Section 4: Strategies on management systems and personal development at the national level

Measure 1   Management systems at the national level

1.1. Encourage the National Commission on the Elderly to act as the coordinator with various organizations, both at the national and international level

1.2.   The National Commission on the Elderly will undertake to revise and update the Second National Plan for Older Persons as needed

1.3.   Set up and develop ageing administrative networks at the local level

Measure 2   *Personnel education and training*

2.1.   Support and promote education and training in health care, and for social workers in elderly care, including to professionals, volunteers and caregivers

2.2.   Evaluate the demand for producing and improving health care and social workers professionals and staff and arrange for further education/training programmes of these personnel according to the current demand for health care services of the country

Section 5:   **Strategies on conducting research for policy and programme development support, monitoring, and evaluation of the Second National Plan for Older Persons**

Measure 1   *Conducting research for the purpose of data collection as a basis for analyses review and development of policy and programme pertaining to older persons*

Measure 2   *Conducting research focusing on policy and programme development, services improvements and other knowledge, which is useful for the improvement of older persons' quality of life*

Measure 3   *Developing mechanisms for continuous monitoring and evaluation of the Second National Plan for Older Persons*

Measure 4   *Developing ageing data processing and information systems*

It is argued that the Second National Plan for Older Persons should have indicators to evaluate/appraise its implementation and development. The Plan should be evaluated on, and monitored for, its overall comprehensive implementation as well as its sectoral approach, by, inter alia, setting up population target indicators with specific timeframe (determined at 5, 10, 15 and 20 years). There are altogether 57 indicators plus 3 overall indices namely:

1. Active Life Expectancy (ALE)
2. Active Life Expectancy/Life Expectancy (ALE/LE)
3. Population Ageing Quality Index (PAQ Index)

Implementation of the Second National Plan for Older Persons (2002–21)

It is generally accepted now that Thailand has a comprehensive long-term plan. The Plan was developed with a holistic approach to prepare persons for old age and security in old age. The next step is to translate the plan into action programmes.

As previously mentioned, the 1997 Thai Constitution supports the rights of the elderly as well as stipulates that the state must provide welfare for the elderly. Thus in order to implement the guidelines stated in the Constitution, the government through legislative procedure, passed The Elderly Act 2003. This law provides for the right of the elderly to be protected from abuse, neglect, unfair treatment, and violence. The elderly will receive support for medical and health services, access to a wide range of information, job training, and job opportunities, accommodation and a suitable living environment, and improved public service systems to facilitate their mobility.

The law also set up the National Commission on the Elderly chaired by the Prime Minister, with the Minister of Social Development and Human Security as the first vice-chairperson. The Commission has the authority to formulate policies and plans for the protection, promotion and support of the status and role, as well as the activities of the elderly, with approval from the cabinet. The Commission has the authority to set up guidelines for implementing those policies and plans. The Bureau of Welfare Promotion and Protection of Children, Youth, the Disadvantaged, Persons with Disabilities and Older Persons, according to the law, will work as the focal point to coordinate with other organizations, activities concerning the elderly. The law also provides tax incentives to adult children who live with, and take care of their parents. We can see that this law fully agrees with and supports the National Long-term Plan.

In order to implement the law and the Long-term Plan, the government has introduced measures to promote saving for old age by providing tax incentives for their contributions to pension schemes, old-age insurance, life insurance, or social security funds. In addition, the government gives tax incentive to adult children who take care of their old-aged parents.

More importantly, survey results indicate that health and finance are the two main problems the majority of the Thai elderly face. The magnitude of these problems will definitely increase as the size of the older population increases.

Currently, the government has set up the "Universal Health Insurance Scheme". Under this scheme, Thai people will receive almost all medical and health services with a 30-baht co-payment. An estimated budget of 100 billion baht will be required for the project to be fully operational and the costs are estimated to rise by 2 per cent annually after inflation (Jitapunkul, Chayovan and Kespichayawattana 2002). This implies that the cost of the scheme will exceed 150 billion baht within 10 years. Meanwhile, however, as older persons have been eligible for the free health care provided by the Ministry of Public Health since 1992, this scheme may possibly add only minimal benefits for them.

Most health care facilities are concentrated in urban areas, while the majority of older persons live in rural areas. Transport costs are another hurdle. To eliminate the accessibility barrier, it is essential to improve the health and social care delivery system, particularly community services and mobile-service units. Additionally, it is crucial that government policies and programmes become more focused with regard to long-term care services and systems. In fact, the Long-term Plan emphasized strengthening informal family care and the development of formal long-term care services based on the principle that older persons should live with their families.

As a matter of fact, economic support for the pension scheme is likely to cover only a very small proportion of the ageing population in developing countries. Thailand, Indonesia, and China reveal a situation more common in low-income countries, in which only civil servants, employees of state-owned enterprises, and a limited number of private sector employees receive pensions (Ogawa 2002). This is also true of provident funds, which cover only workers in the formal sector. The majority of Thai workers — who work in agriculture and the informal sector — are excluded from the pension schemes. Most ageing persons living to advanced ages depend almost entirely on family support during their later years.

CONCLUSION

This chapter reviews the ageing population in Thailand with some detailed analyses of ageing policies and programmes. The evidence shows that a country like Thailand is below the replacement level of fertility and may face labour shortages in the future. Thailand could consider introducing a long-term policy to raise its fertility level and/or a short-term policy on importing foreign workers. Besides these policy options, the government should explore the possibility of redefining the age of elderly persons. Retirement age at 60 was established at a time when life expectancy was much lower and its appropriateness must now be questioned. The government could consider raising the normal retiring age from 60 to 65 years. In addition, the extension of retraining opportunities for older workers, plus better incentives for older persons to continue working, are other policy options.

While most countries in the Asian region, including Thailand, modernize, the family remains a main source of physical, emotional, and financial support for the elderly in the region. It can be seen that to rely solely on the family for the responsibility of caring for the elderly is relatively unrealistic without the government providing support services and welfare aid or facilities. The need for formal programmes as a safety net for older persons is clear.

In fact, increase in life expectancy has brought new challenges to Thailand. The health care system at present is more capable of dealing with acute physical crises rather than treating chronic illnesses often encountered by older persons who need long-term care. In addition, illnesses such as Alzheimer disease and osteoporosis have been discovered only in the past decades because people now live to much older ages. These emerging conditions encountered by a growing number of older Thais probably would require more psychosocial maintenance services rather than advanced medical care. Families in earlier time were more capable of caring for their elders partly because of the presence of stronger family or village networks, but also because of shorter life expectancies. Thus, whether family support remains high or is decreasing, the implementation and extension of formal programmes of social security — both income security and health security — as a safety net for older persons are necessary.

Most Asian countries do not have adequate social security systems in place (ESCAP, 2002a). Although pension systems exist in Thailand, the problem lies with their adequacy and coverage, particularly with reference to those engaged in agriculture and in the informal sector. Therefore, efforts should be directed towards expanding the social security system to include those in agriculture and the informal sector. The government should also examine the adequacy of social security funds to meet the social and economic needs of all elderly.

Although Thailand has established the Second National Plan for Older Persons (2002–21), much remains to be done. To cope with future problems arising from rapid population ageing, the government should make the long-term plan effective. For instance, it normally takes several decades before government old-age pension insurance schemes become mature and operate on a full scale. In this regard, the country could learn and benefit from the experiences of some other Asian countries such as Japan and Singapore. Governments need to formulate suitable policies and allocate reasonable resources to address the growing needs of older persons. The difficulty lies in balancing the need for resources for socio-economic development against that for support for older persons.

The important role of the family in caring and providing in-home health maintenance services should be promoted. Consequently, the government should develop community-based and affordable long-term support systems.

To sum up, the major challenge of Thailand in pursuing its efforts to achieve is the financial constraint. The government has to work with all concerned parties to mobilize resources and allocate reasonable budget to programmes on ageing or older persons. This is in line with the recommendations of the Macao Plan of Action that governments should ensure that a reasonable level of social services be available to older persons, through a coordinated network of governments and civil societies, including the private sector and non-governmental agencies.

Note

[1] With the reform of government organizations, at present it is the Department of Social Development and Welfare, Ministry of Social Development and Human Security.

References

Concepcion, Mercedes B. (1993). "Demographic Situation and Outlook for the ESCAP Region". In ESCAP *The Fourth Asian and Pacific Population Conference, 19-27 August 1992 Bali, Indonesia: Selected Papers*. Bangkok: ESCAP.

Drafting Committee of the Second National Plan for Older Persons, National Commission on the Elderly. *The Second National Plan for Older Persons (2002– 2021)*. Bangkok: National Commission on the Elderly, 2001.

ESCAP. *Ageing in Asia and the Pacific: Emerging Issues and Successful Practices, Social Policy Paper No. 10*. Bangkok: ESCAP, 2002a.

————. *National Policies and Programmes on Ageing in Asia and the Pacific: An Overview of Lessons Learned, Social Policy Chapter No. 9*. Bangkok: ESCAP, 2002b.

Jitapunkul, Sutthichai, Napaporn Chayovan, Sasipat Yodpet and Jiraporn Kespichayawattana. *Ageing in Thailand: 2001 Key Issues and New Challenges*. Bangkok: The Preparatory Committee for the Second World Assembly on Ageing, The National Commission on the Elderly, 2002.

Jitapunkul, Sutthichai, Napaporn Chayovan and Jiraporn Kespichayawattana. "National Policies on Ageing and Long-term Care Provision in Thailand". In *Ageing and Long-term Care: National Policies in the Asia-Pacific*, David R. Phillips and Alfred C.M. Chan, eds. Singapore/Canada: ISEAS/IDRC/TRF/ISEAS, 2002.

Knodel, John and Napaporn Chayovan. "Family Support and Living Arrangements of Thai Elderly". *Asia-Pacific Population Journal* 12, no. 4 (December 1997): 51–68.

Knodel, John and Nibhon Debavalya. "Living Arrangements and Support among the Elderly in South-East Asia: An Introduction". *Asia-Pacific Population Journal* 12, no. 4 (December 1997): 5–16.

Knodel, John, Apichat Chamratrithirong and Nibhon Debavalya. *Thailand's Reproductive Revolution*. Madison: University of Wisconsin Press, 1987.

Knodel, John, Napaporn Chayovan and Siriwan Siriboon. "Familial Support and the Life Course of Thai Elderly and their Children". In *Ageing and Generational Relations: Life Course and Cross-Cultural Perspectives*, Tamara Hareven, ed., pp. 217–40. New York: Aldine de Gruyter, 1996.

National Economic and Social Development Board. *Population Projections for Thailand 2000–2025*. Bangkok, 2003.

Ogawa, Naohiro. "Ageing Trends and Policy Responses in the ESCAP Region", Paper presented to the Fifth Asian and Pacific Population Conference, Senior Official Segment, 11–14 December 2002. Bangkok: ESCAP and UNFPA, 2002.

United Nations. *Report of the Second World Assembly on Ageing, Madrid, 8–12 April 2002*. New York: United Nations, 2002a.

8

FAMILY AND HOUSING CONDITIONS OF THE ELDERLY IN SOUTHEAST ASIA: LIVING ARRANGEMENT AS SOCIAL SUPPORT

Josefina N. Natividad

INTRODUCTION

Population ageing is a phenomenon of the 20th century. During the first half of the last century up to as late as the 1970s, concern with population issues largely centred on high growth rates fuelled by high fertility and falling mortality, the transition stage in the theory of demographic transition. Today at the beginning of the 21st century, the world is starting to face the consequences of the post-transition stage. The confluence of prolonged fertility and mortality declines has produced a population structure whose shape has heretofore been unprecedented in human history. Ageing societies no longer manifest the characteristic pyramid shape of their populations as the proportionate share of age groups have undergone and continue to undergo profound changes (Figure 8.1).

Population ageing is a new phenomenon but individual ageing is not. Everyone ages. If we are lucky we will all reach an advanced age and live to see 70 or 80 or 90. But as we age there are changes in our life course that come with advancing years. We are able to work less, we earn less and we have

FIGURE 8.1
Comparative Population Pyramids of Japan, Pre- and Post-population Ageing

Population Pyramid, Japan 1940

Population Pyramid, Japan 1995

Source: Statistical Handbook of Japan.

to cope with the onset of functional disabilities or declining health that are the natural consequence of physical ageing. Societies have evolved their own ways of dealing with this natural phenomenon. Older people need support; they are also sources of support. They are able to impart wisdom, to pass on their wealth, and are generally an invaluable repository of collective knowledge that is of use to the next generation. The family is normally the safety net that older people rely on to deal with the consequences of a diminished earning capacity and an increased likelihood of health problems and physical disabilities. When life expectancy is not very high in society, the proportion of older people who need to rely on this support network relative to the rest of the population is generally low. Moreover, not too many survive to advanced old age so the period of dependence is normally not so long either.

But when a nation reaches a state of population ageing, this means that a higher share of the total population is now undergoing individual ageing and needs to call on the social safety nets that society must supply. When so many face the prospect of diminished earning capacity and higher health care requirements, the family as an institution may not be able to bear the strain. Moreover, since population ageing is brought on by low fertility in the first place, the pool of family members who may be called upon for support will have diminished as well. Thus the issue of support in old age is a major concern when we study ageing.

AGEING IN SOUTHEAST ASIA

As a whole, Asia is just beginning to experience population ageing, but the process is occurring at a much more rapid pace than has been experienced in Europe and North America. What took more than 50 years to happen in the latter is taking only about to 20 to 30 years in some parts of Asia. However trends in Asia cannot be characterized by a single picture. Within Asia itself, the East Asian countries of Japan, Korea, Taiwan are much more ahead in population ageing than are those in South and Southeast Asia.

Zeroing in on Southeast Asia, we see a picture that is also somewhat varied although there is a general picture that emerges (except for Singapore) which may characterize all. Based on the proportion of total population who are in the age group of 60* and above, the countries that comprise Southeast Asia are at varying stages in their ageing trajectory (Figure 8.2). Although they all started at comparable levels in 1950 (except for Singapore, maybe for reasons related to its history), they appear to be at different stages 50 years later, with Singapore having the highest proportion of elderly, followed by

FIGURE 8.2
Proportion of Population Aged 60+, 1950–2050

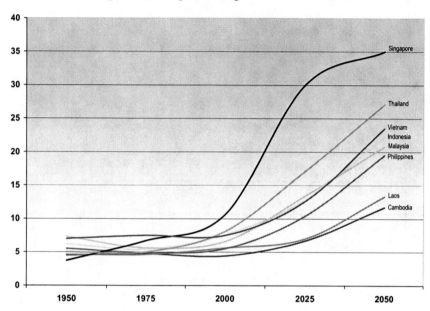

Source: World Population Ageing: 1950–2050, United Nations, 2002.

Thailand and Vietnam. Projecting 25 years and 50 years into the future, the ageing trajectories diverge further.

The main driver of this trend is the fertility rate. Figure 8.3 shows the trend in total fertility rate (average number of children born to a woman) from the past and projected to 2050, a total period of 100 years. While all countries are projected to converge to replacement fertility (TFR=2.1) by 2050, the rates at which the fertility rates have fallen are widely variable. Singapore shows the most dramatic decline in fertility over a 25-year period (1950–1975), from a TFR of 6.4 in 1950 to below replacement at 1.9 only 25 years later, in 1975. For Thailand and Vietnam, the steep decline occurred in the period 1975–2000 although not quite as abruptly as Singapore experienced in the preceding 25-year period. Indonesia also shows significant decline in the last 25 years. For the remaining countries, fertility slowed down but not as quickly.

Another driver of population ageing, although to a less significant degree, is mortality decline. The effect of long-term mortality declines can be seen in rising life expectancies (Figure 8.3). The measurement presented — life

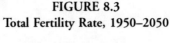

FIGURE 8.3
Total Fertility Rate, 1950–2050

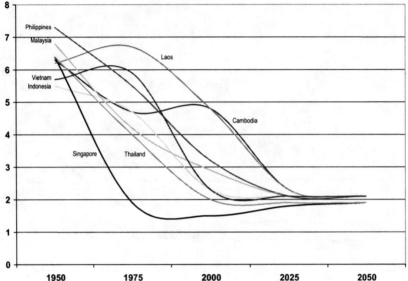

Source: World Population Ageing: 1950–2050, United Nations, 2002.

expectancy at birth — is also influenced by declining fertility, but on the whole, it is a sufficient summary measure of the net effect of declining death rates. Figure 8.3 shows that in 1950, all countries in the Region had low life expectancies at birth (none above 52 years), with the exception of Singapore whose life expectancy even then was 60 years. The 100-year time window reflecting trends, both past and projected, shows that Singapore consistently has the highest life expectancy, although all other countries in the Region are expected to improve in this measurement too.

The change in the population structure brought about by the combined effects of falling fertility and mortality is manifested in the change in dependency ratio — the number of dependents (0–14 years, and 65 and above) per hundred in the working age population (15–64 years). Figure 8.4 shows that over the 100-year time window, with the exception of Vietnam, all countries started out with dependency ratios above 75 dependents per hundred of the working age population. At that time, dependents were mainly the young (0–14). As fertility declined, dependency ratios also declined. It has been pointed out that this demographic window of opportunity, while

FIGURE 8.4
Total Dependency Ratio, 1950–2050

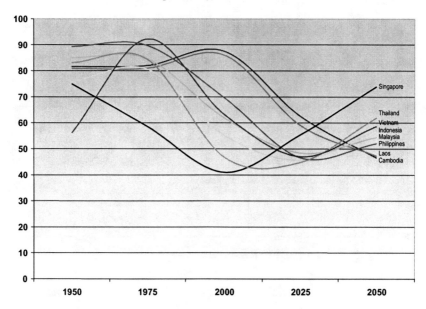

Source: World Population Ageing: 1950–2050, United Nations, 2002.

dependency rates are low, is the best time to put in place the proper policies and infrastructure to prepare for the inevitable ageing of the population that will surely follow.

As ageing starts to manifest itself in most of the countries (projected to the year 2025), the dependency ratio starts to rise again, but with a distinct qualitative difference. The rise is due to the increasing proportion of the elderly (65 and above). Cambodia and Laos, which saw fertility declines later, will experience the same qualitative pattern, but about 25 years later than the other nations. Figure 8.5 shows old age dependency ratios or the proportion of dependent elderly (65 and above) to the working age population. By 2050 it is projected that there will be 1 dependent elderly for every two in the working age in Singapore. The comparative figure in Thailand is 1 dependent elderly for every three in the working ages. The remaining countries will have a lower ratio of old age dependency as a consequence of their undergoing ageing at a slower pace and at a later time.

Finally, with the rising life expectancy among the old as mortality continues to decline, the proportion of older old (75 and above) is also projected to increase. In Figure 8.6, we present the Parent Support Ratios or the proportion of people 85 years and above, to the population 50–64 years. The Parent

FIGURE 8.5
Old Age Dependency Ratio, 1950–2050

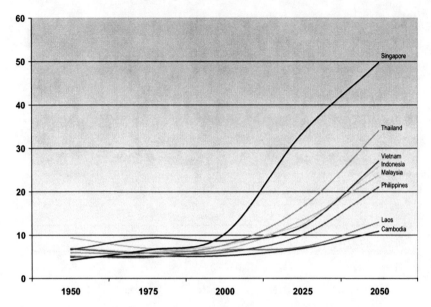

Source: World Population Ageing: 1950–2050, United Nations, 2002.

FIGURE 8.6
Parent Support Ratio, 1950–2050

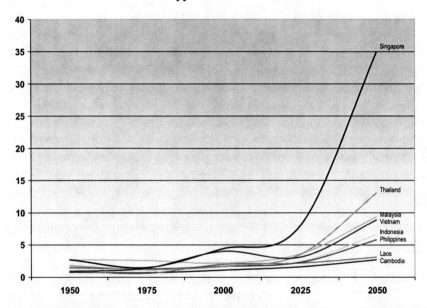

Source: World Population Ageing: 1950–2050, United Nations, 2002.

Support Ratio indirectly measures the proportion of older people who are likely to have a living parent/s. As shown in Figure 8.6 the ratio of 85 and above to the 50–64 year olds in 1950 did not go beyond 3 per hundred at most. The projected cumulative effect of population ageing is such that a hundred years hence, in Singapore, where ageing is occurring at the fastest rate, there will be thirty 85+ year olds for every hundred 50–64 year olds. Roughly a third of the older people in Singapore will have a living parent by 2050. On the other hand, projected parent support ratios are much lower in the other countries, suggesting that mortality declines will not be as dramatic as it has been in Singapore. Overall the total picture in Southeast Asia depicts a region that is only beginning to experience significant ageing except for Singapore, whose patterns of change in fertility and mortality fit more closely with the pattern exhibited in the East Asia Region (Taiwan, Korea, Japan). In fact, among the countries in ASEAN, Singapore appears to be an outlier in population ageing.

SUPPORT NETWORKS FOR THE ELDERLY

For much of the history of these Southeast Asian nations, in fact, of all nations, the proportion of the elderly to the total population has been small. Reliance on informal support systems through family and kinship groups has been the normative standard for coping with the economic insecurity and diminished capacity for full physical functioning that accompanies growing older. But with rising numbers of old people, along with societal changes brought about by modernization — urbanization, migration, higher labour force participation of women who are the traditional caregivers and reduced fertility resulting in fewer members of one's kin network — the question of who will provide support for the elderly is now an issue of very timely concern.

Among ageing societies in the West, formal systems of support for the elderly have evolved over time in a manner consistent with value patterns and preferences that are characteristic of western cultures. The welfare state, for instance, which expanded as these nations modernized, began with the notion of social safety nets for the vulnerable segments of the population: orphans, the mentally ill, the impoverished. The last category included old people with uncertain means of support. Since population ageing took longer to take root in these nations, the institutions that will eventually take care of elderly needs, such as pension systems and health insurance, also took time to evolve. Given the concept of the welfare state and cultural values of personal autonomy and independence, it is not surprising that the formal structures that were finally developed to deal with the ageing issue veered away from reliance on the family as the major pillar of old age support.

In Asia, much of what has been written about as the Asian way of dealing with the ageing issue, is actually from research on East Asian nations which are the "early birds" in the ageing phenomenon: Japan, Hong Kong, Korea, and Singapore. The East Asian model is thought to be rooted in the Confucian tradition of having the family taking up the ultimate responsibility for its members (Chiu 2004). Yet having the family or the kin group play the central role of chief provider of social support in old age is not confined to the countries coming from a Confucian tradition. It is a common pattern in developing societies and is certainly the dominant one in Southeast Asia today, even among nations that are of Malay roots — Malaysia, Indonesia, and the Philippines.

Among the most common indicators of social support extended by the family to older members is the type of living arrangement of the elderly, specifically, co-residence with adult children. Residing in the same household with an elderly member ensures that there is a continuous exchange of social support in all forms — economic, emotional, and social. Much of the research findings on living arrangements in various Southeast Asian nations today examine the extent of co-residence relative to other types of living arrangements that are more common in western ageing societies.

Table 8.1 compares five Southeast Asian nations in terms of living arrangements of the elderly. For three of these countries, Singapore, Thailand and the Philippines, data come from nationally representative samples of the elderly in a four-country comparative study called "Rapid Demographic Change and the Welfare of the Elderly". The fourth country was Taiwan. The data from Vietnam is not nationally representative, but cover "two very important clusters of provinces, including the two most prominent urban centres in Vietnam, and provide considerable rural-urban diversity" (Truong, et al. 1997). Data for Cambodia were derived from household data from the latest Census.

Table 8.1 clearly shows that the dominant living arrangement in all five countries is co-residence with a child (with or without a spouse). For Thailand, Vietnam, and the Philippines, the proportion co-residing increases further when cases of those who live adjacent to a child are included, assuming that living next door is virtual co-residence (Natividad and Cruz 1997; Knodel and Chayovan 1997; Knodel and Debavalya 1997). There is also a significant proportion of elderly in all four countries who live in a three-generation household. Living alone and living with spouse only are rather rare. This picture is in stark contrast to the pattern observed in Europe where in a

TABLE 8.1
Living Arrangements in Selected SEA Countries among those Age 60+

	Philippines[1]	Singapore[2]	Thailand[3]	Vietnam		Cambodia[4]
				North[5]	South[6]	
Living alone	5.5	3.3	4.3	6.9	4.8	2.8
With spouse only	7.9	5.9	11.9	12.5	4.5	7.3
With any child	69.2	87.2	70.9	73.7	81.9	80.5
3-generation household	45.5	36.4	47	57.4	51	45.1

Sources:
[1]   1996 Philippine Elderly Survey.
[2]   1995 National Survey of Senior Citizens.
[3]   1995 Survey of the Welfare of the Elderly in Thailand.
[4]   1997 Socio-economic Survey of Cambodia.
[5]   1996 Red River Delta Survey.
[6]   1997 Institute for Economic Research Survey.

comparative study of five countries, Bulgaria, the Czech Republic, Estonia, Finland, and Romania, the dominant living arrangement among the currently unmarried elderly is living alone (50 to 70 per cent), and among the currently married, living with a spouse only (71–83 per cent). The proportion of those who live with a child ranges from a high of 42 per cent to a low of 12 per cent among the currently unmarried and a range of 12 to 24 per cent among the currently married (de Vos and Sandefur 2002).

Mason (1992), in a review of studies about family change and elderly support in Asia, pointed to two dominant types of family systems: the patrilineal, commonly found in East Asia and the northern part of South Asia, and the bilateral system found in much of Southeast Asia and the southern part of South Asia. The type of family system may also be reflected in gender preference for the co-resident child. Generally there is no difference among the Southeast Asian countries in the gender distribution of unmarried co-resident children. In these countries with still high marriage rates, an unmarried co-resident child is probably not yet expected to leave the parental home and is co-residing with the parent while waiting for marriage. But a pattern of gender preference emerges when analysis is restricted to co-resident ever married children. Married children are more likely old enough and settled enough to be considered providers of social and economic support for the elderly parent. With whom the parent is more likely to reside, is taken to be a sign of gender preference.

Ethnic Chinese from Singapore and Vietnamese show a strong son preference, while Filipinos and ethnic Malays are as likely to co-reside with a married son as with a married daughter, and Thais show a slight preference for a married daughter. The implications of these preferences, where co-residence remains the dominant living arrangement as the population ages quickly, will have an effect on the availability of future family-based support networks in the face of rapidly falling fertility and the changing values of the younger generation. In Japan, for example, where the traditional co-residence arrangement is being met with resistance from daughters-in-law, eldest sons now find themselves handicapped in the current marriage market (Trapaghan and Knight 2003).

While co-residence may be looked upon as a source of social support for the elderly, research findings in this area caution against forming a picture of old people as fully dependent on children. There is enough evidence from survey data on Thailand, Singapore, and the Philippines of a reciprocal support flow in terms of money transfers going from the elderly to their adult children, albeit on a lower magnitude than the flow from adult children to their parents (Biddlecom, Chayovan and Ofstedal 2000). Another form of support that elderly parent extend is grandparenting, especially taking care of co-resident grandchildren (Hermalin, et al. 1997).

Another major benefit of co-residence with children is manifest when the health of the older person starts to falter and functioning is impaired. Co-residence can provide the manpower needed for assistance with instrumental activities of daily living and activities of daily living — activities that enable one to carry on an independent life and to take care of one's personal needs. In Southeast Asia, with the possible exception of Singapore, there is hardly any facility for long-term care, so the function of taking care of the infirm elderly falls in the hands of co-resident kin. Changing patterns of morbidity brought on by the rise of chronic diseases such as diabetes and heart disease, coupled with prolonged life expectancy at older ages, also mean that there will be more frail elderly who will need care. This will likely be provided in a co-resident setting. However amidst a demographic climate of falling fertility, the incidence of co-residence may change in the foreseeable future, given the current trends in urbanization, the declining number of extended families and rising number of nuclear families, the increasing number of women joining the labour force, growing number of older children with living parents, and the question of sustainability will arise.

Finally, one major issue that has not been explored in research on the elderly in Southeast Asia is the physical environment under which the elderly live. Living arrangement is an indicator of social, economic, and emotional support, but cannot indicate what kind of physical environment older people live in. When physical disability sets in, minor impairments in function may result in major inconvenience when the physical environment is inappropriate. Take for example, the ADLs of toileting and bathing. In many Southeast Asian homes, toilets and baths are not elderly-friendly, thus these basic tasks may be especially challenging for older persons even when there are people around to help.

In conclusion, while most of Southeast Asia is still at the tail end of the demographic transition and in the beginning stages of population ageing, there is need to generate reliable data to understand the circumstances of older people and plan ahead on how to deal with the looming greying of the population.

Note

*   The criterion age for the elderly was defined to be 60 years and above in the 1982 World Assembly on Ageing.

References

Biddlecom, A., N. Chayovan and M.B. Ofstedal. "Intergenerational Support Transfers". In *The Well-being of the Elderly in Asia: A Four-Country Comparative Study*, Albert Hermalin, ed. Ann Arbor: The University of Michigan Press, 2002.

Chan, A. "An Overview of the Living Arrangements and Social Support Exchanges of Older Singaporeans". *Asia-Pacific Population Journal* 12, no. 4 (1997).

Chui, E. "An East Asian Model of Housing for Elderly People?". Paper presented at ENHR Conference, Cambridge, 2–6 July 2004.

De Vos, S. and G. Sandefur. "Elderly Living Arrangements in Bulgaria, the Czech Republic, Estonia, Finland, Romania". *European Journal of Population*, 18, no. 1 (2000).

Hermalin, A., C. Roan and A. Perez. *The Emerging Role of Grandparents in Asia.* Paper presented at 1998 Annual Meeting of the Population Association of America, Chicago, 2–4 April 1988.

Knodel, J. and N. Debavalya. "Living Arrangements and Support among the Elderly in Southeast Asia", 1997.

Knodel, J. and N. Chayovan. "Family Support and Living Arrangements of Thai Elderly". *Asia-Pacific Population Journal* 12, no. 4, December.

Natividad, J. and G. Cruz. "Patterns in Living Arrangement and Familial Support for the Elderly in the Philippines". *Asia-Pacific Population Journal* 12, no. 4, December.

Traphagan, J. and J. Knight, eds. *Demographic Change and the Family in Japan's Aging Society*. State University of New York Press, 2003.

Troung, S, et al. *Living Arrangements, Patrilinearity and Sources of Support among Elderly Vietnamese*.

Zimmer, Z. and S.K. Kim. *Living Arrangements and Eocioeconomic Conditions of Older Adults in Cambodia*, Working Papers no. 157. Policy Research Unit Population Council, 2003.

9

QUALITY OF LIFE OF THE ELDERLY IN SINGAPORE'S MULTIRACIAL SOCIETY

Grace Wong

INTRODUCTION

Social definitions of the elderly vary from one society to another. In general, the conventional age set for retirement reflects the social recognition of old age, as well as the socio-economic context of that society. When the socio-economic attributes of society change, the age limit for retirement is also likely to be affected. In Singapore, the official retirement age limit has been raised from 55 to 62 in 1999, but 55 remains the voluntary retirement age since it coincides with the statutory age for Central Provident Fund[1] withdrawal for retirement. In this chapter, the elderly is defined as one who is 55 years and above. This is also the definition employed by the Singapore government when it conducted the national survey of senior citizens in 1995 (Department of Statistics 1995).

Continuing decline in fertility and mortality rates in the past three decades as well as improvements in health care facilities and services have changed the demography of Singapore from a "pyramid-shape" young, post-war baby-boomers population to a rapidly ageing population. In fact, Singapore has the fifth fastest ageing population in the world, growing at a rate of 3.8 per cent and ranking between that of Hong Kong's (4.6 per cent) and Japan's (2.8 per cent) (Kua 1994; Shantakumar 1994). In the 2000 Census of

Population, the elderly aged 60 years and above constituted 10.7 per cent of the population in Singapore. This is projected to increase to about 27 per cent in 2030. In numerical terms, the population of elderly aged 60 years and above in 2000 (348,729) is expected to increase to approximately 898,500 in 2030 (Shantakumar 1994; Department of Statistics 2001). Figure 9.1 shows the projected demographic changes in Singapore from 1990 to 2030. In view of the fact that the elderly will form a significant proportion of Singapore's population, addressing the issues associated with an ageing population has been highlighted as one of the major challenges on the national agenda.

An increase in the proportion of the elderly in Singapore has wide-ranging implications on the country in terms of health care, housing provision and financial support. On the other hand, the quality of life of the elderly themselves is also likely to be affected by the changing socio-demographic structure, as well as the lack of an elderly-friendly environment, and physical infrastructure necessary for an ageing population. To address the multifarious needs and concerns of the elderly adequately, in addition to the Singapore government's efforts, it is also crucial to reflect the elderly population's point of view. Thus, this chapter evaluates the quality of life of the elderly in

FIGURE 9.1
Population Changes in Singapore (1990–2030)

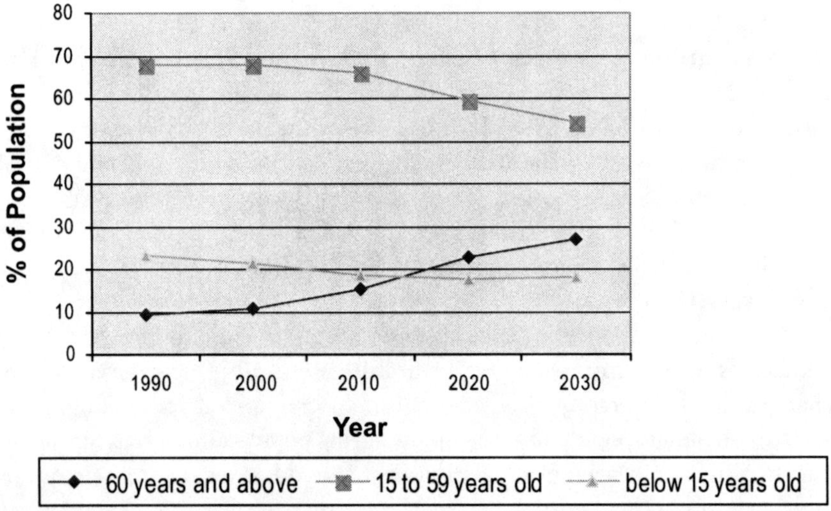

Sources: Compiled from Shantakumar 1994; Department of Statistics, 2001.

Singapore from their perspective, discusses the aspects of life they deem as important, as well as highlights those aspects they are most satisfied or dissatisfied with. As Singapore is a multi-racial society, it is within this context that the study is conducted. In this chapter, the term "quality of life" is used interchangeably with the concept of overall life satisfaction, which is expressed over a spectrum ranging from very satisfied to very dissatisfied.

Over the years, the measurement of quality of life has gradually evolved from applying only objective indicators such as Gross National Product (GNP) and income per capita to employing more subjective and human indicators such as family ties, social network, and religion. Researchers in Singapore have also administered the subjective method of assessment in their quality of life studies, which often entails large cross-sectional surveys so as to reduce any inaccuracy and bias. Although there have been several quality of life studies in the context of Singapore in the past decade, they tend to focus on the population as a whole (for instance, Wang 1993; Kau and Wang 1995; Chua 1997; Foo, Yuen and Chin 1998; Wong and Lim 2001). In their research, Wang (1993), Kau and Wang (1995) as well as Foo, Yuen and Chin (1998) examined the quality of life of Singaporeans aged between 15 and 54. On the other hand, the studies by Chua (1997) as well as Wong and Lim (2001) were geographically restricted to only the residents of a few selected locations in Singapore. In terms of specific population segments, the research by Wong, Foo and Lim (2000) evaluated the quality of life of the expatriate population in Singapore, and the study by Kau and Jung (2000) assessed the life satisfaction of younger Singaporeans aged 23 to 24. It therefore appears that the quality of life studies in Singapore have not focused on the elderly segment of the population who are 55 years and above. As the elderly are at the late stage of the family life cycle, their perspectives and needs are likely to be different from the rest of the population. Thus, this chapter aims to bridge this gap, and at the same time, highlight the likely issues or life domains that have an impact on the quality of life of the elderly in Singapore.

METHODOLOGY

Research Approach

The research approach administered in this study is the subjective method of measurement whereby the quality of life of the elderly is assessed in terms of their overall life satisfaction illustrated over a 5-point Likert scale ranging from "very satisfied" to "very dissatisfied". This method was also adopted in previous studies conducted in the context of Singapore (for instance, Kau and

Wang 1995; Foo, Yuen and Chin 1998; Kau and Jung 2000; Wong, Foo and Lim 2000; Wong and Lim 2001). The value in employing the same method of measurement is that comparisons can be made between different studies on quality of life in Singapore. Similar to the work by Andrews and Withey (1976), Day (1987), Kau and Wang (1995), Foo, Yuen and Chin (1998), Kau and Jung (2000), Wong, Foo and Lim (2000) as well as Wong and Lim (2001), where they formulate their own set of life domains to suit the nature of their quality of life research, this chapter suggests a set of 17 life domains to evaluate the quality of life of the elderly in Singapore. Each domain of life is then rated on a 5-point Likert scale by the elderly to indicate their perception of the importance of, and satisfaction with, that domain.

Domains of Life

As highlighted by Lee (1992), the domains of life contributing to overall life satisfaction could cover a very wide spectrum of aspects, ranging from personal events to world situations, from psychological to social-political well-being, from material to spiritual concerns, as well as from private to public life. It is therefore essential that the domains of life influencing life satisfaction be identified specifically for the population under study. For instance, in their research on the quality of life of Americans, Andrews and Withey (1976) as well as Campbell, Converse and Rodgers (1976) formulated 15 and 17 domains of life respectively. Following on their work, Day (1987) identified 13 separate domains of life, and for each domain, sub-domains were generated which best illustrated the nature of that particular domain. In the Singapore context, Wang (1993) employed a set of 12 life domains while Wong and Lim (2001) administered a set of 18 aspects of life to assess the quality of life of Singaporeans. In general, the domains include family life, personal health, living environment, spiritual life and religion, leisure, working life, material possessions and wealth, social life, self-development, school life and education, consumer goods and services, information and mass media, life within the country as well as public services such as health care and housing provision (Wang 1993; Wong and Lim 2001).

In recent years, a number of health-related measures have been developed to evaluate what has been referred to as "health-related quality of life", which is actually a component of the overall life satisfaction. As the health-related measures, which include the Sickness Impact Profile (SIP) (Bergner, Bobbit, Carter and Gibson 1981) and the Quality of Well-Being (QWB) scale (Brook et al. 1979; Stewart, Ware and Brook 1981), tend to relate health condition for physical functions to quality of life, they assess quality of life largely from the medical perspective. According to Lawton (1983), some health-related measures also evaluate social well-being since physical illness or its treatment could adversely affect the other non-health aspects of life. Although health-related and physical function measures may be especially relevant to the elderly, the concept of quality of life is essentially a multi-dimensional one where the emotional, social, and spiritual aspects of life may even play the role of an antidote.

Drawing from literature and taking into consideration the unique nature of the elderly population, this chapter proposes 17 domains of life which are divided into six major categories, namely, social networks, housing, personal aspects of life, provision of services and facilities, environmental factors as well as leisure.

Social networks, defined as the "set of personal contacts through which the individual maintains his social identity, and receives emotional support, material aid, services and information" (Walker, MacBride and Vachon 1977), are assessed using two life domains: family ties and social life with other elderly. As it is the family and relatives who tend to provide care when the health of the elderly deteriorates (Ward 1983; Hess and Soldo 1985), the sub-domains for family ties include the spouse, children, grandchildren, and relatives. With friends are often the next level of informal caregivers after family and relatives (Penning and Chappell 1987), the sub-domains for social life with other elderly consist of friends, the community, and social activities.

Housing for the elderly is one of the most important aspects because it affects physical health, status, social interaction, access to services, independence, and mobility. Housing is thus evaluated in terms of three domains of life: living conditions, type of housing as well as amenities and facilities. As the elderly are likely to spend more time in the home, but have more difficulty managing it, the sub-domains for living conditions include size of the unit, floor level, and accident hazards. With regards to the type of housing, the sub-domains are basically public or private housing, and specialized housing. The sub-domains identified for amenities and facilities comprise senior citizens' corners, parks, and sports facilities.

Personal aspects of life are examined as personal health, wealth status as well as religion and spiritual life. As health is often related to quality of life by referring to the impact of health conditions on physical function (Kaplan 1988), this domain of life is particularly relevant to the elderly. In the study by Poloma and Pendleton (1990), the religious domain ranked fourth out of eleven aspects of life in predicting overall life satisfaction. It therefore suggests that religion plays a crucial role in affecting one's psychological and emotional well-being, and at times it even acts as a source of mental strength. This is especially applicable to the elderly, as more of them tend to experience incidents of illnesses and bereavements. As financial security in retirement could be an issue for some elderly, the sub-domains of wealth encompass cash, income, assets, and Central Provident Fund withdrawals.

Provision of public services is measured in terms of its role in preserving and enhancing the quality of life of the elderly. The four domains of life illustrating this category include the provision of public transport such as buses, taxis, and the Mass Rapid Transit; health care services such as hospitals, specialist clinics, and doctors; community facilities such as community centres, day care centres and public parks; as well as consumer goods and services where price, variety, and quality are the sub-domains. The level of satisfaction derived by the elderly could determine the effectiveness, efficiency, and quality of these public services in providing for the fast expanding elderly population in Singapore.

Environmental factors are assessed in terms of the physical environment, public safety as well as information and media coverage. The physical environment is illustrated by the elderly-friendly infrastructure and features while the sub-domains of public safety include security, crime rate, and freedom of movement. The information and media coverage domain consists of newschapters, magazines, media, and the Internet, all of which may affect some elderly more than others.

Leisure is important for people of all ages, but is especially so for the elderly since they are likely to be retired and have more time to engage in leisure activities. The two domains of life in this category are the leisure and recreation domain including hobbies, entertainment, sports, relaxation, as well as the arts and culture domain, which is further sub-divided into festivals, performances, and exhibitions.

Questionnaire Design

The research instrument comprised two sections. The first section collected the respondents' personal, employment, household, and housing profile as well as their health condition. The second section listed the 17 domains of life where the respondents were asked to rate, from 1, meaning "very unimportant" to 5, meaning "very important", how important each aspect of life was to them. The elderly were also asked to indicate how satisfied they were with regards to each aspect of life, using the scale from 1, meaning "very dissatisfied" to 5, meaning "very satisfied". In the second section, there were two questions regarding the overall life satisfaction of the elderly, one was positioned at the beginning and the other at the end. The purpose was to allow the elderly to take into consideration all 17 aspects of life, and then provide an answer to the same question. By averaging the answers to both questions, possible measurement errors and inaccuracies would be reduced. For those elderly who provided low satisfaction scores for any of the domains of life, they were additionally asked to state their reasons. As Singapore is a multi-racial society with 80.0 per cent of its elderly being Chinese (Department of Statistics 2001), a Mandarin version of the questionnaire was also administered in the study.

Sample

The sample consisted of 1,519 ambulant elderly aged 55 years and above who were either Singapore citizens or permanent residents. Random stratified sampling was administered according to the elderly ethnic distribution in the 2000 Census of Population in Singapore. The method of data collection was via personal interviews with the elderly in their own homes as well as in public areas such as community centres, senior citizens' corners, and parks. The sample survey, which was conducted in July 2001, covered the entire island of Singapore with its 20 public housing new towns and numerous private housing estates. A total of 1,800 questionnaires were disseminated, but only 1,519 were completed and usable, thus registering a response rate of 84 per cent.

Statistical Analysis

Analysis of Variance between groups ANOVA tests were employed to examine the relationships between the demographic characteristics of the elderly and their overall life satisfaction scores. To assess the perception of the elderly with regards to the importance of, and satisfaction with, each of the 17 domains of life, the means and standard deviations were computed for each aspect. Analyses across race and age categories were also conducted to compare the similarities and differences between the various races and age groups of the elderly in Singapore.

RESULTS

Profile of Respondents

In the sample, 44.2 per cent of the elderly surveyed were males and 55.8 per cent, females. The sample comprised 77 per cent Chinese, 13.1 per cent Malays, 9.9 per cent Indians, and others. 41.2 per cent of the elderly respondents were between 55 to 59 years old while about half of them belonged to the age group 60 to 79 years. In terms of marital status, although 78.1 per cent of the sample were married, widowhood was higher among elderly females with 35 per cent, compared with only 6 per cent for elderly males. About half of the sample (56.9 per cent) had either nil or primary education with the younger age groups being better qualified than their older counterparts, and with elderly males having slightly higher qualifications than elderly females. The majority of the elderly respondents (68.9 per cent) were Buddhists with only 8.7 per cent Christians, 7.7 per cent Muslims, 4.8 per cent Catholics, and 9.9 per cent either practising Hinduism or not having any religion.

More than three-quarters of the elderly respondents lived in public housing with 21.8 per cent residing in 3-room or smaller apartments, and another 54.8 per cent living in 4-room or larger units. Yet another 13.1 per cent of the sample resided in private apartments/condominiums while the remaining 10.3 per cent lived in either private terrace, semi-detached, or detached houses. The average household size of the elderly respondents comprised 3.6 persons with the majority (67.1 per cent) living in households of three to five persons. It is additionally observed that while the elderly aged 55 to 59 years tended to live in smaller households of four persons and fewer, those aged 60 years and above generally had larger households comprising six or more persons. Although the majority (64.2 per cent) of the sample lived together with their spouses and children, 2.7 per cent of the elderly respondents lived alone while another 2.9 per cent lived with only their spouses. Those elderly respondents who either lived alone or with only their spouses were found to be mainly between 70 and 79 years. While 94.3 per cent of the 55 to 59 age group generally had only two generations under one roof, all the elderly respondents in the 80 and above age group lived together with three or more generations.

Half of the sample had a monthly personal disposable income of less than S$1,000.[2] Out of this poorest group of elderly respondents, 80.7 per cent received their incomes from family members or relatives. Only 15.4 per cent of the sample had incomes above S$3,000 and these elderly respondents were likely to be from the 55 to 59 age group who were probably still in employment before the official retirement age limit of 62. Out of the 40.4 per cent of the elderly respondents who were still working, 26.7 per cent consisted of females and 73.3 per cent were males. Other than family and salary, the elderly respondents' other sources of income included income generated from assets (16.6 per cent) such as shares, interest, and investments, as well as retirement-related finances (9.6 per cent) such as Central Provident Fund savings, retirement benefits, and government pensions. Financial support from the family and relatives (58.3 per cent) was the major source of income for the elderly respondents especially where females (79.3 per cent) were concerned, compared with only 20.7 per cent for males. This observation is closely related to the employment pattern between male and female elderly. It was further found that while only 29.6 per cent of the elderly respondents aged 55 to 59 years received income from their families and relatives, all elderly respondents aged 80 and above did so.

Following the discussion on income, it is observed that 59.6 per cent of the sample was economically inactive, that is, they were either retired or not working. Most of the elderly respondents who were still working, tended to be holding higher skilled jobs in administrative, managerial, professional, and technical fields (22.4 per cent), followed by services and sales occupations (11.3 per cent), and clerical and secretarial work (6.7 per cent). The proportion of the sample that were economically inactive was found to rise with age, from 40.3 per cent among the elderly aged 55 to 59 years, to a high of 74 per cent for those aged 70 years and above. The employment status of male elderly also differed from that of females, whereby within the most economically active age group (55 to 59 years), only 29 per cent were females compared with 71 per cent males.

In their self-evaluation of their own health condition, 83 per cent of the elderly respondents considered themselves to be in "good", "very good" or "excellent" health. Those who assessed their health to be "fair" or "poor" seemed to be mainly from the older age groups. In terms of gender, more (88.5 per cent) male elderly respondents regarded themselves to be in good health compared with 79.2 per cent among females.

Overall Life Satisfaction

When the responses of the two questions on overall life satisfaction of the elderly were averaged to reduce bias and inaccuracy, the resulting ratings still ranged from 1 to 5, but with a gap of 0.5 instead of 1, see Table 9.1. In general, the sample indicates that they were rather "satisfied" with their life at a mean value of 3.82. The elderly respondents aged 70 to 79 years appeared to be more satisfied (3.96) compared with their younger (3.81) and older (3.77) counterparts.

Using the ANOVA test, pegged at a significance level of 0.05 ($p < 0.05$), the survey found only three demographic characteristics, namely, the level of education, monthly disposable income, and type of housing, to be statistically significant in influencing the overall life satisfaction scores of

TABLE 9.1
Overall lLife Satisfaction by Age Group

Satisfaction level	Score	55 to 59 (n = 628)	60 to 69 (n = 536)	70 to 79 (n = 233)	80 & above (n = 122)
Very dissatisfied	1.0	–	–	–	–
	1.5	–	–	–	–
Dissatisfied	2.0	–	–	–	–
	2.5	–	7.4%	–	–
Neither satisfied nor dissatisfied	3.0	24.4%	13.3%	–	–
	3.5	10.5%	11.5%	30.6%	48.7%
Satisfied	4.0	50.6%	46.8%	56.0%	51.3%
	4.5	9.8%	21.0%	–	–
Very satisfied	5.0	4.7%	–	13.4%	–
Mean*		3.82	3.81	3.96	3.77

Note: *Overall mean = 3.82; standard deviation = 0.51.
Source: Author's survey.

the elderly respondents, see Table 9.2. In general, the elderly with higher education level and larger housing were observed to be more satisfied with their quality of life. In terms of income, the elderly in the highest income group were the most satisfied followed by those in the lowest income category. Although it appears that the Chinese (3.80) elderly tend to be less satisfied compared with their Malay (3.95) and Indian (3.93) counterparts from the ANOVA results, the difference between the means was not significant, see Table 9.2.

Importance of Various Aspects of Life

When the elderly respondents were asked to rate the importance of the 17 domains of life, they indicated that "personal health condition" (4.36) was the most important aspect followed by "family ties" (4.26), "public safety" (4.22), "health care" (4.20), and "public transportation" (3.94), see Table 9.3. When examined in terms of age, the elderly aged 55 to 59 years rated "personal health condition" (4.56), "health care" (4.48), and "public safety" (4.43) as the three most important aspects of life. The next age group (61 to 69 years) indicated that they were also concerned with "personal health condition" (4.38) but differed in that they selected "family ties" (4.26) and

TABLE 9.2
Comparison of Overall Life Satisfaction by Demographic Stratification

Demographic Characteristics	%	Mean*	F-value	p
Age group			0.74	0.53
55 to 59	41.2	3.82		
60 to 69	34.9	3.81		
70 to 79	15.5	3.96		
80 and above	8.4	3.77		
Gender			3.67	0.06
Male	44.2	3.73		
Female	55.8	3.91		
Race			0.80	0.47
Chinese	77.0	3.80		
Malay	13.1	3.95		
Indian and others	9.9	3.93		
Highest level of education attained			3.31	0.02
Primary and below	56.9	3.77		
Secondary	24.1	4.01		
Vocational/junior college/polytechnic	12.6	3.60		
Tertiary	6.4	4.07		
Monthly disposable income			5.42	0.00
Less than S$1,000	51.3	3.98		
S$1,000 to S$1,999	21.2	3.46		
S$2,000 to S$2,999	12.1	3.96		
S$3,000 to S$3,999	9.4	3.81		
S$4,000 to S$4,999	3.9	3.80		
S$5,000 and above	2.1	4.00		
Religion			0.75	0.54
Christianity	8.7	3.89		
Buddhism	68.9	3.73		
Muslim	7.7	3.92		
Catholicism	4.8	3.93		
Others	9.9	4.11		
Occupation			1.41	0.20
Manager	8.6	3.97		
Professional	6.6	3.55		

continued on next page

Administrator	4.6	4.20		
Technician and skilled worker	2.6	3.73		
Clerical and secretarial	6.7	3.84		
Services and sales	11.3	3.80		
Others	43.4	3.81		
Retired	16.2	3.78		
Type of housing			3.59	0.00
3-room and smaller public housing	21.8	3.97		
4-room public housing	23.9	3.62		
5-room public housing	18.2	3.58		
Executive public housing	12.7	4.30		
Private apartment/maisonette	13.1	3.83		
Private terrace house	1.8	4.49		
Private semi-detached house	3.0	4.01		
Private detached house	5.5	3.88		
Household size			0.64	0.63
1 to 2	3.5	4.01		
3	15.1	3.73		
4	30.0	3.90		
5	22.0	3.78		
6 and above	29.4	3.80		
Type of living arrangements			0.41	0.86
Alone	2.7	4.00		
With spouse	2.9	4.02		
With children	4.1	3.82		
With spouse and children	64.2	3.85		
With children and grandchildren	13.5	3.79		
With spouse, children & grandchildren	12.6	3.72		

Notes: *Overall life satisfaction score = 3.82.
Source: Author's survey.

"public transportation" (4.22) as their second and third most important aspects of life. For those elderly aged 70 to 79 years, "family ties" (4.26) was the most important aspect, followed by "personal health condition" (4.13), and "social life with other elderly" (4.09). In the oldest age group (80 years and above), the responses tended to cluster within a narrow range from a mean value of 2.82 to 3.83. To this group of very-old elderly, "health care" (3.83), "family ties" (3.75), and "physical environment" (3.67) were highlighted

TABLE 9.3
Importance of Various Aspects of Life as Rated by the Elderly

Aspect of life	Ratings*						Mean	Standard Deviation
	1.0 (%)	2.0 (%)	3.0 (%)	4.0 (%)	5.0 (%)	N.A. (%)		
Family and social aspects								
Family ties	0.0	0.0	10.2	52.1	37.7	0.0	4.26	0.62
Social life with other elderly	0.0	4.1	24.3	61.6	7.2	2.8	3.63	0.89
Personal aspects								
Wealth	0.0	5.4	28.6	47.8	18.2	0.0	3.77	0.81
Health	0.0	2.6	10.6	36.0	50.8	0.0	4.36	0.76
Religion and spiritual life	1.8	3.1	26.3	47.0	20.3	1.5	3.79	0.93
Provision of services and facilities								
Public transportation	1.9	1.1	15.4	63.9	17.7	0.0	3.94	0.74
Health care	0.0	2.5	6.2	61.5	29.8	0.0	4.20	0.67
Consumer goods and services	6.9	24.1	52.9	16.1	0.0	0.0	3.78	0.77
Community facilities	0.0	3.4	44.9	38.8	11.2	1.7	3.51	0.90
Housing								
Amenities and facilities	0.0	3.8	40.1	46.8	8.1	1.2	3.54	0.80
Type of housing	0.0	6.8	45.2	39.0	9.0	0.0	3.50	0.78
Living conditions	0.0	9.4	41.4	31.3	17.9	0.0	3.57	0.89
Environment								
Physical environment	0.0	7.0	28.3	43.4	21.3	0.0	3.78	0.88
Public safety	0.0	2.2	7.1	58.3	32.4	0.0	4.22	0.65
Information and media coverage	0.0	5.7	37.7	33.8	22.1	0.7	3.72	0.94
Arts and culture								
Leisure and recreation	0.0	9.8	47.5	28.3	13.8	0.6	3.42	0.87
Arts and culture	1.9	26.9	43.7	24.3	3.2	0.0	2.92	0.95

Note: *1 = very unimportant; 2 = unimportant; 3 = neither important nor unimportant; 4 = important; 5 = very important; N.A. = not available.
Source: Author's survey.

as the three most important domains in their quality of life. With regards to race, despite being a multi-racial society, all races indicated the importance of family ties, personal health condition, health care services, and public safety as the more important domains of life.

Satisfaction with Various Aspects of Life

From the mean values of the satisfaction scores indicated by the sample (see Table 9.4), the elderly respondents were generally more satisfied with their family life (4.01), followed by public transportation (3.86), public safety (3.86), health care (3.83) as well as religion and spiritual life (3.79). While all age groups were similarly satisfied with family ties and religion, the elderly aged 55 to 69 years tended to be more contented with the physical environment and public transportation system, while those aged 70 years and above were more satisfied with health care services, housing amenities such as senior citizens' corners, as well as their own wealth situation. In terms of race, all races were generally more satisfied with family ties, religion, and health care services than the other aspects of life. The two domains of life that the elderly respondents were most dissatisfied with were leisure and recreation (3.42) as well as arts and culture (3.32). This dissatisfaction seemed to be more obvious among the older categories of elderly aged 70 years and above, as well as among Malays, Indians, and other races. The main reasons provided by the respondents as to why they were dissatisfied with the arts and leisure scene in Singapore, included a lack of variety of programmes, events, and activities that were suitable for the elderly, as well as a limited number of elderly-friendly public spaces such as parks and exercise areas.

DISCUSSION

With the population in Singapore ageing rapidly in the next few decades and the elderly dependency ratio increasing from 15.8 per cent in 2000 to approximately 50.0 per cent in 2030 (Shantakumar, 1994; Department of Statistics, 2001), it is one of the government's objectives to promote a physically and mentally healthy elderly population, which can integrate into the community and continue to contribute to society rather than become a burden on the family or country (Ministry of Community Development, 1999). As life satisfaction often provides a good indication of one's future mental health (Green et al., 1992; Baruffol, Gisle and Corten, 1995), the way the elderly view their quality of life in Singapore has become of interest and importance. At present, the elderly in Singapore

TABLE 9.4
Satisfaction with various aspects of life as indicated by the elderly

Aspect of life	Ratings* 1.0 (%)	2.0 (%)	3.0 (%)	4.0 (%)	5.0 (%)	N.A. (%)	Mean	Standard Deviation
Family and social aspects								
Family ties	0.0	2.2	18.2	58.4	21.2	0.0	4.01	0.68
Social life with other elderly	0.0	2.1	26.8	64.6	6.5	0.0	3.75	0.62
Personal aspects								
Wealth	1.9	6.8	32.5	50.7	8.1	0.0	3.55	0.85
Health	2.7	2.0	31.7	56.2	7.4	0.0	3.66	0.75
Religion and spiritual life	0.0	0.0	32.3	51.8	14.3	1.6	3.79	0.81
Provision of services and facilities								
Public transportation	0.0	3.0	21.7	57.3	18.0	0.0	3.86	0.88
Health care	1.8	6.5	9.5	71.4	10.8	0.0	3.83	0.77
Consumer goods and services	0.0	6.1	50.6	31.2	12.1	0.0	3.47	0.78
Community facilities	0.0	0.0	63.6	22.2	13.0	1.2	3.42	0.86
Housing								
Amenities and facilities	0.0	2.1	37.9	44.3	13.6	2.1	3.62	0.89
Type of housing	0.9	2.1	45.7	37.0	14.3	0.0	3.65	0.77
Living conditions	2.7	4.0	45.7	39.8	7.8	0.0	3.47	0.81
Environment								
Physical environment	0.7	4.3	45.7	38.4	10.9	0.0	3.54	0.79
Public safety	2.2	0.0	21.8	63.7	12.3	0.0	3.86	0.70
Information and media coverage	0.0	2.1	41.2	43.5	12.6	0.6	3.66	0.78
Arts and culture								
Leisure and recreation	0.0	2.9	56.9	32.8	6.9	0.5	3.42	0.75
Arts and culture	0.0	6.5	58.6	27.1	7.2	0.6	3.32	0.87

Note: *1 = very dissatisfied; 2 = dissatisfied; 3 = neither satisfied nor dissatisfied; 4 = satisfied; 5 = very satisfied; N.A. = not available.
Source: Author's survey.

are relatively satisfied with their life at a mean value of 3.82 for the overall life satisfaction index.

When examined in terms of age, the chapter highlights that even at this late stage of the life cycle, the elderly often have to undergo major lifestyle changes, which have considerable impact on their life satisfaction. For instance, the lower satisfaction level registered by the elderly aged 55 to 69 years (3.81) could be largely due to adjustment problems after retirement, such as the "empty nest" syndrome, loss of regular income, establishing new friendships with other elderly, and managing their leisure time, which many of them do not know how to do after working for the most part of their lives. However, when the elderly are more settled into their retirement lifestyles, they appear to be more satisfied as shown by the age group from 70 to 79 years (3.96). When the elderly enter the oldest age group of 80 years and above, they again become less satisfied (3.77), basically because of health-related reasons. Although there are limits to what the government or voluntary welfare organizations could implement to influence the health condition of the elderly, these authorities could assist the elderly in their adjustments after retirement by providing appropriate social networks and community services as well as pre-retirement public education on financial security, planning, and investments.

The one-way ANOVA tests reveal that three demographic characteristics play a significant role in contributing to the overall life satisfaction scores of the elderly. The elderly with higher education levels, drawing higher monthly disposable incomes, and living in larger housing tend to be more satisfied. As these elderly generally have more financial security after retirement, it could be inferred that financial security does not only provide daily sustenance, but also a sense of confidence, dignity, and independence that is crucial to life satisfaction. This finding therefore emphasizes the importance of financial security in old age and pre-retirement planning. In its Report on the Ageing Population, the Inter-Ministerial Committee established by the Singapore government in 1999, states that the onus to plan for retirement financial security is on the individual rather than on the family and nation, although family members should form the next level of financial support (Ministry of Community Development, 1999). With the recent establishment of a multitude of new financial investments, savings as well as insurance schemes and funds, the future elderly in Singapore are likely to be better equipped financially than the present cohort.

Besides the financial impact associated with the three demographic characteristics, the level of education, monthly disposable income, and type of housing are also related to the socio-cultural environment. It is observed that despite being in the lowest income group and living in the smallest and cheapest housing, the elderly in these categories expressed higher satisfaction levels compared with some of the elderly who were in a better financial situation. There are therefore some elements in the quality of life that outweigh the financial aspects. The study further highlights that regardless of race, the elderly from the poorest category tended to be more satisfied with their family ties and religion. It can thus be inferred that the poorest elderly are likely to have lower education, with little or no income of their own, and are receiving financial support from their families. Although the financial contribution given to these lowest income elderly by their families may be relatively smaller, the strength of the psychological support and commitment of their families have provided them with considerable satisfaction in their quality of life. This conclusion is additionally reinforced by the perception of the elderly with regards to the importance of the various aspects of life. "Family ties" is considered the most important aspect by the elderly while "wealth" is ranked at only the eighth position out of a total of 17 domains of life (see Table 9.3).

In a multi-racial Asian society where most traditions and cultures are similar in perpetuating the concept of family cohesion, and where the Singapore government emphasizes participation of the family in supporting the elderly (Ministry of Community Development, 1999), the life satisfaction of the elderly is more likely to be influenced by the country's overall socio-cultural context rather than by any individual culture or race. The financial and socio-cultural implications of the three significant demographic characteristics have upheld this hypothesis. In further support of this hypothesis, the ANOVA results also indicate that although Chinese elderly tend to be less satisfied compared with the elderly of minority races, the difference between the races is not significant.

The impact of Singapore's socio-cultural environment on the elderly population's perception of importance with regards to the various aspects of life is evident in this research. In general, the elderly in Singapore view "personal health condition", "family ties", "public safety", "health care services", and "public transportation" as the five most important domains of life. These five aspects coincide with the Singapore government's agenda to promote cohesion within the family, integration among the various strata of society, continuing employment of the elderly, financial security, a healthy lifestyle as well as elderly-friendly housing and infrastructure (Ministry of Community Development 1999). In contrast, racial influences on the perception of the elderly appear to be insignificant with all races indicating the same aspects, that is, "family ties", "personal health condition", "health care services", and "public safety", as the more important domains of life. In terms of quality of life implications, it can be seen that strained family relations, poor health care services, anxiety about safety as well as mobility and transportation difficulties could lead to considerable physical and psychological health problems, which would in turn lower the life satisfaction for the elderly.

Comparisons with other quality of life researches conducted in Singapore on the local population (Kau and Wang 1995; Foo, Yuen and Chin 1998; Wong and Lim 2001) as well as the expatriate population (Wong, Foo and Lim 2000) show similar the importance rankings of "personal health condition" and "family ties". Thus, it can be inferred that regardless of age, race, and nationality, one is likely to place personal health condition and family life as the two most important priorities in life.

Although the ANOVA tests conclude that age is not a significant variable in influencing the perception of the elderly, it is interesting to highlight some salient similarities and differences among the various age groups. First, all age groups similarly consider their "personal health condition" as well as the availability and access to "health care services" as very important. This is understandable since health problems are likely to increase as one reaches the late stages of the life cycle, and hence the issue of health care also becomes of greater concern. While the younger elderly aged 55 to 69 years tend to place higher importance on mobility aspects such as "public safety" and "public transportation", the older elderly aged 70 years and above are generally more concerned with "family ties", "social life with other elderly", and the surrounding "physical environment". This observation reflects the different lifestyles of the elderly, with the younger age groups leading more mobile, active, and independent lives, and the older ones being more confined to their immediate surroundings and more dependent on their families and friends for support.

With regards to the satisfaction scores of the individual aspects of life, the elderly tend to be more satisfied with "family ties", "public transportation", "public safety", "health care services" as well as "religion and spiritual life" in descending order. As these five most satisfied aspects coincide with the six most important domains of life ranked by the elderly, the major concerns of the elderly in Singapore appear to be generally satisfied at the present time, which explains the elderly's positive outlook with their quality of life (3.82).

Although age and race are found to be insignificant in the ANOVA tests, this by no means implies that they are irrelevant in the life satisfaction of the elderly. For instance, the younger elderly aged 55 to 69 years, who are probably more active and independent, seem to be more satisfied with the "physical environment" and "public transportation system". On the other hand, the older elderly aged 70 years and above, who are likely to be frailer and less mobile, are generally more contented with "health care services" and the "housing amenities" near their homes. In terms of race, other than their common satisfaction with "family ties", there are slight variations in that the Chinese elderly are generally more contented with "public transportation" and "public safety", while the Malay elderly are more satisfied with "religion" and "health care services", and the Indians and other races are more contented with their "personal health condition" and "wealth" situation. As these observations would require further in-depth analyses into the lifestyles of the individual races before any conclusions can be drawn, it suffices to only highlight these differences in the context of this chapter.

The two domains of life that the elderly are most dissatisfied with are "leisure and recreation" facilities as well as the "arts and culture" scene in Singapore. This dissatisfaction seems to be more pronounced among the older categories of the elderly aged 70 years and above, as well as among Malays, Indians, and other races. The main reasons for their dissatisfaction include a lack of variety of programmes, events, and activities that are suitable for the elderly, as well as the limited number of elderly-friendly public spaces such as parks and exercise areas. As Singapore has been actively providing for a young, post-war baby-boomers population since the 1960s, the majority of its housing stock, physical infrastructure, as well as leisure and recreation facilities are not suitable for an elderly population. Similarly, with the arts and culture scene, the bulk of the programmes and activities is targeted at the majority of the population, which comprises mostly Chinese, and the young and working population. This therefore explains the relatively higher dissatisfaction indicated by the elderly, especially those in the older age groups and minority races.

CONCLUDING REMARKS

This chapter has detailed an exploratory research, which evaluates the quality of life of the ambulant elderly in Singapore by using the concepts of overall life satisfaction and life domains. The domains of life have been specially formulated to suit the unique nature of the elderly population as well as the multi-racial society in Singapore. With the subjective method of assessment where the perception of the elderly are clearly reflected, policy-makers and service providers from both the public and private sectors will be able to gain a better insight on the type of initiatives, services, and facilities that could improve the built environment, socio-cultural context, as well as the quality of life for the elderly in Singapore. By examining the levels of satisfaction associated with each aspect of life, policy-makers and service providers are also better able to review and refine their existing measures, policies, products and services, which target the elderly population in Singapore. Finally, from the knowledge of the emphasis given to the various domains of life by the elderly, policy-makers and service providers could be more efficient and effective in providing for the rapidly ageing population in Singapore by focusing on those aspects that matter most in the lives of the elderly.

Notes

[1] The Central Provident Fund (CPF) is a compulsory savings fund into which all employees contribute 20 per cent of their salary and employers are expected to contribute a similar sum. With the occurrence of the Asian economic crisis, employers currently provide only 16 per cent of the employee's salary. Although CPF is basically a savings scheme for retirement, it can also be applied for the purchase of housing, education and health care services.

[2] At the time of writing, US$1.00 = S$1.70.

References

Andrews, F.M. and S.B. Withey. *Social Indicators of Well-being: Americans' Perceptions of Life Quality*. New York: Plenum Press, 1976.

Baruffol, E., L. Gisle and P. Corten. "Life Satisfaction as a Mediator between Distressing Events and Neurotic Impairment in a General Population", *Acta Psychiatrica Scandinavica* 92, no. 1 (1995): 56–62.

Bergner, M., R.A. Bobbit, W.E. Carter and B.S. Gibson. "The Sickness Impact Profile: Development and Final Revision of a Health Status Measure", *Medical Care* 19 (1981): 787–805.

Brook, R.H., J.E. Ware Jr., A. Davies-Avery, A.L. Stewart, C.A. Donald, W.H. Rogers, K.N. Williams and S.A. Johnston. "Overview of Adult Health Status Measures Fielded in Rand's Health Insurance Study", *Medical Care (Supplement)* 17, no. 7 (1979): 1–131.

Campbell, A., P.E. Converse and W.L. Rodgers. *The Quality of American Life: Perceptions, Evaluations and Satisfaction*. New York: Russell Sage Foundation, 1976.

Chua, P.M. "Quality of Life Indicators in Singapore New Towns", unpublished academic exercise, School of Building and Real Estate, National University of Singapore, Singapore, 1997.

Day, R.L. "Relationships between Life Satisfaction and Consumer Satisfaction". In *Marketing and the Quality of Life Interface*, A.C. Samli, ed., pp. 289–311. New York: Quorum Books, 1987.

Department of Statistics. *Report of the National Survey of Senior Citizens*. Singapore: Department of Statistics, 1995.

————. *Census of Population 2000*. Singapore: Department of Statistics, Singapore, 2001.

Foo, T.S., B. Yuen and K.H. Chin. "Measuring the Quality of Life of Singaporeans", unpublished research report, Center for Real Estate Studies, National University of Singapore, Singapore, 1988.

Green, B.H., J.R. Copeland, M.E. Dewey, V. Sharma, P.A. Saunders, I.A. Davidson, C. Sullivan and C. McWilliam. "Risk Factors for Depression in Elderly People: A Prospective Study", *Acta Psychiatrica Scandinavica* 86, no. 3 (1992): 213–17.

Hess, B.B. and B.J. Soldo. "Husband and Wife Networks". In *Social Support Networks and Care of the Elderly*, W.J. Sauer and R.T. Coward, R.T., eds., pp. 67–92. New York: Springer, 1985.

Kaplan, K.H. "Assessing Judgement", *General Hospital Psychiatry* 9 (1988): 202–08.

Kau, A.K. and K. Jung. "Quality of Life in Singapore: The View of a New Generation". In *Proceedings of the Second International Conference on Quality of Life in Cities*. Singapore, 2000.

Kau, A.K. and S.H. Wang. "Assessing Quality of Life in Singapore: An Exploratory Study", *Social Indicators Research* 35 (1995): 71–91.

Kua, E.H. *Aging and Old Age among Chinese in a Singaporean Urban Neighborhood*. Singapore: Singapore University Press, 1994.

Lawton, P. "Environment and Other Determinants of Well-being in Older People", *The Gerontologist* 23 (1983): 349–57.

Lee, P.S. "The Meaning of Satisfaction in the Quality of Life Studies". In *The Development of Social Indicators Research in Chinese Societies*, pp. 129–46. Hong Kong: The Chinese University of Hong Kong, 1992.

Ministry of Community Development. *Report of the Inter-Ministerial Committee on the Aging Population*, Ministry of Community Development, Singapore, 1999.

Penning, M.J. and N.L. Chappell. "Ethnicity and Informal Supports among Older Adults", *Journal of Aging Studies* 1, no. 2 (1987): 145–60.

Poloma, M.M. and B.F. Pendleton. "Religious Domains and General Well-being", *Social Indicators Research* 22 (1990): 255–76.

Shantakumar, G. *The Aged Population of Singapore, Census of Population 1990, Monograph No. 1*. Singapore: Department of Statistics, 1994.

Stewart, A.L., J.E. Ware, and R.H. Brook. "Advances in the Measurement of Functional Status: Construction of Aggregate Indexes", *Medical Care,* vol. 19 (1981): 473–87.

Walker, K.N., A. MacBride and M.L.S. Vachon. "Social Support Networks and the Crisis of Bereavement", *Social Science and Medicine,* vol. 20 (1977): 365–69.

Wang, S.H. "Life Satisfaction in Singapore: An Exploratory Study", unpublished academic exercise, Faculty of Business Administration, National University of Singapore, Singapore, 1993.

Ward, R.A. *Limitations of the Family as a Supportive Institution in the Lives of the Aged.* Lanham: University Press, 1983.

Wong, G.K.M., T.S. Foo and L.Y. Lim. "Quality of Life of Expatriates in Singapore". In *Proceedings of the Second International Conference on Quality of Life in Cities.* Singapore, 2000.

Wong, G.K.M. and L.Y. Lim. "Quality of Life of Lower Income Inner City Residents in Singapore", unpublished research report, Center for Real Estate Studies, National University of Singapore, Singapore, 2001.

10

LIFE EVENTS, STRESS AND LIFE SATISFACTION AMONG OLDER ADULTS IN MALAYSIA

Ong Fon Sim

INTRODUCTION

It is widely acknowledged that the number of elderly in Malaysia has been increasing. It is projected that by year 2020 the proportion of those aged 60 years or older will likely constitute 9.5 per cent of the total population (Department of Statistics 2000). In the past, studies on the elderly in Malaysia tended to focus on health and health care, sociological and demographic perspectives, as well as some attempts to understand active ageing and the well-being of elderly (e.g. Mohd Noor 1997, Poi 1998, Yassin 2001, Da Vanzo and Chan 1994). However, research on the effects of life events and stress on consumer behaviour in terms of how older people cope as consumers when facing life events was scarce (Ong and Md Nor 2004).

The ageing processes and experiences over the life span are different for different people and people of identical age cannot be assumed to have shared the same experiences or moved through the same ageing process (Moschis 1994). Ageing and age-related behaviours are multidimensional in nature. Several studies conducted in the West reveal that people tend to make changes in their behaviour as consumers during periods of life transitions (e.g. Andreasen 1984; Price and Curasi 1996; Lee et al. 1998, 2001, Mathur et al. 2003). One of the explanations for such behavioural changes can be linked to the perspective of stress and role transitions, and or the adjustments that individuals make in order to handle difficult situations and solve problems (Lazarus and Folkman 1984; Stone et al. 1988; Murrell et al. 1988, Mathur et al. 2003). Since major life events are usually stressful, the occurrence of such events makes demands on the individual which require adjustments in the individual's usual behaviour patterns (Thoits 1995).

Andreasen's (1984) focused on how individuals experiencing life events undergo changes in consumer behaviour based on the concept of lifestyle changes. According to him, households may decide to change their interests and priorities in marginal or significant ways, and this leads to changes in lifestyles. In the same study he examined the relationship between life events, changes in consumption behaviour, and satisfaction with product. Several other research that examined the effects of life events on brand and store preference changes includes Lee et al. (1998 and 2001); Mathur et al. (1999 and 2003).

Objectives

This chapter focuses on the direct effects of life events on life satisfaction and the indirect effects of life events through stress. The specific objectives are (a) to test the direct effect of life events on life satisfaction, (b) to examine the relationship between life events experienced and coping as measured by changes in consumption-related lifestyles, (c) to test the indirect effect of life events on stress, and (d) to examine the moderating effect of self-esteem on the relationship between life events and consumption-related lifestyle changes, as well as between life events and stress.

THEORETICAL BACKGROUND AND HYPOTHESES

Life events have been variously classified. Major events such as death of a spouse or a close family member, marriage, and a major illness or accident, may take place at various stages of our life. Some of these major events also involve role change or transition that requires further adjustments (e.g. Lee et al. 2001). Although negative events may have a stronger impact and are usually viewed as stressors, positive events are more frequently experienced compared with negative events, and could be stressful too (Reich and Zautra 1988, Block and Zautra 1981; Vinokur and Selzer 1975; Zautra and Simons 1979). Lee et al. (2001) classified life events into expected and unexpected life events. Some of the life events are age-related and hence, are to be expected while the non-normative ones are beyond expectations (Lee et al.

2001). For example, the sudden death of a spouse is a non-normative event, but retirement is a life event that is anticipated since it follows the chronology of age. Regardless of the nature of life events, such occurrences usually evoke stress, or are associated with some kind of adjustment.

Life events impact individuals differently, so we would expect people to cope differently. Coping refers to thoughts and actions that enable the individual to handle difficult situations, solve problems, and reduce stress (Lazarus and Folkman 1984; Stone et al. 1988; Murrell et al. 1988). Coping has been broadly defined as "...cognitive and behavioural efforts to manage specific external or internal demands that are appraised as taxing or exceeding the resources of a person" (Lazarus 1984, p. 141). Coping efforts are conceived of as responses to external stressors, such as illness, divorce or bereavement, to overcome the person-environment imbalance rather than responses to unconscious conflicts (McCrae 1984). Coping is not a homogeneous concept and it can be described in terms of strategies, tactics, responses, cognitions, or behaviour (Schwarzer and Schwarzer 1996). For the purpose of this chapter, coping is defined as comprising changes in consumption-related lifestyles in response to life events and/or stress. Here, we argue that coping does not need to be a consequence of stress, but rather it could simply be the direct effect of the occurrence of life events which require life adjustments.

Coping from the perspective of consumer behaviour has received interest from researchers in the West (Lee et al. 1998, 2001, Mathur et al. 2001, 2003). According to Mathur et al. (2001), little systematic research can be found to answer the question of which aspects of consumer behaviour reflect the efforts on the part of consumers to handle stress, even though previous researchers have explicitly or implicitly suggested consumer behaviour as coping mechanisms. Houston (1987) reports methods such as seeking pleasurable activity, listening to music, watching television, going to movies, using drugs and alcohol as coping strategies. Andreasen (1984) reported a positive relationship between level of stress and lifestyle changes that include eating out, participation in sports, and exercising. Mathur et al. (2001*a*) provided a good review of other studies that suggested the use of consumption activities as coping mechanisms.

Lee et al. (1998) propose that changes in patronage behaviour are due to (1) the perspective of role transitions and (2) stress theory and research. Research results support the notion that changes in patronage behaviour may be viewed as outcomes of stress, mediated through changes in the consumption of products and services as a result of the experience of life events (Lee et al. 1998). Coping strategies from this perspective are measured from the changes in brand and store preference changes, as well changes in consumption-related lifestyles.

The Direct Effect of Life Events on Life Satisfaction

Appendix 10.1A shows the framework developed for the purpose of this study. Due to the occurrence of life events and changes in physical capacity, which could be potentially stressful, older individuals may be more vulnerable to stress and experience reduced life satisfaction (Chiriboga and Cutler 1980; cf. Geis and Klein 1989). Hence, it is expected that higher levels of recent life changes would be negatively related to life satisfaction. Geis and Klein (1989) found in their study of older participants that those who experienced higher levels of life changes reported lower life satisfaction.

H1: The larger the number of life events older adults experience, the lower their level of life satisfaction.

Indirect Effects of Life Events: Effects on Consumption-related Lifestyles and Stress

Indirect Effect on Consumption-related Lifestyles

In our life course, certain life events are major ones that involve transitions into new roles which result in new demands. For example, marriage, divorce, death of spouse, and retirement are transitional events that make new demands on the individual for new behavioural and emotional responses that require adaptation (Lee et al. 2001). Retirement usually involves a change in lifestyle. Retirement also means a transition of one's role in society from the work role (as an employee in the formal sector) to a loss in work role (retired person with no formal engagement) (George 1992). The retirees are socialized to the "retiree" role, which may be defined as a "leisure" role, even though the retiree role is not explicitly defined (Moschis 1992). Related to this role change is a change in the activities, from those that are typical of an employed person to activities that reflect greater availability of leisure time. Studies (e.g. Burnett, 1989 Lumpkin 1984) find retirees to show many differences in activities from those non-retirees.

Besides retirement, other life events that could bring about changes in lifestyles are: birth of a child, widowhood, divorce, marriage, loss of a job, an improvement in financial position, etc. The occurrence of life events does not only create stress, but also raises the probability of the occurrence of other events (Lee et al. 1998). Past research supports the positive relationship between life events and changes in consumption-related lifestyles, brand and patronage preferences (Andreasen 1984; Lee et al. 2001; Mathur et al. 2001*b*).

H2: The larger the number of life events older adults experience, the greater their propensity to engage in consumption-related lifestyle changes.

Indirect Effect of Life Events on Stress

While discrete life events cause acute stress, these events also lead to chronic strains. Life events not only cause people to adjust to new demands or conditions experienced, but also affect them indirectly through the exacerbation of role strains (Mathur, et al. 2001*a*). In most cases, the occurrences of life events bring about stress. Stress forces an individual to adjust his/her behaviour in order to restore the person-environment equilibrium (e.g. Norris and Murrell 1984; Thoits 1995).

For the purpose of this chapter, two types of stress, acute stress and chronic stress were examined. Acute stress measures stress that stems from the appraisal of a life event that an individual has experienced. Since the same event could be appraised differently by different individuals, the degree of acute stress is expected to differ among individuals. It has also been argued that a positive event is also likely to bring about acute stress due to the additional demands caused by the event (Reich and Zautra 1988).

Chronic stress refers to "continuous and persistent conditions in the social environment resulting in a problematic level of demand on the individual's capacity to perform adequately in social roles" (Wheaton 1990, p. 210). Because of the nature of chronic stress, we would expect the individual undergoing chronic stress to readjust his/her behaviour patterns (Thoits 1995). Chronic stress is relevant in older adults since research in the past shows that chronic life strains exert a great influence on their psychological well-being (Mathur et al. 2001*a*). In addition, several studies supported the positive relationship between the experience of life events and chronic stress (Lee et al. 1998; Mathur et al. 2001a and 2001*b*).

H3: The larger the number of life events older adults experience, the greater their level of stress.

Direct and Indirect Effects of Stress

In responding or reacting to stress, people engage in changes in attitude and/or behaviour. The interconnectedness of life events, stress, and the circumstances in which the event took place, triggers a chain reaction that could require a change in behaviour including consumer behaviour (Moschis

2007). Previous research suggests that loss of a spouse or a close family member may lead to increased alcohol consumption, cigarette smoking, and psychotropic medication use to reduce stress (Zisook, Shuchter and Mulvihill 1990; Valanis, Yeaworth, and Mullis 1987; Mor, McHorney, and Sherhood 1986). Hence, changes in behaviour could cause changes in consumption-related lifestyles. From the perspective of consumer behaviour, several studies report the positive relationship between chronic stress and changes in lifestyle. According to Andreasen (1984), life status changes are positively associated with changes in several consumption-related lifestyles. Listening to the music, watching a movie, drinking alcoholic beverages, eating, shopping, travelling, or simply spending money on things that bring pleasure are some of the examples of coping strategies. Other studies that support the positive relationship between the experience of life events and changes in consumption-related lifestyles include Lee et al., (2001); Mathur et al., (2001*a*) and (2001*b*). Besides the possible changes in consumption-related lifestyles, individuals experiencing stressful episodes are expected to experience dissatisfaction with life (Andreasen 1984).

H4 (a): The higher the level of stress older adults experience, the greater the likelihood of changes in their consumption-related lifestyles.

H4 (b): The higher the level of stress older adults experience, the lower their level of life satisfaction.

Direct Effects of Consumption-related Lifestyles

Previous studies had not considered the effect of changes in consumption-related lifestyles on life satisfaction. Hypothesis H5 is formulated based on the findings drawn from the study of Andreasen (1984). Andreasen hypothesized that the more the change in brand preferences, the more the satisfaction with product and service purchases. In the same vein, since consumption-related lifestyle changes are initiated in order to reinstate one's equilibrium due to external or internal demands, such changes should improve one's life satisfaction.

H5: The greater older adults change their consumption-related lifestyles, the higher their level of life satisfaction.

Effects of Self-esteem

Self-esteem is a construct that refers to a positive or negative attitude towards a particular object, namely, the self (Rosenberg 1965, p. 30). The measurement for self-esteem was adopted from Rosenberg's self-esteem scale (1965, p. 31), which expresses the feeling that one is "good enough" if the level of self-esteem is high. Hence, a person with high self-esteem is an individual who respects himself, considers himself worthy, and at the same time, recognizes his limitations and expects to grow and improve. Low self-esteem, on the other hand, implies self-rejection, self-dissatisfaction, and probably self-contempt as well. It is obvious that an individual with low self-esteem tends to experience stress, which impairs performance. In contrast, persons who have strong efficacy deploy their attention and effort to the demands of the situation and are spurred to greater effort by obstacles (Bandura 1982). Additionally, perceived self-efficacy helps to account for the level of physiological stress reactions and other diverse phenomena.

Following from this argument, we expect an inverse relationship between self-esteem and level of stress. According to Myers (1990) self-esteem is the single most important factor in determining happiness. We would expect older adults with a high level of self-esteem to experience a greater level of life satisfaction.

H6 (a): The higher the level of older adults' self-esteem, the lower their level of stress.

H6 (b): The higher the level of older adults' self-esteem, the higher their level of life satisfaction.

In response to life events and stress, people tend to employ different mechanisms to cope with the situation or new demands. One popular approach to understanding the differences in coping behaviours is to focus on coping resources (Mathur et al. 1999). Although common coping resources are social support, locus of control and self-esteem, only self-esteem and locus of control have been suggested as predictors of specific types of coping strategies (Thoits 1995). Since an individual's appraisal of situational demands is influenced by personality resources (self-esteem and locus of control), Thoits (1995) reasons that individuals with high levels of self-esteem are likely to use problem-focused coping strategies, which include activities that focus on altering one's environment when faced with stress. On the other hand, people with low self-esteem tend to cope by engaging in emotion-focused strategies, which are thoughts and actions directed at regulating one's emotions (Lazarus and Folkman 1984). Mathur et al.'s study (1999) supports the notion that older adults who score low on self-esteem are more likely to use emotion-focused coping compared with those who score high on the self-esteem scale.

H7: **When experiencing stressful life events, older adults with low self-esteem are more likely than those with high self-esteem to engage in emotion-focused consumption-related lifestyle changes.**

METHODOLOGY

<u>Measurement of Variables</u>

Life Events Measurement

A total of 17 major life events were included for the purpose of this study (Appendix 10.2A). While life event scales typically consist of several dozen items, shorter versions of these scales containing as few as 15 items have been found to be as effective (Chiriboga 1989). The suggestions of Aneshensal (1992), Chiriboga (1989), Cohen (1988), and Pearlin (1989) were followed, and life events that were particularly relevant to older people were included. Although some concerns were expressed regarding the decrease in recall ability with time, this is not a major disadvantage because all the events included in this study are major life events that are salient and important to individuals (Jenkins 1979). For analysis, an index of life events was computed by adding the number of life events that was reported by the respondents. A summary score could range from 1 to 17. The life event index had a mean of 2.41 (SD = 1.41).

From a psychometrics standpoint, the various events are not expected to be an estimate of a single underlying construct and therefore, should have nothing in common (Herbert and Cohen 1996, p. 304). Hence we did not expect our composite measure of life events to display internal validity or consistency because each event may occur independently from other events and there is no necessary expectation that the experience of one event increases the likelihood of another (Herbert and Cohen 1996).

Stress

Acute stress is the extent of stress one experiences as a result of the occurrence of a particular event. The respondent was required to appraise the level of stress associated with the life event that they experienced instead of relying on a predetermined weighting system (Chatters and Taylor 1989), as different people tend to assess event-related stress differently. Although it was possible to speculate that some events would always be evaluated as more stressful than others, for example, the death of a spouse, a moment's reflection will indicate that even in these cases, assumptions will not be universally valid (Andreasen 1984). There are also a number of objective events, such as divorce, for which no imputation of the favourableness of the effect is possible. Acute stress was measured using a three point response format, with 1 = "very stressful", 2 = "somewhat stressful", and 3 = "not stressful at all". The items used in this scale were similar to those used in previous studies (Lee et al. 2001; Mathur et al. 2003). The mean score of this scale was 2.0 (SD = 0.41), which represents the score relative to the number of events older adults had experienced during the previous year.

Chronic Stress

Chronic stress refers to persistent or recurrent demands, which require readjustment over a prolonged period of time (e.g. disability injury, chronic illness) (Thoits 1995). The measure used for this variable was a single-item scale which has been used in previous psychological and consumer studies (e.g. Lee et al. 2001; Norris and Murrell 1984). The respondents were asked to indicate how stressful their life had been in the past 12 months, with responses measured on a seven-point scale, indicating "extremely more stressful than usual" (1) to "not at all stressful" (7). In order to validate this measure, a global depression scale was used to test the validity of the chronic stress scale. This measure was found to be highly reliable as previous research has shown that an outcome of stress is depression (Norris and Murrell 1984; Cohen 1988; Lee et al. 2001). We asked respondents to indicate how depressed they had been in the past 12 months, with responses measured on a seven-point scale varying from "extremely more depressed than usual" (1) to "not at all depressed" (7). The mean score for chronic stress was 3.66 (SD 1.69) and the mean score for depression was 3.29 (SD = 1.75).The study found that chronic stress and depression was strongly correlated ($r = .0.753$, $p <0.001$), providing evidence of nomological validity.

Consumption-related Lifestyles

Lifestyle is defined as a "mode of living that is identified by how people spend their time (activities); what they consider important in their environment (interests); and what they think of themselves and the world around them (opinions)" (Assael 1987, p. 261). Activities which reflect what people do are behavioural, are more objective and have stronger impact than interest and opinions. Things that older people do in order to deal with life are indirectly a measure of the mechanisms used to cope with life changes. This study has adopted a list of consumption-related lifestyle changes, which reflects a series of activities that respondents might engage in more often than usual, in order to deal with the occurrence of specific life events (Appendix 10.3A). From a psychometrics standpoint, the various lifestyle changes are not expected to be an estimate of a single underlying construct and therefore, should have nothing in common (Herbert and Cohen 1996, p. 304). Hence we did not expect our composite measure of consumption-related lifestyle changes to display internal validity or consistency. The mean score was 2.45 (SD= 1.51). The number of coping strategies employed by the older adults relative to the number of life events experienced produced a mean score of 2.38 (SD = 1.52).

Self-esteem
The Rosenberg Self-Esteem Scale (RSE) (Rosenberg 1965) is a 10-item measure of global self-regard. It is the most widely used measure of self-esteem and requires respondents to rate all the 10 items on a four point Likert-type scale (1 = strongly agree, 4 = strongly disagree). Statements that were negatively worded were reversely scored. Responses were totalled to generate scores ranging from 10 to 40. The mean self-esteem score was 30.33 (SD = 4.28). Cronbach's alpha coefficient of 0.73 indicated acceptable reliability of this scale and compared favourably with alphas based on U.S. samples (Amato and Sobolewski 2001; Thoits and Hewitt 2001).

Life Satisfaction
Life satisfaction was measured using a one-item scale by asking respondents to indicate their level of satisfaction with life in the past 12 months. The respondents were asked to circle the number that best describes how, on the whole, they feel about their life on a six point Likert-type scale with "1 = very satisfied" and "6 = very dissatisfied". The response was then reversely scored. The measure of life satisfaction was intended to test the negative relationship between life events experienced and life satisfaction as found in the study of Geis and Klien (1989). The desirability of using such a scale was suggested by several studies that appeared in leading scientific journals (e.g. Amato and Sobolewski 2001; Thoits and Hewitt 2001). The mean score for life satisfaction was 4.66 (SD= 0.96).

Emotion-focused strategies refer to actions, both cognitive and behavioural, an individual may take to manage his or her emotions in response to stressful events (Lazarus and Folkman 1984). Because we were primarily interested in the effects of stress on consumer behavior and the consequences of engaging in specific consumption activities on the person's well-being, we measured this variable by asking respondents to indicate if they engaged in 21 different consumption-related activities "more often than usual", for 17 of the life events that they indicated that they had experienced in the previous 12 months. From a list of 21 consumption-related activities that was developed based on previous research (Andreasen 1984; Lee et al. 2001; Mathur et al. 2003), the following nine were classified as emotion-focused strategies: praying or engaging in religious activities, travelling, watching television, exercising or participating in sports, performing tai-chi/qi-gong (a form of breathing and movement exercise), using tranquilizers, drinking alcoholic beverages, smoking, and listening to music. In order to arrive at an index of emotion-focused coping strategies, the number of activities checked by respondents was adjusted by the number of life events that respondents reported that they had experienced. The average number of emotion-focused strategies was 1.15 (SD = .73). We had no expectations that this scale would demonstrate psychometrics properties and display internal validity or consistency.

Sampling
Non-probability quota sampling was used as the sampling method since the use of random sampling is not possible in Malaysia due to the absence of a mailing list that is representative of the Malaysian population, in particular, of the older people. The use of non-probability sampling is considered acceptable and appropriate since the objective of this research was not to estimate population parameters, but to study relationships (Kessler and Neighbors 1986; Mathur et al. 1999).

Based on the structure of the Malaysian population, care was taken to ensure that adequate samples were drawn from the three major ethnic groups: Malays, Chinese, and Indians. In addition to the ethnic composition, the gender factor was also taken into account in data collection. This is to ensure that there were sufficient numbers of male and female for analyses. For the purpose of this study, older adults are defined as comprising those aged 50 or older since many studies in the past have adopted the age of 40 years or older as older adults (Silver 1997). Samples were drawn from older adults residing in urban areas in Penang, Kuala Lumpur/Petaling Jaya, Johor Baru, Kuantan, and Kota Baru. Types of dwellings were used as a proxy for social economic status so that respondents were not drawn from a biased socio-economic background. Training sessions were conducted for the interviewers, and interviews were conducted using the appropriate language, mainly English, Malay which is the national language, and Chinese. A total of 645 respondents participated in the survey. Of this number 478 had experienced a life event in the past three years so the analyses are based on life events that occurred in the recent past. The remaining 167 were dropped from the analyses.

Sample

The sample was made up of about 44 per cent (N = 209) of respondents below 60 years old, about 37 per cent (N = 178) in their 60s, and the remaining (N = 91) in the age group of 70 and above. Consistent with the Malaysian Population Census that there are more females than males among the older age groups, the sample for this study had slightly more than 50 per cent females. As the largest ethnic group in this country, the Malays made up about 45 per cent (N = 215) of the sample while the Chinese formed 29 per cent (N = 136) of the sample. The remaining 26 per cent (N = 127) were Indians. The composition of the sample by ethnicity differed from the targeted sample due in part to the urban nature of the population as well as the life event criterion that determined eligibility for inclusion in the analyses. In terms of religion, about 45 per cent were Muslims since 45 per cent of the sample consisted of Malays. About one-fifth of the respondents were Buddhists. Hinduism was the religion for about 22 per cent of the respondents. About 7 per cent of the sample were Christians. In terms of educational achievement, about 18 per cent of the sample had no formal education while 37 per cent had only primary school education, and about 30 per cent had secondary school level of education. Less than 10 per cent of the respondents had university education or professional qualifications. (See Table 10.1)

In terms of their employment status, more than half were retired or unemployed. A small percentage was retired, but continued to work either on a full-time or part-time basis. Monthly income for more than one-third of the sample stayed below RM1,000. About 13 per cent had income of RM4,000 or more. The income level is characteristic of an urban population. The majority of the respondents was married, which was reflected in the living arrangements reported by the respondents. About two-thirds of them lived with their spouses and/or with children. Only six per cent lived alone. Slightly more than 40 per cent had 4–6 children while 36–37 per cent had three children or fewer.

RESULTS

Direct Effect of Life Events

In testing the relationship between the number of life events experienced and life satisfaction, the Pearson Correlation was used. The Pearson correlation was significant, ($r = -.102$, $p < .026$), providing an initial support to the inverse relationship between the number of life events experienced and life satisfaction. However, controlling for the influence of self-esteem and stress, we found the resulting partial correlation showing an absence of the

TABLE 10.1
Demographic Characteristics of Respondents

Demographic Characteristics of respondents
N = 478 (%)

Age		Religion	
50 – 54	111 (23.2)	Islam	217 (45.4)
55 – 59	98 (20.5)	Buddhism	106 (22.2)
60 – 64	90 (18.8)	Hinduism	102 (21.3)
65 – 69	88 (18.4)	Christianity	35 (7.3)
70 and above	91 (19.0)	Others	18 (3.8)
Sex		**Education**	
Male	228 (47.7)	No formal education	88 (18.4)
Female	250 (52.3)	Primary school	173 (36.2)
		Form 3, LCE, SRP or	
Ethnicity		equivalent	79 (16.5)
Malay	215 (45.0)	Form 5/SPM	68 (14.2)
Chinese	136 (28.5)	Form 6/Diploma	31 (6.5)
Indian	127 (26.6)	Graduate/Professional Degree	39 (8.2)
Income		**Employment Status**	
Less than RM1,000	169 (35.4)	Retired or not employed	262 (54.8)
RM1,000 – RM1,999	118 (24.7)	Retired and employed	
RM2,000 – RM2,999	78 (16.3)	part-time	39 (8.2)
RM3,000 – RM3,999	50 (10.5)	Retired and employed	
RM4,000 – RM4,999	23 (4.8)	full-time	33 (6.9)
RM5,000 – RM5,999	6 (1.3)	Employed part-time	74 (15.5)
RM6,000 or above	34 (7.1)	Employed full-time	70 (14.6)
Marital Status		**Number of Children**	
Married	64 (13.4)	3 children or fewer	174 (36.4)
Married with children	324 (67.8)	4 – 6 children	210 (43.9)
Widowed	78 (16.3)	7 children or more	94 (19.7)
Single or divorced	12 (2.5)		
Living Arrangements			
Living alone	28 (5.9)	Living with spouse and	
Living with spouse only	58 (12.1)	married children	123 (25.7)
Living with spouse and		Living with children only	94 (19.7)
child/children	175 (36.6)		

Source: Based on my survey.

hypothesized relationship ($r = -.064$, not significant) (Table 10.2). Hypothesis H1 was therefore not supported.

Indirect Effects of Life Events
The findings supported the indirect effects of life events through changes in consumption-related lifestyles and stress. As hypothesized, the larger the number of life events experienced by older adults, the greater the changes in their consumption-related lifestyles. The Pearson correlation showed $r = .517$ ($p < .001$) and partial correlation, controlling for the influence of chronic and acute stress, further lent support to the hypothesis. Hence, H2 was supported (Table 10.2).

Similarly the indirect effect of life events on chronic stress was supported using the Pearson Correlation, $r = .243$ ($p < .001$). When the measure of acute stress was used, the relationship was also supported with the Pearson correlation value at $r = .114$ ($p < .013$). Controlling for the effect of self-esteem on the relationship between life events experienced and stress, we found the results showed support for the hypothesis when chronic stress was applied, although it was just marginally significant when using the measure of acute stress. Hypothesis H3 was therefore supported (Table 10.2).

Direct Effect of Stress and Consumption-related Lifestyles
When the direct effect of chronic stress on consumption-related lifestyles was tested, the Pearson correlation showed a significant relationship ($r = .143$, $p < .002$) between chronic stress and changes in consumption-related lifestyles. After controlling for the effect of the occurrence of life events, we found the partial correlation showing the relationship was not significant. However, the Pearson correlation did not show a significant relationship when the measure of acute stress was used ($r = 0.72$, not significant). H4 (a) was therefore not supported. This suggests that changes in consumption-related lifestyles had no relationship with acute stress, which stems from the subjective appraisal of life events, while chronic stress which represents ongoing strain and is longer-term in nature produced an effect on changes in consumption-related lifestyles. Research results supported Hypothesis H4 (b) which tested the positive relationship between stress, using both chronic and acute stress, and life satisfaction as indicated by the Pearson Correlation and partial correlation, and controlling for the possible influence of self-esteem and the number of life vents experienced (Table 10.2). The Pearson correlation showed $r = -.262$ ($p < .001$) for chronic stress and $r = -.261$ ($p < .001$) when the measure of acute stress was used.

TABLE 10.2
Results of Hypotheses Testing

	Independent Variable	Dependent Variable	Pearson Correlation		Partial Correlation		
			Correlation Coefficient	Sig.	Partial-Correlation Coefficient	Sig.	Variables Controlled
H1	Number of life events	Life satisfaction	-.094	$p < .017$	-.064	ns	Self-esteem Chronic stress Acute stress
H2	Number of life events	Consumption-related lifestyle changes	.517	$p < .001$	.512 .511	$p < .001$ $p < .001$	Chronic stress Acute stress
H3	Number of life events	Stress: – Chronic stress – Acute stress	.243 .114	$p < .001$ $p < .013$	.170 .114	$p < .004$ $p < .057$	Self-esteem
H4 (a)	Stress: (i) Chronic stress (ii) Acute stress	Consumption-related lifestyle changes	(i) .143 (ii) .072	$p < .002$ ns	-.041 -.011	ns ns	Number of life events
H4 (b)	Stress: (i) Chronic stress (ii) Acute stress	Life satisfaction	(i) -.262 (ii) -.261	$p < .001$ $p < .001$	-.222 -.245	$p < .001$ $p < .001$	Self-esteem and number of life events
H5	Consumption-related lifestyle changes	Life satisfaction	.038	ns	.022	ns	Number of life events, Self-esteem and stress
H6 (a)	Self-esteem	Stress: (i) Chronic stress (ii) Acute stress	(i) -.150 (ii) -.089	$p < .001$ ns	-.160 -.092	$p < .001$ $p < .045$	Number of life events
H6 (b)	Self-esteem	Life satisfaction	.395	$p < .001$	.371 .387	$p < .001$ $p < .001$	Life events, chronic stress and acute stress

Source: Based on my survey.

Testing the relationship between changes in consumption-related lifestyles and life satisfaction showed an absence of relationship ($r = .038$, not significant) suggesting that changes that were initiated when experiencing a major life event has more to do with reducing the stress that ensued, rather than improving life satisfaction. Hypothesis H5 was therefore not supported (Table 10.2).

Results supported the inverse relationship between self-esteem and chronic stress with the Pearson correlation producing $r = -.150$ ($p < .001$). Controlling for the influence of occurrence of life events, we found the partial correlation supporting the hypothesized negative relationship (Table 10.2). However, when the measure of acute stress was used, the hypothesized relationship was not supported. Using partial correlation to test the relationship between self-esteem and acute stress, we found the results showed significance when controlling for life events, indicating that the support for the negative relationship between self-esteem and acute stress was due to the influence of life events. Hypothesis H6 (a) was therefore partially supported.

Hypothesis H6 (b) was strongly supported, i.e. the stronger the level of self-esteem, the higher the level of life satisfaction as indicated by the Pearson correlation that showed $r = .395$ ($p < .001$). The partial correlation, with life events and stress factored in, lent further support to the hypothesized relationship (Table 10.2).

In order to test H7, the respondents were classified into two groups based on the median of the self-esteem score. Respondents who had self-esteem scores of 30 or less were classified as low on self-esteem (N = 191) while scores of more than 30 made up the high esteem group (N = 287). Using the t-test, we found the results showed no significant differences between the group with low self-esteem and that with high self-esteem. The group with low self-esteem engaged less on emotion-focused coping strategies ($\overline{X}$ = 1.06, SD = 0.68) while those with high self-esteem had more such coping strategies ($\overline{X}$ = 1.16, SD = 0.71). Hypothesis H7 was, therefore, not supported.

<u>Moderating Effect of Self-esteem</u>
In testing the moderating effect of self-esteem on the relationship between life events and stress; and between life events and adoption of consumption-related lifestyles, the procedures suggested by Baron and Kenny (1986, p. 1175) were applied. The first test involved the Pearson correlation in which the correlation between life events and stress for the low self-esteem group was compared with the strength of the correlation for the group with high self-esteem. Z-transformation was performed to test the significance of the correlations. Results showed that self-esteem did not produce any moderating

effect on the relationship between life events and stress, or between life events and consumption-related activities since the Z-transformation was not significant. The findings are summarized as follows (Table 10.3):

TABLE 10.3
The Moderating Effect of Self-esteem

Moderating Variable	Pearson Correlation		Z-transformation	
Self-esteem	Life events and chronic stress	Life events and consumption-related lifestyles	Life events and chronic stress	Life events and consumption-related lifestyles
High (N=287)	$r = .181$ $(p < .006)$	$r = .571$ $(p < .001)$	Z = 0.678 (not significant)	Z = 0.287 (not significant)
Low (N-191)	r = .142 $(p < .025)$	$r = .471$ $(p < .001)$		

Source: Based on my survey.

Regression analysis as suggested by Baron and Kenny (1986) was performed to test the moderating effect of self-esteem on the relationship between life events and chronic stress; and between life events and consumption-related lifestyles. The dependent variable was regressed on the independent variable, the moderator, and the product of the moderator, and the independent variable. For a moderating effect to take place, the product of the moderator and the independent variable has to be significant. In this study, chronic stress was regressed on life events, self-esteem, and the product of life events, and self-esteem. Self-esteem failed to produce a moderating effect as the product of self-esteem and life events did not emerge as significant in the regression analysis (Baron and Kenny 1986).

Self-esteem and Selected Variables: A Comparison among Older Adults
Although the study failed to establish the moderating effect of self-esteem, it would be interesting to examine if older adults with high self-esteem differed from those with low self-esteem in handling or dealing with the occurrence of life events. Table 10.4 shows the findings.

TABLE 10.4
Comparing Older Adults with High and Low Perceived Self-esteem

	Self-Esteem		
	High (N= 287)	Low (N= 191)	t-Test
Number of Life Events	2.43	2.43	Not significant
Acute Stress	1.98	2.00	Not significant
Chronic Stress	3.48	3.92	Not significant
Coping as measured by average changes in consumption- related Lifestyles	2.57	2.26	Not significant
Life Satisfaction	4.86	4.35	$p < .001$

Source: Based on my survey.

There was no significant difference with respect to the number of major life events experienced between the high and the low groups. In addition, there was also an absence of significant difference with respect to acute stress that stemmed from the experience of life events, the number of coping strategies engaged to deal with the occurrence of life events, and chronic stress. The only significant difference was found with respect to life satisfaction in which the low group had a significantly lower level of life satisfaction compared with the group with high self-esteem. In summary, it is interesting to note that although the occurrence of major life events is non-discriminative and the appraisal of life events was not significantly different between the two groups, they differed in life satisfaction.

Understanding Factors that Influence Life Satisfaction
This study further analysed the factors underlying life satisfaction. A regression analysis was conducted to further illuminate the relationship between life satisfaction (the dependent variable) and variables that might impact on it. Table 10.5 shows the analysis. The regression model is presented as follows:

$$Y_i = \alpha_0 + \beta_1 E_i + \beta_2 G_i + \beta_3 S_i + \beta_4 P_i + \beta_5 M_i + \beta_6 C_i + \beta_7 X_i + \beta_8 L_i + e_i$$

where:

Y = life satisfaction;
E = number of life events;
G = chronic stress;

S = acute stress;
P = perceived Self-esteem;
L = consumption-related lifestyles;
M = 1 if ethnic group is Malay, 0 if otherwise;
C = 1 if ethnic group is Chinese, 0 if otherwise;
X = 1 if male and 2 if female; and
e = error term

TABLE 10.5
Relationships between Life Satisfaction and Explanatory Variables

Explanatory Variables	Dependent Variable: Life satisfaction
Intercept	8.078 ($p < .001$)
Number of life events	.013 (*ns*)
Chronic stress	-.154 ($p < .001$)
Acute stress	-.175 ($p < .001$)
Consumption-related lifestyles	.035 (*ns*)
Self-esteem	.354 ($p < .001$)
Malays	.063 (*ns*)
Chinese	.031 (*ns*)
Gender	-.033 (*ns*)

Note: Table entries are standardized regression coefficients, $R^2 = .171$
Source: Based on my survey.

When all the independent variables were analysed simultaneously, chronic stress and acute stress, as well as self-esteem, were significant variables that predicted life satisfaction. The regression analysis shows that what matters most for life satisfaction among older adults in Malaysia were the level of stress and self-esteem.

CONCLUSION

Findings from this study failed to show the direct effect of life events on life satisfaction and that life event was not a predictor variable for life satisfaction. Similarly, changes initiated in consumption-related lifestyles were also not predictor variables for life satisfaction. Coping mechanisms initiated (as seen in changes in consumption-related lifestyles) when faced with the occurrence of life events were intended more for restoring the imbalance resulting from the occurrence of life events or for stress reduction, than for improving life satisfaction. The findings that supported the hypothesized relationship between life events and changes in consumption-related lifestyles show that individuals do initiate changes even in the absence of stress. For example, "an improvement in financial status", an event that is universally seen as a positive event and not stressful, is likely to bring about changes in consumption-related lifestyles. This is consistent with findings of past studies (e.g. Lee et al. 2001; Mathur et al. 1999).

Although self-esteem was not a moderator, older adults with a higher level of perceived self-esteem were significantly different from those low in perceived self-esteem in terms of chronic stress, life satisfaction, and changes in consumption-related lifestyles. This is consistent with the assertion of Myer (1990) that self-esteem is the single most important factor in predicting happiness.

References

Amato, P.R. and Sobolewski J.M. "The Effects of Divorce and Marital Discord on Adult Children's Psychological Well-Being". *American Sociological Review* 66 (December 2001): 900–21.

Andreasen, A.R. "Life Status Changes and Changes in Consumer Preferences and Satisfaction". *Journal of Consumer Research* 11 (December 1984): 784–94.

Aneshensel, C.S. "Social Stress: Theory and Research". *Annual Review of Sociology* 18 (1992): 15–38.

Assael, H. *Consumer Behavior & Marketing Action*, 3rd edition. Belmont, California: Wadsworth, Inc., 1987.

Bandura, A. "Self-efficacy Mechanism in Human Agency". *American Psychologist* 37, no. 2 (February 1982): 122–47.

Baron, R.M. and D.A. Kenny. "The Moderator-Mediator Variable Distinction in Social Psychological Research: Conceptual, Strategic, and Statistical Considerations". *Journal of Personality and Social Psychology* 51, no. 6 (1986): 1173–82.

Block, M. and A. Zautra. "Satisfaction and Distress in a Community: A Test of the Effects of Life Events". *American Journal of Community Psychology* 9 (1981): 165–80.

Burnett, J.J. "Retirement Versus Age: Assessing the Efficacy of Retirement as a Segmentation Variable". *Academy of Marketing Science* 17, no. 4 (1989): 333–43.

Chatters, L.M. and Robert J. Taylor. "Life Problems and Coping Strategies of Older Black Adults". *Social Work* 34 (1989): 313–19.

Chiriboga, D.A. "The Measurement of Stress Exposure in Later Life". In *Aging Stress and Health*, K.S. Markides and Cary L. Cooper, eds., pp. 13–41. New York: Wiley and Sons, 1989.

Cohen, L.H. *Life Events and Psychological Functioning: Theoretical and Methodological Issues*. Newbury Park, California: Sage Publications, Inc., 1988.

Da Vanzo J. and Chan J. "Living Arrangements of Older Malaysians: Who Co-reside with Their Adult Children?". *Demography* 31, no. 1 (February 1994): 95–113.

Department of Statistics Malaysia. Population and Housing Census of Malaysia 2000.

Geis J.A. and H.A. Klein. "The Relationship of Life Satisfaction to Life Change among the Elderly". *The Journal of Genetic Psychology* 151, no. 2 (1989): 269–71.

George, L.K. "Stress, Social Support, and Depression over the Life-course". In *Aging, Stress, and Health*, K.S. Markides and C.L. Cooper, eds., pp. 241–67. New York: John Wiley and Sons, 1989.

Jenkins, C.D., M.W. Hurst and R.M. Rose. "Life Changes: Do People Really Remember?". *Archives of General Psychiatry* 36 (1979): 379–84.

Lazarus, R.S. and S. Folkman. *Stress, Appraisal and Coping*. New York: Springer, 1984.

Lee, E., G.P. Moschis and A. Mathur. "A Study of Life Events and Patronage Behavior". *Asia Pacific Advances in Consumer Research* 3 (1998): 147–53.

————. "A Study of Life Events and Changes in Patronage Preferences". *Journal of Business Research* 54 (2001): 25–38.

Kessler, R.C. and H.W. Neighbors. "A New Perspective on the Relationships among Race, Social Class, and Psychological Distress". *Journal of Health and Social Behavior* 27 (June 1986): 107–15.

Lumpkin, J.R. "The Effect of Retirement versus Age on the Shopping Orientations of Older Consumers". *The Gerontologist* 24, no. 6 (1984): 622–27.

———— and J.B. Hunt. "Mobility as an Influence on Retail Patronage Behavior of the Elderly: Testing Conventional Wisdom". *Academy of Marketing Science* 17, no. 1 (1989): 1–12.

Mathur, A. and G.P. Moschis. "Socialization Influences on Preparation for Later Life". *Journal of Marketing Practice: Applied Marketing Science* 5, no. 6 (1999): 1–11.

———— and E. Lee. Stress and Consumer Behavior Coping Strategies of Older Adults. *Journal of Marketing Practice: Applied Marketing Science*, 5, no. 6/7/8 (1999): 233–47.

————, G.P. Moschis and E. Lee (2001*a*). "Consumer Stress-Handling Strategies: Theory and Research Findings". *Journal of Psychology and Marketing*, (July 2001*a*): 1–36.

————, G.P. Moschis and E. Lee. "A Study of Changes in Brand Preferences". In *Asia Pacific Advances in Consumer Behaviour. Association for Consumer Research*, P. Tidwell and T. Muller, eds. Valdosta: G.A. 4, 133–39, 2001*b*.

McCrae, R.R. "Situational Determinants of Coping Responses: Loss, Threat, and Challenge". *Journal of Personality and Social Psychology* 46, no. 4 (1984): 919–28.

Mohd Noor, N.A. "Health Care of the Elderly in Malaysia". In *Proceedings for the National Day for the Elderly*, P.C. Tan and S.T. Ng, eds., pp. 223–33. Kuala Lumpur: National Council of Senior Citizens Organisations, Malaysia, 1997.

Moschis, G.P. "Consumer Behavior in Later Life: Multidisciplinary Contributions and Implications for Research". *Journal of the Academy of Marketing Science* 22, no. 3 (1994): 195–204.

―――. "Stress and Consumer Behavior". *Journal of the Academy of Marketing Science* (2007, in press).

―――. *Marketing to Older Consumers*. CT: Quorum Books, 1992.

Murrell, S.A., F.H. Norris, and C. Grote. "Life Events in Older Adults". In *Life Events and Psychological Functioning: Theoretical and Methodological Issues*, L.H. Cohen, ed., pp. 96–122. Newbury Park, California: Sage Publications, 1988.

Myers, J.K., J.J. Lindenthal and M.P. Pepper. "Life Events, Social Integration and Psychiatric Symptomatology". *Journal of Health and Social Behavior* 16, no. 4 (December 1975): 421–29.

Norris, F.H. and S.A. Murrell. "Protection Function of Resources Related to Life Events, Global Stress, and Depression in Older Adults". *Journal of Health and Social Behavior* 25 (December 1984): 424–37.

Ong F.S. and M.N. Othman. "Life Events and Brand Preference Changes among Older Adults: Does Ethnicity Matter?". In *Proceedings of the Inaugural Conference of the Academy of World Business, Marketing and Management Development: The Challenge of Inter-Disciplinary Perspectives and Globalization in the 21ˢᵗ Century*, Paper No. 28, 2004.

―――. "A Study of Life Events, Stress and Coping Strategies among Older Adults in Malaysia: Implications for Marketers". In *Proceedings of the Tenth Asia Pacific Management Conference: Sustainable Growth in the e-Ea*, pp. 621–36. Daejeon, Korea, 2004.

Pearlin, L.I. and C. Schooler. "The Structure of Coping". *Journal of Health and Social Behavior* 19, no. 1 (March 1978): 2–21.

―――. The Sociological Study of Stress. *Journal of Health and Social Behavior* 30, no. 3 (September 1989): 241–56.

Poi P. "The Physiology of Ageing: Understanding Your Body". In *Proceedings for the National Day for the Elderly*, P.C. Tan, S.T. Ng and G.K. Chwee, eds., pp. 27–35. Kuala Lumpur: National Council of Senior Citizens Organisation, Malaysia, 1998.

Price, L.L. and C.F. Curasi. "If One Thing Doesn't Get You, Another Will: Old Age Transitions and Market Vulnerabilities". Paper presented at the *Association for Consumer Research Conference*. Tuscon, AZ, 1996.

Reich, J.W. and J.A. Zautra. "Direct and Stress-Moderating Effects of Positive Life Experiences". In *Life Events and Psychological Functioning: Theoretical and*

Methodological Issues, L.H. Cohen, ed., pp. 149–81. Newbury Park, California: Sage Publications, Inc, 1988.

Rosenberg, M. *Society and the Adolescent Self-Image*. Princeton, New Jessey: Princeton University Press, 1965.

Schwarzer, R. and C. Schwarzer. "A Critical Survey of Coping Instruments". In *Handbook of Coping: Theory, Research, Applications*, M. Zeidner and N.S. Endler, eds., pp. 107–32. New York: John Wiley and Sons Inc, 1996.

Silvers, C. "Smashing old Stereotypes of 50-Plus America". *Journal of Consumer Marketing* 14, no. 4 (1997): 303–09.

Stone A.A., L. Helder and M.S. Schneider. "Coping with Stressful Events: Coping Dimensions and Issues". In *Life Events and Psychological Functioning: Theoretical and Methodological Issues*, L.H. Cohen, ed., pp. 182–210. Newbury Park, California: Sage Publications, Inc, 1988.

Thoits P.A. "Stress, Coping, and Social Support Processes: Where Are We? What Next?". *Journal of Health and Social Behavior*, Extra Issue, 1995, pp. 53–79.

―――― and L.N. Hewitt. "Volunteer Work and Well-Being". *Journal of Health and Social Behaviour* 42, no. 2 (June 2001): 115–31.

Valanis, B., R.C. Yeaworth and M.R. Mullis. "Alcohol Use among Bereaved and Non-bereaved Older Persons". *Journal of Gerontological Nursing* 13 (1987): 26–32

Vinokur, A. and M.L. Selzer. "Desirable versus Undesirable Life Events: Their Relationship to Stress and Mental Distress". *Journal of Personality and Social Psychology* 32, no. 2 (1975): 329–37.

Wheaton, B. "Life Transitions, Role Histories, and Mental Health". *American Sociological Review*, April 1990, 209–23.

Yassin Z. "Healthy Lifestyle in Older Women". Paper presented at the National Seminar on Women and Ageing in Malaysia, Kuala Lumpur, 26 May 2001.

Zautra, A.J. and L.S. Simons. "Some Effects of Positive Life Events on Community Mental Health". *American Journal of Community Psychology* 7 (1979): 441–51.

Zisook, S., S.R. Shuchter and M. Mulvihill. "Alcohol, Cigarette, and Medication Use during the First Year of Widowhood". *Psychiatric Annals* 20, no. 6 (June 1990): 318–26.

Appendix 10.1A: A Framework of Life Events, Stress, and Life Satisfaction

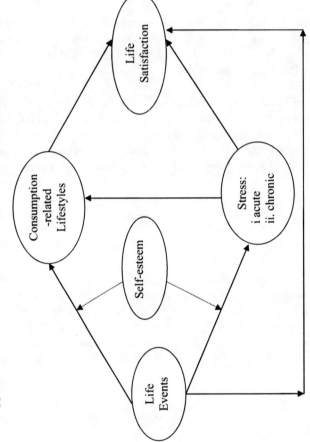

Appendix 10.2A: List of Major Life Events

1. Birth of the first grandchild
2. Change jobs
3. Chronic illness or condition diagnosed
4. Death of spouse
5. Death of a close family member
6. Divorce/separation
7. Family member's health a lot worse than before
8. Financial status a lot worse than usual
9. Last child moved out of household
10. Lost job/business or forced to retire
11. Major conflict with family member or co-worker
12. Major improvement in financial status
13. Marriage of an adult child
14. More responsibility for aged relative
15. Moved to a different place
16. Retirement
17. Serious injury or major operation

Source: Adapted from Lee, E., Moschis, G.P. and Mathur, A. (2001): p. 36.

Appendix 10.3A: List of Consumption-related Lifestyles

1. Buying insurance
2. Praying/engaging in religious activities
3. Learning new skills
4. Travelling
5. Watching television
6. Taking up a new hobby
7. Engaging in charitable activities
8. Reading
9. Exercising or participating in sports
10. Tai Chi/Qi Gong
11. Renovating or refurbishing home
12. Using tranquilizer
13. Shopping
14. Meditation/yoga
15. Volunteering
16. Drinking alcoholic beverages
17. Gardening
18. Eating out
19. Smoking
20. Listening to music
21. Buying gifts

Source: Various sources including author's.

11

MULTIGENERATIONAL FAMILIES IN SINGAPORE

Kalyani K. Mehta[1] and Thang Leng Leng

INTRODUCTION

The maintenance of close relational ties within multigenerational families has long been a cultural ideal in Asian families. In the discussion of the concept of the Asian family discussed in sociological literature, the high level of interdependence which is maintained even after adult children are married seems to be a distinguishing factor. Research that has studied the life course perspective among Asian populations has highlighted the concept of the "traditional contract" between generations (Bengston 1992). Antonucci's (1990) concept of generalized reciprocity, which refers to exchanges that take place over the lifespan of two generations, are observed to be very much alive in Singapore today (Mehta 1999). This exchange of reciprocal ties between older parents and their adult children has been studied in anthropological and sociological literature as "filial piety". (Thang 2000)

The topic of grandparenting has received much attention in recent years (Hayslip and Kaminski 2005; Minkler and Fuller-Thomson 2005; Landry-Meyer and Newman 2004). A recent study on filial piety in Singapore by Goransson (2004) traces the trends in changes in the operationalization of filial piety in the Singapore context presently. Discussing the impact of the non-welfare system of Singapore on family dynamics in the context of Chinese Confucian tradition, she concludes that although "[t]he prevalence of filial piety, seniority, and solid intergenerational ties in notions of Chinese

216

culture suggest that familial support and care of elderly would be somehow in-built in the minds of Chinese people", "[i]n practice however, the image proves to be problematic." (ibid., p. 20). From Goransson's illuminating study, it is therefore important to conduct in-depth qualitative research to "listen to the ground" in order to fully understand the Singaporean reality.

FOCUS OF CHAPTER

This chapter will limit the "Asian family" to the three major ethnic groups in Singapore, that is, the Chinese, Malays and Indians. The chapter reports on the qualitative findings of part of a larger research project titled "Grandparenting in Selected Asian Societies", funded by the National University of Singapore. While the larger research covers five countries, this chapter is restricted in scope to Singapore only.[2]

Living arrangements determine to a large extent the nature and support available to the members residing in the household. As another study showed, there are benefits and strains involved in co-residential living (Mehta, Osman and Lee 1995). According to the Census 2000, 5.6 per cent of all households were multigenerational in Singapore in the year 2000. Among the major ethnic groups, the Malays had the highest proportion of multigenerational households. Prior to discussion of the findings, we need to take a look at the policy framework of Singapore's approach to families and old age care. Unlike in many developed countries and newly industrialized countries where the government takes major responsibilities in providing health care financing, it is a matter of individual responsibility in Singapore.

The family is expected to be the main provider if the individual needs assistance in old age, and the government steps in only as the last resort. Housing and economic policies provide incentives for, and facilitate intergenerational living. Thus in this way the government promotes interdependence within Singaporean families. Moreover, the Asian cultural values of "filial piety" and "repaying debt to parents" are promoted and preserved by the government; one example is the provision that a person can use his/her Medisave to pay for the hospitalization expenses of his/her parents or grandparents. This, in turn, also paves the way for the state to assume minimal responsibility for senior Singaporeans. National policies for the elderly in Singapore have been described elsewhere (Mehta 2002; Teo 1994). Although the ideology embedded in the policies is that the multigenerational family is highly valued, and the tangible and intangible benefits are immeasurable, few systematic studies, however, have actually been conducted, taking into account the views of the three generations.

METHODOLOGY

A qualitative methodology was applied using originally designed questionnaires. The questions are related to the meaning of grandparenting from the viewpoint of the grandparent as well as the grandchild; level of satisfaction with relationships with members of the household; whether the relationship of the link parent with his/her parent affects the grandparent-grandchild relationship; roles and functions of the grandparent; activities that grandparent and grandchild participate in; description by grandchild and link parent of their vision of the kind of grandparent they would be in future. The literature on intergenerational relationships shows that if the grandparent has been involved in nurturing the grandchild, their relationship is likely to be closer. We have analysed the impact of this factor in the study.

Families were identified through personal contacts, supplemented by snowballing technique. Each case (or multigenerational family) would have to be agreeable to three interviews i.e. the grandparent, link parent and grandchild generation. This chapter discusses the initial findings of ten families, that is, thirty interviews. The following table summarizes the breakdown according to ethnicity, age, gender, marital status, and living arrangements. The remaining interviews with five more families have been completed and the researchers are currently analysing the findings. Most of the interviews were held in the homes of the families, and the average time taken for all three interviews was about 3 hours. The questionnaires have been translated into Mandarin and Malay. As the Indian families were fluent in English the need to translate into Indian languages did not arise.

FINDINGS AND DISCUSSION

An Exploration of the "Practice" of "Interdependence"

Interdependence gives agency to older persons, perceiving them in an active role as a provider, and not only a recipient in the intergenerational relationships. Earlier research in the Singapore context has informed us of the exchanges that occur on a daily basis in local families (Mehta et al. 1995; Mehta 1999; Mehta and Teo 2000; Chan 1997). The types of commodities/services exchanged vary from financial, household chores, food, child minding, and social support. Reciprocity is the theme that runs through the daily lives of families, as this is not only economical but also practical. The caveat is that exchanges terminate when relationships turn sour. Equity balance, in terms of the exchanges that occur, is affected when the health of older parents or parents-in-law deteriorates, and they are

TABLE 11.1
Qualitative Data
3 Generations in 10 Families: Grandparents/Middle/Grandchildren

S #	Living Arrangement From grandparent perspective	Ethnicity	Grandparent (1)			Middle generation (2)			Grandchildren (3)		
			Gender	Age	Mar status	Gender	Age	Mar status	Gender	Age	Mar status
A	3-gen	Indian	M	81	M	M	52	M	M	18	S
B	son only	Chinese	F	68	W	F	43	M	F	14	S
C	3-gen	Indian	M	93	W	M	50	M	F	18	S
D	alone/maid	Chinese	M	78	W	F	42	M	F	14	S
E	3-gen	Indian	M	76	M	M	42	M	M	17	S
F	spouse only	Indonesian	M	77	M	M	46	M	F	18	S
G	3-gen	Indian	M	71	M	F	43	M	M	16	S
H	spouse only	Chinese	F	64	M	F	39	M	M	13	S
I	3-gen	Indian	M	81	M	M	57	M	F	22	S
J	3-gen	Chinese	F	86	W	M	58	M	F	22	S

Source: Original tabulation from qualitative data of 10 multigenerational families.

unable to perform their functions or contributions towards the family unit any more. This is when distress in the intergenerational relationships may occur, although human beings are creative in substituting one form of contribution with another, depending on their resources.

From the viewpoint of the middle or sandwich generation, juggling the caregiving responsibilities towards the older generation and the younger generation can be described as a "balancing act" (Balancing act, 7/9/1992). The same article discusses the caregiving challenges experienced by the "sandwich" generation in the United States as becoming a domestic crisis in future, given the demographic ageing of the population. What about the situation in Singapore? Can we expect the essence of "filial piety" to continue, in the midst of transforming social values and economic pressures? One main difference between the American and Singaporean value system is that in the former, autonomy or independence is given premium emphasis by individuals, while in the latter, the authors believe, interdependence is highly valued. It follows that the Singaporean societal and familial coping strategies in dealing with the reality of an ageing population would differ from that of the American. Nevertheless, tensions and strains within the family and community are unavoidable.

Qualitative data are indeed highly suitable in giving us insights on family dynamics and human responses to unprecedented challenges. The authors now turn to the findings of the research to shed light on the nature of interdependence and factors that influence it.

Nature of Interdependence

We explored this topic by asking how each generation perceives their role in their relationship and interaction with the older/younger generation in the family.

CHILD CARE

It is common to confine interdependence only to the provision and reception of physical care. This is shown in the qualitative data, when it was asked across generations whether physical care was provided by grandparents/parents/children to the other generation. A grandmother describes her role thus:

> I: So if you observe from the past and now, last time you were saying you were more excited, but now you're like, "It's okay."…you have your own things to accomplish, how has it changed?
>
> H1: How has it changed? I suppose now you know what is grandparenting already, it's not easy, it's your time they want, you have to do, and you're on the go all the time…when the 3 girls come, you want to go and look after them. They come here for the night, they have dinner, you bath them, you wash them, and the parents after dinner will just, all asleep, will just carry them home. So it's quite tiring, I find it tiring, I'm getting along.

Grandparents, irrespective of gender, see their role as "taking care of grandchildren physically" but only when the grandchildren were small; they see their roles as reversed once their grandchildren grow up.

In a sense, the interdependence in physical help has a time lag, which also runs in a circle of three generations — of grandparents taking care of grandchildren when they were young, and the parents taking care of the grandparents when they become old. Thus the Singaporean local scenario is somewhat different from that in the United States or Britain where grandparents are depended on, when the middle generation has difficulties, or is unable to nurture the children due to castration, poor health, or divorce

(Hayslip and Kaminski 2002; Minkler and Fuller-Thomson 2005; Landry-Meyer and Newman 2004).

FINANCIAL

Financial interdependence also takes a "time lag" perspective, where grandparents find it natural for their children to take care of their financial needs in old age because they have provided for them when they were young. It is sometimes referred to as "filial piety" or the continuation of the traditional contract between generations (Thang 2001; Mehta and Ko 2004).

This idea of adult children providing for grandparents (i.e. older children providing for their ageing parents) is well established, partly due to the "forced" interdependence mentioned earlier as a result of a lack of pensions in Singapore for the public (except for some categories of civil servants).

TRANSMITTING OF VALUES AND CULTURES

The role of grandparents as the transmitter of values and cultures is well recognized in the literature. Grandparents are recognized as the "wardens of culture" — guiding, preserving, and transmitting knowledge, experiences, and skills to the next generation to "help craft the new myths on which acculturation should be based" (Guttman 1985). The quote below of a grandchild illustrates this:

> I: One of their roles is teaching you religious knowledge?

> E2: They gave me directions. My father, basic lineage, if you're born a Hindu, explores what religion is all about and applies it to your life. Basically, faith is something that…faith does not…I can't put faith in you. Faith is you have to get connected. He's never been forceful, a strong administrator like you must do this, you must do that, you must do this. Flexibility can be applied, options can be exercised. But one thing is that, if born in a religion, seek fullness in the religion for this life. One thing he always tell us, "Don't go into any (religious) conversion as far as you can."

EMOTIONAL

Respondents expressed the joy of having grandchildren, especially that at the arrival of grandsons (and first-born) which is in accordance with Asian tradition, especially Chinese and Indian traditions, where there is a preference for sons.

"… in our Asian mind, it is something to have a male son, a male grandson. I don't believe in it. But it is an Asiatic mind. People think that oh I've got a grandson so I am proud. Naturally I am very happy. At that time my father-in-law was alive, and still my mother-in-law, she's 94. It's her grandson's son… you know Asiatic society, so in our society we've got very close family relationship." (A1, Indian)

The emotional satisfaction is further enhanced by the success of grown-up grandchildren.

In the interviews, grandparents who have retired from gainful employment, or have retired from their active roles in the family, speak constantly of their "doctor grandson", "lawyer granddaughter", and could not conceal their sense of pride in the achievements of their grandchildren.

A granddaughter who was interviewed, spoke of the favouritism she noticed her grandmother shows towards her elder brother who is now a medical doctor.

"It's the way when my brother comes back, "oh, you are back…" (she would say lovingly) and she is very proud of him. He is a doctor, that's why she is very proud of him, because she is the one who took care of him when he was young." (J3)

SPENDING TIME TOGETHER (LEISURE)

When asked what common activities grandparents and grandchildren do together, most mentioned watching TV together. Some families also go for overseas trips together when possible. Taking meals together on weekends is also another common activity as illustrated below.

F1: The whole place is in a mess, the floor is strewn with all those toys inside there, everything is everywhere, but we do have a family reunion on Sunday nights unless it is impossible, unless I have a function, unless somebody is away or not well you know. But let's say out of 52 weeks, 52 Sundays a year, we would say, have more than 85% of that.

I: Okay, and what I usually see with such events is as the grandchildren starts [sic] to get older at about John and Beth's age, they have activities on their own and they start to drop out sometimes.

F1: They do, they do. But for example, I just told you, I'm in very close touch with both Beth and John, despite their growing you know, their age. Now John is coming to 19 already you know. But the funny...I won't say funny, the nice thing is that, you know when he comes to our house, he still kisses me on the cheek.

I: Wow!

F1: And before he goes, he still kisses me as well on the cheek, also Beth.

OTHERS

In Singapore, it is not uncommon for Chinese older and younger generations to have different religions, typically, the older believe in Buddhism or Taoism; while the younger may accept Christianity. In some families, the religions practised by all three generations were the same for example, Indian and Malay families, where Hinduism and Islam were practised respectively. In general, grandparents saw themselves in a supportive and mentoring role.

Factors Affecting the Extent of Interdependence

Living arrangements

In Singapore, it is the norm for children to stay with parents before they are married. Due to a government housing policy in purchasing public flats, whereby grants are available to those who are married, it has also become a norm for young couples to purchase their own flats and move out upon marriage. A Singaporean can also use his/her Central Provident funds to purchase a Housing Development Board (HDB) flat, a policy which facilitates home ownership.

It is generally observed that those who are living in the same household with the older generation tend to be closer in their relationship with them, compared with children and grandchildren who are living apart from their grandparents. However, some exceptions exist, such as the case of one grandchild who was closer with her maternal grandmother although she was living together with her paternal grandmother.

Two factors had a bearing on the nature of the grandchild-grandparent relationship. The first factor was the gender of grandparent — grandchildren seemed to be closer to grandmothers compared with grandfathers. This supports existing literature on the subject (e.g. Spitze and Ward 1998). Another variable that had a bearing on the closeness of relationship between the grandparent and grandchild was whether the grandparent had looked after the child when he/she was young. The authors found it useful to interpret the findings using the life course perspective. If a grandparent had cared for a grandchild when the latter was young, it was found that the grandchild was closer to the grandparent when he/she had grown up. Brown (2003) also had a similar finding in her study in the American context, wherein the caregiving given by the grandparent was a strong predictor of a close grandchild-grandparent bond.

ROLE OF THE MIDDLE GENERATION IN PROVIDING THE LINK FOR ALL GENERATIONS

The interviews revealed that the middle generation plays an important role in facilitating and offering more opportunities for the alternate generations to communicate and interact. This is especially significant in nuclear family settings nowadays, as illustrated in the following example.

> "I think, like you said, we actually act as a bridge between them and give them the closeness to share during the later half of their lives, without this link, I feel that the grandparents would be very lonely, the grandchildren would be very, very [lonely]…they wouldn't actually be adequate in that sense to understand the rapport that you have or can have with the grandparents." (B2)

The role of the middle generation in the intergenerational relationship also impacts in other ways, for example, the interaction between the middle and the older generations serves as a guidepost and role model for the younger generation on how they should relate to the older generation.

> "it does affect [me], because my parents are very filial to my grandmother, so they are kind of like my role model. Like, this is what we should do with older people." (J3)

The interviews show that, although the middle generations often stress the independence of the relationship between the middle and old generations from that between the older and younger generation, the younger generation find it difficult to be indifferent when the relationship between the middle and older generations is strained.

For example, while the middle generation does not perceive any influence of the middle generation on alternate generation, the younger generation of the same family thinks differently, "because I am close to my mother... how she thinks of my grandpa will affect me. I mean... she and my grandpa are all right. She takes care of him and everything...but you know...sometimes my grandpa has his hang-ups and so it gets on everyone's nerves. But they're all right...

I: ok... so you do get affected by what your mother says about your grandpa?

C3: ya... I feel it when my mother gets frustrated with my grandfather sometimes." (C3)

On the other hand, some grandchildren also feel that their presence serves to promote closeness between the middle and older generations, as the grandchildren become a topic of conversation, and mutual concern of both generations (D3).

Grandchildren can be seen as magnets drawing together link parents and grandparents. They are frequently the focus of discussions between link parents and grandparents.

SOCIAL AND CULTURAL CHANGES

Asian families, especially urban families, have experienced drastic changes in the past few decades. This is especially felt in Singapore, a small island with swift social changes in the 40 years post independence. With the dramatic rise in literacy rates, the increase in the number of nuclear households, and the highly competitive work culture, the possibilities of older grandchildren finding the time to chat with their grandparents seems to be reducing. This was observed when the grandchildren and grandparents commented that when the grandchildren were in primary school, they spent more time with their grandparents, but with increasing school workload, the time spent together is drastically reduced. This may seem logical, given the increase in school work in secondary school, and the growing importance of peers in the lives of teenagers. Regardless of this, the grandparents do miss the company of the grandchildren they doted on, who have grown up.

Future cohorts of elders are predicted to be better educated, and alternative models of grandparenting are emerging, according to our research. The present cohort of older Singaporeans above the age of 75 years find it hard to contribute, or participate in, certain activities such as computer games. The few activities in which they can join their grandchildren include playing board games or watching television together. Due to their language limitations, for instance, many do not speak English, they have difficulties communicating with their grandchildren. Future baby boomer cohorts of grandparents are highly likely to have enhanced language capabilities, computer and IT skills, and hence their ability to participate in a wider range of activities is predicted.

Although there will be grandparents who are better educated, they may think twice about looking after grandchildren on a daily basis. The new baby boomer grandparents are likely to have plans for retirement such as travelling, working on a freelance basis, and volunteering in voluntary welfare organizations. It is predicted that there could be tensions in future intergenerational relations due to the expectations and needs of each generation.

Effects of Globalization on Family

Among the families that we interviewed, many had grandchildren studying in Australia and the United Kingdom, and children working in Indonesia and the United States. How would close emotional ties be maintained? Would the love between generations withstand the test of time?

IMPLICATIONS AND FUTURE CHALLENGES

The roles of grandparents may change as some may find themselves displaced, with their skills and capabilities inadequate for today's world. Their response may be to withdraw into their own "shell" and perhaps go down the spiritual path.

Others may learn new ways of keeping abreast with the changes, for example, through learning the use of computers and the internet, having mobile phones and learning how to use the Short Messaging System (or SMS). Some grandparents realize the need to learn from the young about things that they are unfamiliar with in today's world, and this initiative serves as an opportunity for intergenerational communication. One respondent sees the need to care for the older parents as including both the physical as well as cognitive aspects, as his father is educated, and desires to stay in touch with the modern world. The family had emigrated from India about a decade ago and the ageing parent is now living with his son and daughter-in-law in Singapore.

> "… it's both a physical as well as a intellectual level because now he finds too many things which are strange to him. He says, "Hey, I don't understand all this, what do you mean?" He will send me an e-mail:

"What does this mean?" He has had more intellectual shocks here…rather than earlier, and the reason is that in India, while we were still there and here, it is always [sic] faculty around him. He was able to grasp because he has a scientific mind, that was what he graduated in, with physics, chemistry and stuff like that and he was a teacher in the beginning so he has that mindset, he's a very alert person normally, and he was very curious, so he picked up all these things very easily, so it wasn't that he was a stranger to technology. But once his faculties degraded so very suddenly over here, then he started, sort of becoming more and more alienated with technology. So its [sic] not that suddenly the level of technology here shot up, I don't think that's an issue, but because of that, now even intellectually, he feels more handicap [sic] that, "Hey, I don't know what's going on." Then again, there was [sic] too many times when he said, "No no, I don't understand what you say." He would have heard everything, and in terms of language, he's understood what you meant but in intellectual terms, he didn't understand and he will want, of all people in the world, he will want me to go and explain it to him. So the relationship now is that if I says [sic] it, then that's the way it is. If somebody else says it: "No I don't understand what you say." So you know that the role has changed only after [sic] his handicap here. (C2)

FUTURE TRENDS

The study suggests that we should expect changes in the nature of interdependence and its practice. Most of the grandchildren voiced the view that they would be different from their grandparents when asked to project themselves as a grandparent in future. With better education and some financial preparation, future grandparents may be less financially dependent on children and, therefore, may be in a position to decline the link parents' request or expectation to care physically for grandchildren on a daily basis.

The cultural context also plays an important role in a) whether grandparents are called upon to babysit the grandchildren, and b) which set of grandparents would be more likely to get involved. The cultural choices may be mediated by variables such as geographical proximity, closeness of relations, and whether the grandparents are still working.

When grandparents are the primary caregivers, for instance, when the link parent is divorced and is therefore highly dependent on the co-residential grandparent for child-minding, intergenerational programmes will be required to educate and support the grandparents.

From a sociological viewpoint, it would seem that the cyclical nature and timing of care predicts that when children get married and move out of the family of origin, there is some distancing of relationships (Grandpa's at home but lonely, 6/5/2004). Then, when grandchildren arrive, opportunities for the closing of the distance arise, and they meet more often, sharing knowledge, experiences, and engaging in an exchange of resources. As the elders become older, the link parents have to be prepared to be primary caregivers to their parents and this may bring them closer, or distance them because of the weight of the burden of eldercare. This cyclical nature of family dynamics is not necessarily universal. Through migration, the untimely death of older or middle generations, terminal illness and severing of relationships for a variety of reasons, the cycle of family care can be interrupted, and substitutes may be found. However, Asian cultures tend to idealize the multigenerational family, and individuals strive to maintain harmony between the generations because they realize the tangible and intangible benefits for all generations. The modernization of Singapore society is one version of the "idea of multiple modernities" (Tu Wei-Ming 2000, p. 256), in which traditions and modernization are interwoven into the daily lives of families, and individuals find creative ways to blend apparent paradoxes.

Notes

[1]   The authors wish to acknowledge the funding provided by the National University of Singapore (R-107-000-040-112), which made this research project "Grandparenting in selected Asian Societies" possible.
[2]   A shorter version of this chapter has been published in a special issue of the Journal of Intergenerational Relationships.

References

Antonucci, T.C. "Social Supports and Social Relationships". In *Handbook of Aging and Social Sciences*, 3rd edition, by R.H. Binstock and L.K. George, eds. (California: Academic Press, 1990).

Bengston, V. *The New and Emerging "Contract" between Generations*. Paper presented at the Conference on Chronic Illness, Formal/Informal Care, and Medical Problems among Chinese and American Elderly (Academia Sinica: Institute of European and American Studies, Taipei, Taiwan, 1992).

Brown, L.H. "Intergenerational Influences on Perceptions of Current Relationships with Grandparents". *Journal of Intergenerational Relationships* 1, no. 1 (2003): 95–112.

Chan, A. An Overview of the Living Arrangements and Social Support Exchanges of Older Singaporeans, *Asia-Pacific Population Journal* 12, no. 4 (1997): 1–16.

Goransson, K. *Filial Children and Ageing Parents: Intergenerational Family ties as*

Politics and Practice among Chinese Singaporeans. Working paper in Social Anthropology, Lund University, 2004.

Gutmann, D. "Deculturation and the American Grandparent". In *Grandparenthood*, V. Bengston and J. Robertson, eds. (Beverley Hills, Calif.: Sage Publications, 1985).

Grandpa's at home, but lonely. *Straits Times*, 6/05/04, p. 3.

Hayslip, B. Jr. and P.L. Kaminski. "Grandparents Raising their Grandchildren: A Review of the Literature and Suggestions for Practice". *Gerontologist* 45, no. 2 (2005): 262–69.

Landry-Meyer, L. and B.M. Newman. "An Exploration of the Grandparent Caregiver Role. *Journal of Family Issues* 25 (2004): 1005–25.

Mehta, K. "Intergenerational Exchanges: Qualitative evidence from Singapore". *Southeast Asian Journal of Social Science* 27 (1999): 111–22.

———, M. Osman and A. Lee. "Living Arrangements of the Elderly in Singapore: Cultural Norms in Transition". *Journal of Cross-Cultural Gerontology* 10 (1995): 113–43.

——— and H. Ko. Filial Piety Revisited in the Context of Modernizing Asian Societies, Geriatrics and Gerontology International vol 4, no. 4 (2004): 577–78.

——— and P. Teo. Voices of the Heart: Widows and Widowers in Singapore. Singapore: Humanities Press, 2000.

———. "National Policies on Ageing and Long-term Care in Singapore: A Case of Cautious Wisdom?". In *Ageing and Long-term Care: National Policies in the Asia-Pacific*, D. Phillips and A. Chan, eds. (Singapore/Canada: Institute of Southeast Asian Studies/International Development Research Centre, 2002).

Minkler, M. and Fuller-Thomson, E. African American Grandparents Raising Grandchildren: A National Study Using the Census 2000 American Community Survey. *Journal of Gerontology and Social Sciences* 603, no. 2 (2005): 882–92.

Spitze, G. and R.A. Ward. "Gender Variations". In *Handbook of Grandparenthood*, M.E. Szinovacz, ed. (Westport, CT: Greenwood Press, 1998).

Teo. P. "The National Policy on Elderly People in Singapore". *Ageing and Society* 14 (1994): 405–27.

Thang, L.L. "Aging in the East: Comparative and Historical Reflections". In *Handbook of the Humanities and Aging* (Second edition), T. Cole, R. Kastenbaum and R. Ray, eds. (New York: Springer Publishing Company, 2000).

Tu Wei-Ming. "Multiple Modernities: A Preliminary Enquiry into the Implications of East Asian Modernity". In *Culture Matters: How Values Shape Human Progress*, L.E. Harrison and S.P. Huntington, eds. (New York: Basic Books, 2000), pp. 256–66.

12

SUPPORT TRANSFERS BETWEEN ELDERLY PARENTS AND ADULT CHILDREN IN INDONESIA

Sri Harijati Hatmadji and Nur Hadi Wiyono

INTRODUCTION

The success of Indonesia's population policy, particularly the family planning programme, has resulted in lowering the fertility rate as indicated by the decrease in the total fertility rate (TFR) from 5.6 in 1967 to 2.3 in 2000. Conversely, the combination of low fertility with rising life expectancies has resulted in accelerating the population ageing process. An Indonesian population census shows that there is a significant increase in the proportion of elderly from 4.5 per cent of the total population in 1971 to 7.2 per cent in 2000. Compared with other developed countries (North America, Europe and Japan), the proportion of Indonesian elderly is lower, however, in terms of absolute numbers, the number of Indonesian elderly in 2000 was about 14 million, close to the number of older people in the Netherlands in 2001, which was about 16 million. It is projected that the proportion of the elderly will increase to 12.7 per cent, or equal to 37 million in 2025 (Demographic Institute 1999).

The industrialization process has led to changes in family relations in Indonesia. For example, because industrialization provided various wage employment to many household members, the proportion of households getting income from family businesses, such as from farms and shops, had decreased. Instead, more households had come to rely on income from wage employment, either from formal or informal jobs. The relation between parents (elderly) and adult children are less inter dependent in part because the children are more independent as they have their own income. Finally, since industrialization largely took place in the urban areas, it has led to the migration of young people to the cities. Therefore, according to Mason (1992), the effect of industrialization on the situation of the elderly may be less co-residence with adult children in the rural areas.

Some studies on Asia have shown that the proportion of elderly who co-reside with adult children has decreased over time. The decreasing proportion of co-residence does not necessarily mean an erosion of support and care of the elderly by family members (Mason 1992). In Asia, including in Indonesia, family support remains high.

Like in other developing countries, in Indonesia the increasingly ageing population has raised some issues, such as how to care for older persons, the government's efforts to cope with the problem, and how families look after older persons. This chapter will look at how adult children support older persons and how older persons support their children, with special focus on intergenerational transfers.

The organization of the chapter is as follows: Part I looks briefly at the motivation behind the transfers, Part II examines how transfers between parents and children take place, and Part III deals with the government's policy towards the elderly.

MOTIVATION AND DIRECTION OF TRANSFERS

In an in-depth case study of Malaysia, Lillard and Willis (1997) identified the different motives for intergenerational transfers. One of the old age security hypotheses emphasized the problems of individuals having to find reliable outlets for saving for old age in developing countries, "where financial institutions are primitive, property rights are insecure, the currency is subject to inflation, and [the] government social security system, private pension, and health insurance are non existence [sic]" (p. 115). Facing those conditions, individuals will rely on the investment in their children whom they hope would take care of their parents in future. "Although children themselves are risky investment — they may die, be the wrong sex, be economic failure, or be disloyal — according to this hypothesis they represent the only chance for common people in poor countries to have any security in old age" (ibid., p. 115).

The old age security hypothesis thus shows a long-term mechanism of saving by parents. There is another model of transfers that focuses on the short-term, which hypothesizes that transfers reflect an exchange of money for time. For instance, elderly parents may care for the grandchildren in return for money from adult children, or able-bodied adult children may perform chores for their parents in return for money.

Another intergenerational transfers hypothesis developed by Becker (1974), called the altruism hypothesis, argues that the fact that family members have altruistic feelings towards one another would explain many aspects of family behaviour. An example of this hypothesis is the family investment in the children's human capital; the more altruistic the household head, the more he finances investment in his children's education through gifts, and the less he requires repayment from them (Lillard and Willis, 1997, p. 117). Altruism may also lead the children to transfer resources to their ageing parents, particularly if the parents have instilled a strong sense of filial responsibility in their children (Frankerberg, Lillard, Willis, 2002).

A study conducted in several Asian countries found varying motivations for transfers depending on the country and data. Table 12.1 presents motivations for transfers in selected Asian countries which employed different methods and data.

There are two types of intergenerational transfers: money and time. Money transfers involve people in different generations through either inter or intra household transfers. Two activities can be considered as time transfer: household assistance and personal assistance. Household assistance includes all kinds of household help (e.g. repairs, cleaning, maintenance, yard work), while personal care assistance refers to help with basic tasks such as bathing, dressing, eating, and toileting. Time transfer has an economic value that can be purchased by money. Other types of transfers that can be valued by money is goods transfer (George 1998).

Having reviewed studies of intergenerational transfers in the United States, George (1998) concluded that time and money transfers have different directions. The dominant direction of money transfers throughout adulthood is from parents to children, although transfers from adult children to elderly parent still exist. Time transfer, however, takes the opposite direction — from adult children providing a lot of assistance to their elderly parents.

Lee (2003) summarizes research on transfer flows in different forms of societies, i.e. hunter-gatherer, agriculture, and industrialized societies. The direction of transfer was calculated from average ages of production and consumption in a population. In the hunter-gatherer society, people continued

TABLE 12.1
Motivation for Transfers in Selected Asian Countries

Country	Author(s)	Data	Method	Result
Indonesia	Raut & Tren (2001)	IFLS	Tobit	Support altruistic model
Indonesia, Malaysia	Frankerberg, Lillard, & Willis (J. Marr & Fam 2002)	IFLS, MFLS	Probit	No single motive
Malaysia	Lillard, & Willis (Demography 1997)	MFLS	Probit	No single motive
Taiwan	Lee, Parish, Willis (Am. J. Soc 1994)	Family & Women Survey	Heckman	Support altruistic model & bargaining model
Rep. of Korea	SJ Kang & Y Sawada (Developing Econ 2003)	KHPS	Fixed Effect Logit, Random effect Tobit	Support altruistic model

Note: – IFLS: Indonesia Family Life Survey
— MFLS: Malaysia Family Life Survey
— KHPS: Korean Household Panel Survey
Source: Modified from Lee (2004).

to produce resources in excess of their consumption into old age, transferring the surplus to the children, and grandchildren. In addition, food was an important resources. Therefore, the direction of transfer of food was strongly downwards, from older to younger people. In an agriculture society, property rights were established and the ownership of land, dwelling, livestock, and other goods was common. Many old people owned property that was a source of power and control. Similar to the hunter-gatherer society, the net direction of resource transfers, was also strongly downwards, from older to younger people. In the industrialized society, education became increasingly important in terms of enhancing life-chances and led to the gradual demise of child labour. A calculation of average ages of production and consumption for individuals in the United States around 1900 shows that the net direction has shifted from downward to upward flows.

INTERGENERATIONAL TRANSFERS IN
THE INDONESIAN CONTEXT

Industrialization, urbanization, and migration have brought about the decrease of co-residence between elderly parents and adult children. Rising incomes and education, cost of living, and the need for privacy, have also contributed to the decrease of co-residence. However in Indonesia, the family has traditionally played a significant role in supporting the elderly by co-residing with the elderly. From Table 12.2, regardless of the survey location, we can see that 29.8 per cent of the elderly live with his/her spouse and his/her adult child and 19.5 per cent lived with spouse and adult child/in-law, and only 1.5 per cent of the elderly lived alone.

TABLE 12.2
Number and Proportion of Elderly by
Type of Co-residence and Location of Survey

Co reside with	Reg Central Lampung	Mun Bogor	Regency Sukoharjo	Mun Pasuruhan	Total	
					n	%
Alone	1	2	2	1	6	1.5
Spouse	8	14	26	11	59	14.8
Spouse & adult child	29	29	33	28	119	29.8
Spouse & child in law	26	20	5	27	78	19.5
Adult Child	1	3	6	3	13	3.3
Adult child/in-law	4	4	6	6	20	5.5
Others	31	28	22	24	105	26.3
Total	100	100	100	100	400	100

Source: Wirakartakusumah, 1994.

Recent research done on elderly households in two villages in Yogyakarta found that only a small proportion (4 per cent) of them lived alone and 11 per cent lived together with only their spouse (Keasberry 2002). The study also found that almost half of the sample (48.1 per cent) lived with spouse and "other(s)" and about a third only lived with "other(s)". Keasberry defined other(s) as lived with parents, siblings, nephews/nieces, great-grandchildren, and child's parents-in-law (*besan*).

With whom are the Indonesian elderly most likely to live? Wirakartakusmah et al. (1995) found that the married elderly are less likely to live with married children, in other words, non-married elderly are more likely to live with married children. It is generally believed that elderly people prefer to live with a daughter. This is because household chores such as preparing meals, washing, cleaning the house, are considered female tasks, therefore, it is easier for the elderly who need help to ask a daughter or daughter-in-law, if she/he lives with them rather than with a son. The Keasberry (2002) study found that elderly males have a significant preference for living with daughters and mothers have a significant preference for living with sons.

Based on an ethnographic study in five different ethnic groups in Indonesia, Abikusno (2002) found that children from different ethnic groups adopt different care for their parents. Among the Batak (an ethnic group in North Sumatra, most daughters provided additional assistance and care for their parents compared with sons. However parents felt ashamed accepting it. In Java and Bali, the eldest son is economically responsible for his older parents, and daughters are in charge of care giving, especially those living nearby. Among the Bugis (an ethnic group in South Sulawesi), the responsibility for taking care of parents is given to employed children, especially those living with parents.

In the Indonesian socio-economic context, older persons are either giving support to, or receiving support from, their children. The absence of a social security scheme for the majority of old persons has led to their working to meet the needs of their daily lives. A study on the consequences of ageing in Indonesia found that 58 per cent old persons rely on their income and 27 per cent receive support from their children or children-in-law, 19 per cent either receive support from pensions, or husband/wife's income (Table 12.3) (Wirakartakusmah, 1999). Schroder-Butterfill (2003) in her study in Kidul Villlage, East Java, among 200 respondents, found a similar result — one in ten elderly people in the study community was in poor health and the majority continued to work or have income from pensions or the land.

Using the 1993 Indonesia Family Life Survey (IFLS), Mundiharno (1999) found that 62 per cent of adult children were giving transfers to their elderly parents who lived alone, while only 21 per cent of adult children were receiving transfers from parents who lived alone (Table 12.4). The proportion of adult children giving transfers to parents living alone is higher than those giving transfers to parents living with a spouse and with a child/child-in-law. How much was transferred (in Rupiah, Rp) by children to their parents? The average monetary sum given by adult children to their parents who lived

TABLE 12.3
Percentage of Source of Elderly Support by Region

Source	Central Lampung (Sumatra)	Bogor (West Java)	Sukoharjo (Central Java)	Pasuruhan (East Java)	Total (%)
Own income/salary	79	37	76	42	58.5
Husband/wife's income/salary	35	15	17	11	19.5
Pension	9	32	7	29	19.3
Husband/wife's pension	6	8	1	7	5.5
Insurance	0	0	0	1	0.2
Savings	0	3	1	1	1.3
Rent	9	3	1	1	5.5
Adult children/in-law	12	30	31	37	27.5
Grandchildren	0	3	1	5	2.2
Other relatives	1	3	2	1	1.3
Friends	0	0	0	1	0.2
Charity organizations	0	1	0	0	0.2
Garden/livestock	16	1	4	2	5.7

Source: Wirakartakusumah, 1994.

TABLE 12.4
Proportion of Adult Children Who Give/Receive Transfer to/from
Their Parents by Co-residence Type

Reside/co-reside with	Giving Transfer to Parents		Receiving Transfer from Parents	
	% "Yes"	N	% "Yes"	N
Alone	61.9	506	20.9	507
Husband/wife	51.1	4,134	29.7	4,134
Child/child in-law	55.7	5,206	26.2	5,204
Others*	58.8	2,580	23.6	2,582
Total	55.6	7,376	26.1	7,378

Note: Others include co residing with parents/parents in-law, grandchildren, brothers/sisters.
Source: Mundiharno, 1999.

alone was Rp 623,355 annually, which was higher than those giving money to parents who did not live alone. Adult children also received money from their parents averaging Rp 111,253 annually (Table 12.5).

TABLE 12.5
Average Valued-money Transfer Given to/Received from
Parents by Co-residency Type

Reside/co-reside with	Giving Transfers to Parents		Receiving Transfers from Parents	
	Rp	N	Rp	N
Alone	623,355	282	111,253	87
Husband/wife	264,495	1,942	304,597	1,110
Child/child in-law	514,134	2,701	329,556	1,204
Others*	735,705	1,419	538,368	516

Note: Others include co residing with parents/parents in-law, grandchildren, brothers/sisters
Source: Mundiharno, 1999.

These figures indicate that the family still plays a role in supporting the elderly, although some elderly have to work to meet the needs of their daily life and to support their children. A qualitative study in East Java (Schroder-Butterfill 2003) found that elderly people are not considered a "burden" of the family but, in fact, some of them are the economic backbone of the family.

Another qualitative study on Yogyakarta and North Sumatra by Beard and Kunhariwibowo (2001) found that some of the respondents acknowledged that they supported their adult children who co-resided with them. "This generally occurred when the adult child had not yet married, had not started working, and/or had never left home to establish [sic] an independent household… Or …it also occurred when [the] adult children was married but [had] not yet moved away and established an independent household" (p. 26).

What are the determinants of adult children giving or receiving transfers to/from parents? With regard to adult children giving transfers, using the 1993 IFLS data, Mundiharno (1999) found that characteristics of adult children such as age, income, marital status, and living distance from the parents were statistically significant in determining the giving of transfers (money or materials) to their parents. For example, the higher the income of adult children, the higher the likelihood of their giving transfers to their parents. Unmarried children are less likely to give transfers to their parents. Usually unmarried children receive transfers from their parents because they do not have any income. Adult children characteristics such as education, sex, and location (urban-rural) statistically do not determine whether or not they give transfers to their parents. In the Indonesian context, children are expected to respect their parents, regardless their education, location, or sex. Social norms prescribe that children who ignore and do not care for their parents are subject to social sanction (Wirakartakusumah, 1999).

With regard to gender, for example, there is statistically no difference between male children and female children in giving transfers. Parent characteristics such as education, living distance, frequency of meetings, working status, age, and having severe diseases, were statistically significant in determining if adult children are giving transfers to their parents. For example, the negative sign of the education coefficient shows that the more educated parents would be less likely to receive transfers from their adult children. Adult children whose parents have severe disease are more likely to give transfers.

With regard to adult children receiving transfers, the study found that adult children characteristics such as education, sex, location, marital status, age, and income were statistically significant in determining receiving transfers. Parent characteristics such as education, living distance, frequency of meetings, marital status, working status, and having severe diseases were also statistically significant in determining of parents were receiving transfers from adult children. (See Table 12.6)

Besides money and material support, elderly people also receive time support in the form of instrumental activities of daily life (IADL) support

TABLE 12.6
**Determinants of Giving Transfer to and Receiving from Elderly
(Multivariate Logistic Regression)**

	Giving transfers to elderly			Receiving transfers from elderly		
	Param (β)	Sig	Odd ratio	Param (β)	Sig	Odd ratio
Intercept	-2.2369	0.0001		-2.3569	0.0001	
Characteristics of children						
Education						
No schooling	n.a.					Rf
Elementary school	n.a.			0.2167	0.0020	1.242
Junior high school	n.a.			0.3593	0.0001	1.432
Sex						
Female	n.a.					
Male	n.a.			-0.2481	0.0001	0.780

continued on next page

TABLE 12.6 — *continued*

	Giving transfers to elderly			Receiving transfers from elderly		
	Param (β)	*Sig*	*Odd ratio*	*Param (β)*	*Sig*	*Odd ratio*
Residence						
Urban	n.a.					Rf
Rural	n.a.			0.2333	0.0002	1.263
Marital status						
Married			Rf			Rf
Not Married	-0.2915	0.0056	0.747	0.6828	0.0001	1.979
Age (years)						
<20			Rf			Rf
20–39	1.5124	0.0054	1.663	-0.5280	0.0033	0.590
40–59	0.6092	0.0013	1.839	-0.9593	0.0001	0.383
60+	0.3532	0.0966	1.424	-1.4886	0.0001	0.226
Income	0.0305	0.0001	1.031	-0.0160	0.0001	0.984
Parents characteristics						
Education						
No schooling			Rf			Rf
Elementary school	-0.1040	0.0660	0.901	0.2631	0.0001	0.301
Distance of living						
Same village	1.5318	0.0004	4.627	2.0553	0.0001	7.810
Different village			Rf			
Frequency of meeting						
Never meet			Rf			Rf
Ever meet	1.3088	0.0001	3.702	1.6602	0.0001	5.260
Marital status						
Married	n.a.			0.1491	0.0128	1.161
Not Married	n.a.					Rf
Working status						
Work			Rf			Rf
Looking for work	0.977	0.2334	2.656	-0.3855	0.6434	0.680
Other	0.3395	0.0001	1.404	-0.5308	0.0001	0.588
Age	0.0205	0.0182	1.021	n.a.	n.a.	
Severe diseases						
Have severe diseases	0.2645	0.0001	1.303	0.2336	0.0005	1.263
Don't have severe diseases			Rf			Rf

Note: n.a. = not applicable, rf = reference group.
Variables statistically not significant have been excluded from the model. Giving transfers to and receiving from elderly is done by non co-resident adult children. Transfers from co-resident children are not included in the model.
Source: Mundiharno (1999).

such as shopping, cutting wood, fetching water, boiling water, cooking meals, doing the laundry, sweeping the yard, cleaning the house, and feeding livestock. Keasberry's study (2002) in two villages in Yogyakarta found that on average elderly people can perform the IADL without difficulty. Table 12.7 shows who usually gives support for the different IADLs. The elderly who need IADL support mostly receive support from female household members i.e., a daughter (42.6 per cent) and daughter-in-law (11.2 per cent), with some support coming from male household members i.e. son (8.8 per cent) and son-in-law (10.0 per cent). Female household members usually provide support such as sweeping the yard and doing the laundry and males mostly provide help with heavier tasks such as cutting wood and feeding livestock.

THE GOVERNMENT POLICY ON ELDERLY PEOPLE

In response to the growing ageing population and the implications of this on health, social life, and social security, the government has launched programmes that aim to increase support for and contribution to the elderly, involving government sectors at all levels, NGOs (non-governmental organizations), the private sector, and unions. In 1999, the Ministry of Population launched the *National Plan of Action for Family and Community Activities in Support of the Elderly*. The National Plan has three objectives: a) to formulate a strong policy on efforts to maintain and strengthen family support for the elderly population, b) strongly comprehend problems on the elderly population, and c) to strengthen inter-sector cooperation on the elderly population. Basically, the goals of the policies are to encourage elderly people to be healthy, self reliant, productive, prosperous both mentally and physically, so that the life of the elderly will not be a burden to their families and the community at large (Ministry of Population/NFCB (1999).

In the year 2000, the revised National Plan of Action for Elderly Welfare was adopted. It stated that in the future social welfare programmes for the elderly will be directed to: a) promoting the elderly well-being and social security system, b) improving the health service system, c) strengthening family and community support, d) improving the quality of life, and e) developing special facilities. Details of the programmes are listed below.

a) Promoting the Elderly Well-being and Social Security System includes:
    — Promoting the quality of life of older person by increasing their level of social welfare and institutionalizing related activities,
    — Maintaining the existing higher level of social life.

TABLE 12.7

Primary Source of Support for Instrumental Activities of Daily Life (IADL) %

Source of IADL Support	Instrumental Activities of Daily Life (IADL)									Total of support received[a]	
	Shop daily (N=42)	Cut wood (N=37)	Fetch water (N=28)	Boil water (N=29)	Cook meals (N=32)	Do laundry (N=26)	Sweep yard (N=16)	Clean house (N=19)	Feed livestock (N=20)	freq	%
Female hhd member											
– wife	2.4	–	3.6	6.9	3.1	3.8	–	–	5.0	7	2.8
– daughter	52.4	13.5	39.3	44.8	53.1	57.7	5.3	47.4	25.0	106	42.6
– daughter-in-law	23.8	2.7	7.1	10.3	15.6	15.4	12.5	5.3	–	28	11.2
– grand daughter	9.5	2.7	3.6	3.4	9.4	11.5	6.3	15.8	10.0	19	7.6
– other kin	4.8	–	–	–	6.3	–	6.3	–	–	5	2.0
Male hhd member											
– husband	–	10.8	3.6	6.9	–	3.8	6.3	10.5	10.0	13	5.2
– son	2.4	21.6	17.9	3.4	3.1	3.8	–	5.3	20.0	22	8.8
– son-in-law	–	35.6	10.7	10.3	3.1	–	–	–	25.0	25	10.0
– grandson	–	5.4	3.6	3.4	–	–	–	–	–	4	1.6
– other kin	–	5.4	10.7	3.4	–	–	–	10.5	5.0	9	3.6
Non hhd member											
– daughter	–	–	–	–	–	3.8	–	5.3	–	2	0.8
– son	2.4	–	–	–	–	–	–	–	–	1	0.4
– other kin	–	–	–	6.9	6.3	–	6.3	–	–	5	2.0
– neighbourhood/friend	2.4	2.7	–	–	–	–	6.3	–	–	3	1.2
Total	100	100	–	100	100	100	100	100	100	249	100

Note: a = the support for the different instrumental activities of daily life might be given by the same source.
hhd = household
Source: Keasberry (2002).

b) Improving Health Service includes:
   — Increasing the health status and quality of life of older person through promotion of healthy life behaviour,
   — Prioritizing elderly health service through disease prevention, without disregarding curative and rehabilitation services,
   — Complimentary health service for the impoverished elderly through the existing procedures.
c) Strengthening Family and Community Support includes:
   — Promoting and guiding members of families to observe and respect the interest and welfare of older members of the family,
   — Promoting and guiding community, social agencies, non-government organizations and the private sector on service for the elderly,
   — Promoting, reinforcing and socializing national behaviour and norms to show respect for the elderly in their daily life,
d) Improving Quality of Life includes:
   — Providing for potential older persons to promote their knowledge and skills at work or hobbies through formal or non-formal education and training,
   — Providing access and opportunity for potential and productive elderly to keep working, according their ability, knowledge, and experience.
e) Developing Special Facilities
   — Establishing provisions on special facilities and privileges for older persons to perform their daily activities at work and travelling, such as providing lifetime identity cards, access to public facilities, discounts on health services etc.
   — Improving facilities, research and development,
   — Promoting organization and work mechanisms and observing laws and regulation.

In addition, to cope with the neglected and non-potential[1] elderly, the government provides home care in selected cities in Indonesia. There are 157 home care (Panti Sosial Tresna Werdha) centres supported by the government. The government also established an Integrated Service Post (Posyandu) for elderly people that gives services such as medical check-ups (blood tension and urine checking) and exercise.

CLOSING REMARKS

In Indonesia, adult children giving transfers (money, materials and time) to elderly parents is common since tradition prescribes that children are expected to respect their parents. However there are also a reverse transfers from elderly parents to adult children because some children do not have their own income or their own independent homes.

A major problem of the elderly in Indonesia is the absence of social security for the majority of the elderly population. Social security was enjoyed by those who worked in formal sectors (government and private sector), and these constitute only less that 2 per cent of the population. Compared with other countries such as Singapore (77 per cent) and Malaysia (36 per cent), social security coverage is low (Kertonegoro, 1999). Therefore, family support is still an important source for elderly although this support could be undermined by modernization and migration. In the future a social security system should be established to cover elderly people. On 19 October 2004 President Megawati signed the new Law on National Social Security System which cover six programmes: health insurance, old-age security, pension, safety work insurance, death insurance. The law would be a base to develop a programme to protect elderly people.

Note

[1]   The Welfare Elderly Law (No 13/1998) distinguished between potential and non-potential elderly. Potential elderly are elderly aged 60 year and above who are still active and able to work to produce goods and services. Non-potential elderly are dependent elderly because they do not work to meet the needs of their daily life.

References

Abikusno, Nugoho. "Sociocultural Aspect of the Aged: A Case Study in Indonesia", in *Asia Pacific Journal Clinical Nutrition* 11, no. 3 (2002).

Beard, Victoria A. and Yacobus Kunhariwibowo. "Living Arrangements and Support Relationship among Elderly Indonesians: Case Studies from Java and Sumatra". *International Journal of Population Geography* 7 (2001): 17–33.

Becker, Gary. "Theory of Social Interaction", *Journal of Political Economy* 82 (1974): 1063–1093.

Demographic Institite. *Indonesian Population Projection 2000–2025*. Jakarta, 1999.

Frankenberg, Elizabeth, Lee A. Lillard and Robert J. Willis. "Patterns of Intergenerational Transfers in Southeast Asia", in *Journal of Marriage and the Family* 64, no. 3 (Aug. 2002); Academic Research Library.

George, Linda K. "Intergenerational Transfers: Who Gives and Who Gets" in *Journal of Financial Service Professional* 52, no. 2 (Mar. 1998); Academic Research Library.

Lillard, Lee A. and Robert J. Willis. "Motives for Intergenerational Transfers: Evidence from Malaysia", *Demography* 34, no. 1 (1997): 115–34.

Lee, Sang-Hyop. Materials for Workshop of Economic Aspect of Population Aging, the 35th Summer Seminar on Population, East-West Center, Honolulu, Hawaii, 2004.

Lee, Ronald. "Demographic Change, Welfare, and Intergenerational Transfers: A Global Overview". Paper was prepared for Rencontres Sauvy at Villa Mandragone, Frascati, Rome, 2003.

Mundiharno, *Determinant Sosial Ekonomi Intergenerational Transfer, Analisis Data IFLS I*, Thesis Program Kependudukan dan Ketenagakerjaan, Universitas Indonesia, 1999.

Mason, Karen Oppenheim. "Family Change and Support of the Elderly in Asia: What Do We Know?" in *Asia Pacific Population Journal* 7, no. 3 (1992).

Ministry of Population/NFCB. *National Plan of Action for Family and Community in Support of the Aged*. Jakarta, 1999.

Keasberry, Iris N. *Elder Care, Old-Age Security, and Social Change in Yogyakarta, Indonesia*. Ph.D. thesis Wagenangen University. Wagenangen, 2002.

Kertonegoro, Sentanu. "The Role of Social Security for People's Welfare: A Study of Social Security Scheme in Indonesia" in *Journal of Population* 5, no. 2 (1999).

Schroder-Butterfill, Elizabeth. Pillars of the Family: "Support Provided by the Elderly in Indonesia". Paper presented in the 2002 IUSSP Regional Population Conference, Bangkok, Thailand, 2003.

Wirakartakusumah, Djuhari. *Local Policy Development on Consequences of Aging: Indonesia Case*. Asian Population Studies Series No. 131, Bangkok: ESCAP, 1994.

Wirakartakusumah, Djuhari. *Determinant of Work and Co-residence of the Elderly in Indonesia*. Unpublished report. Demographic Institute, FEUI, 1995.

INDEX

Printed in the United States
123703LV00002B/239/P